EXCALIBUR BY TINI HOWARD VOL. 2. Contains material originally published in magazine form as EXCALIBUR (2019) #7-12. First printing 2020. ISBN 978-1-302-92146-0. Published by MARVEL WORLDWIDE, INC., a subsidiary of MARVEL ENTERTAINMENT, LLC. OFFICE OF PUBLICATION: 1290 Avenue of the Americas, New York, NY 10104. © 2020 MARVEL No similarity between any of the names, characters, persons, and/or institutions in this magazine with those of any living or dead person or institution is intended, and any such similarity which may exist is purely coincidental. **Printed in Canada.** KEVIN FEIGE, Chief Creative Officer; DAN BUCKLEY, President, Marvel Entertainment; JOHN NEE, Publisher; JOE QUESADA, EVP & Creative Director; TOM BREVOORT, SVP of Publishing; DAVID BOGART, Associate Publisher & SVP of Talent Affairs; Publishing & Partnership; DAVID GABRIEL, VP of Print & Digital Publishing; JEFF YOUNGQUIST, VP of Production & Special Projects; DAN CARR, Executive Director of Publishing Technology; ALEX MORALES, Director of Publishing Operations; DAN EDINGTON, Managing Editor; RICKEY PURDIN, Director of Talent Relations; SUSAN CRESPI, Production Manager; STAN LEE, Chairman Emeritus. For information regarding advertising in Marvel Comics or on Marvel. com, please contact Vit DeBellis, Custom Solutions & Integrated Advertising Manager, at vdebellis@marvel.com. For Marvel subscription inquiries, please call 888-511-5480. **Manufactured between 9/25/2020 and 10/27/2020 by SOLISCO PRINTERS, SCOTT, QC, CANADA.**

10 9 8 7 6 5 4 3 2 1

Vol. 2

Writer: **Tini Howard**
Pencilers: **Marcus To** (#7-8) **&**
                         Walton Santos (#8-12)
Inkers: **Oren Junior** (#7),
                         Sean Parsons (#8),
                         Marcus To (#8-12),
                         Roberto Poggi (#8) **&**
                         Victor Nava (#8)
Color Artist: **Erick Arciniega**
Letterers: **VC's Cory Petit** (#7-10) **&**
                         Ariana Maher (#11-12)

Cover Art: **Mahmud Asrar &**
                         Matthew Wilson

Head of X: **Jonathan Hickman**
Design: **Tom Muller**
Assistant Editor: **Annalise Bissa**
Editor: **Jordan D. White**

Collection Editor: **Jennifer Grünwald**
Assistant Managing Editor: **Maia Loy**
Assistant Managing Editor: **Lisa Montalbano**
Editor, Special Projects: **Mark D. Beazley**
VP Production & Special Projects: **Jeff Youngquist**
SVP Print, Sales & Marketing: **David Gabriel**
Editor in Chief: **C.B. Cebulski**

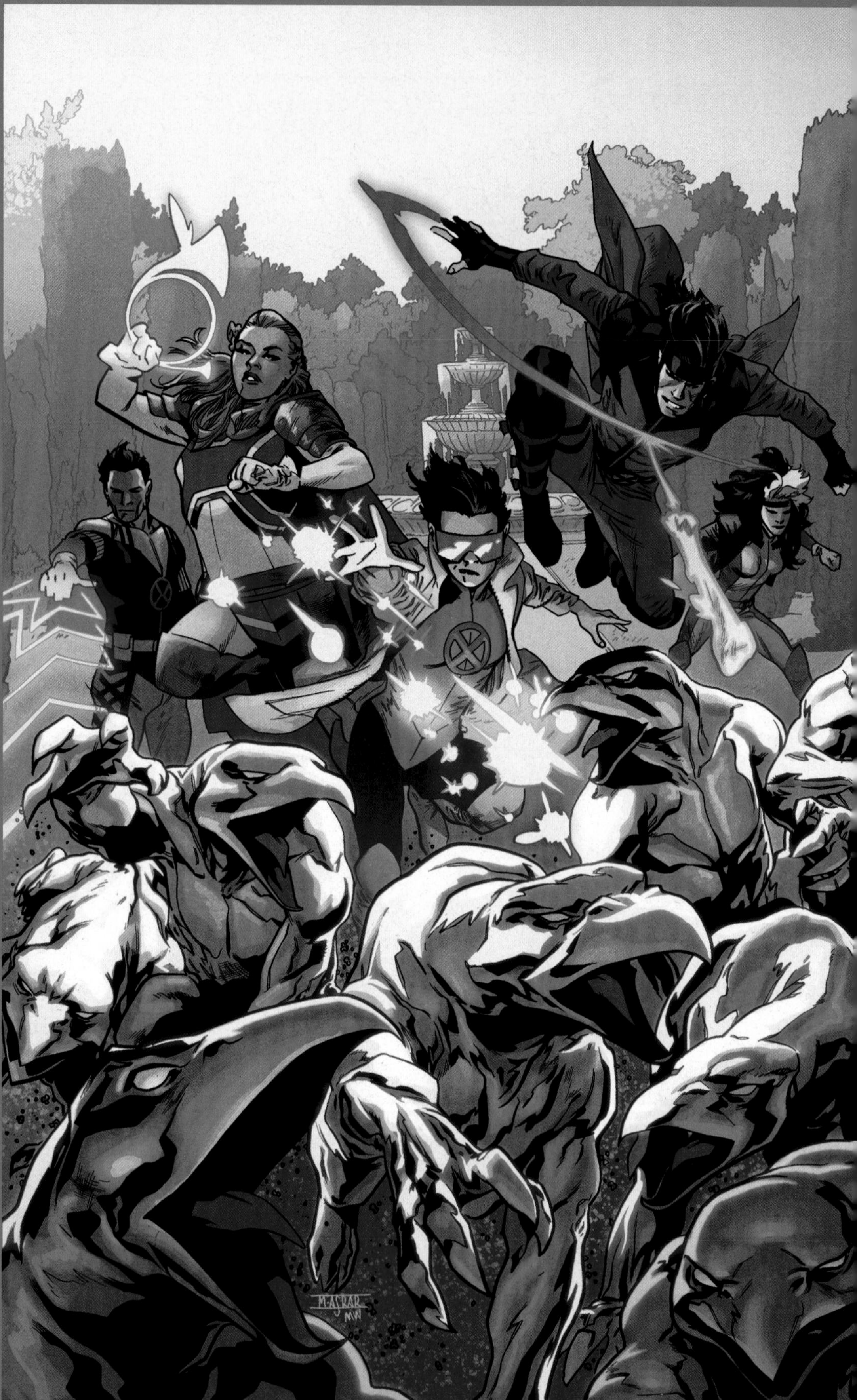
M.ASRAR
MW

The Unspeakable
and the Uneatable

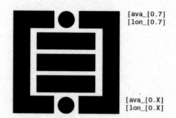

[ava_[0.7]
[lon_[0.7]

[ava_[0.X]
[lon_[0.X]

THE HUNT IS ON

EXCALIBUR reigns! With evil sorceress Morgan Le Fay defeated and Brian Braddock freed from her clutches, Apocalypse has maneuvered his pick for king onto the throne: Jamie Braddock! Jamie may be a mad choice...but Apocalypse always has his reasons.

And despite no longer being possessed, Brian's time under Morgan Le Fay's sway changed him -- into a man who unwillingly wields the Sword of Might...

Gambit

Rogue

Rictor

Jubilee

Shogo

Captain Britain

Pete Wisdom

Apocalypse

Jamie Braddock

Exodus

[ava_[0.7]...]
[lon_[0.7]...]

[Tally....HO.]

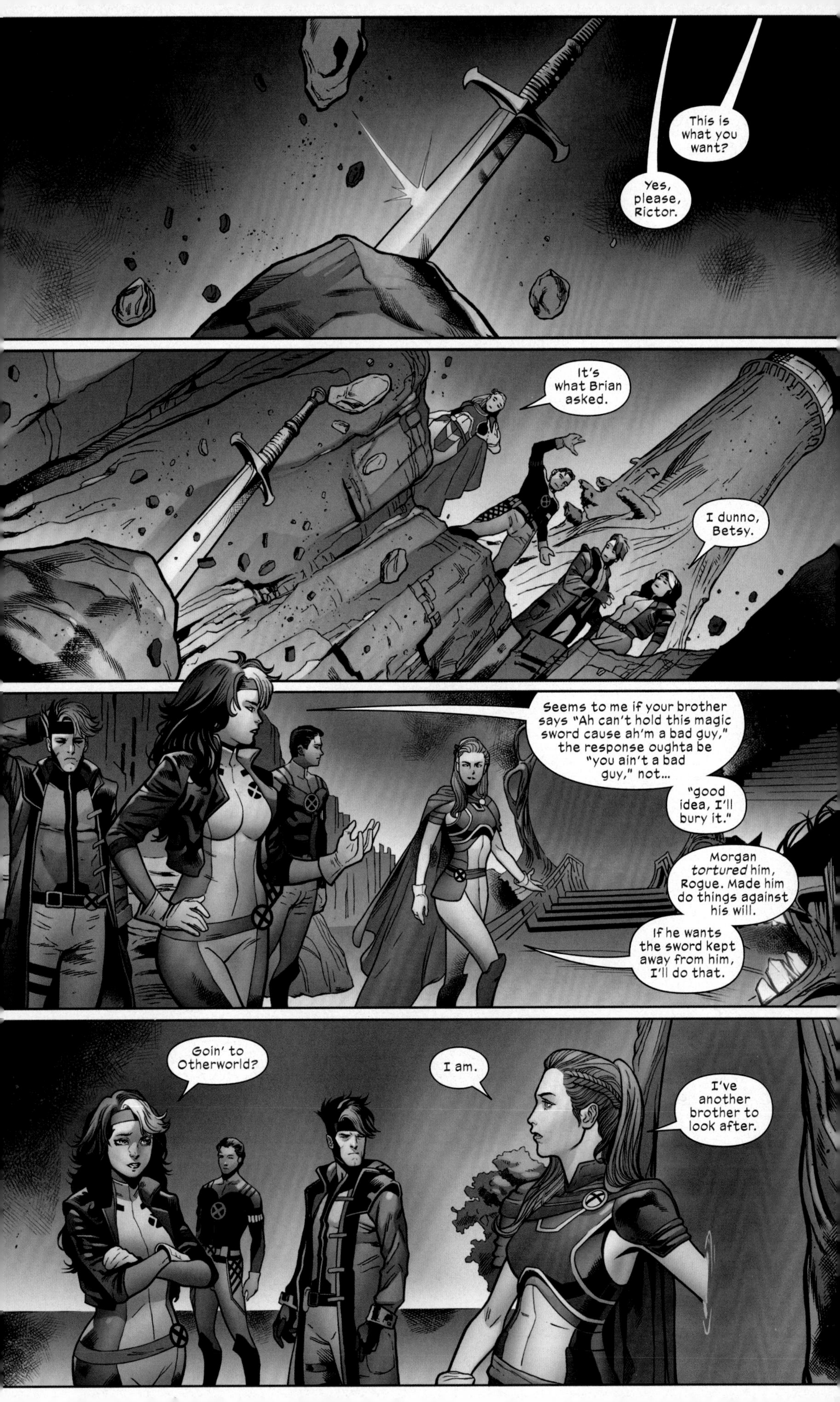
This is what you want?
Yes, please, Rictor.
It's what Brian asked.
I dunno, Betsy.
Seems to me if your brother says "Ah can't hold this magic sword cause ah'm a bad guy," the response oughta be "you ain't a bad guy," not...
"good idea, I'll bury it."
Morgan *tortured* him, Rogue. Made him do things against his will.
If he wants the sword kept away from him, I'll do that.
Goin' to Otherworld?
I am.
I've another brother to look after.

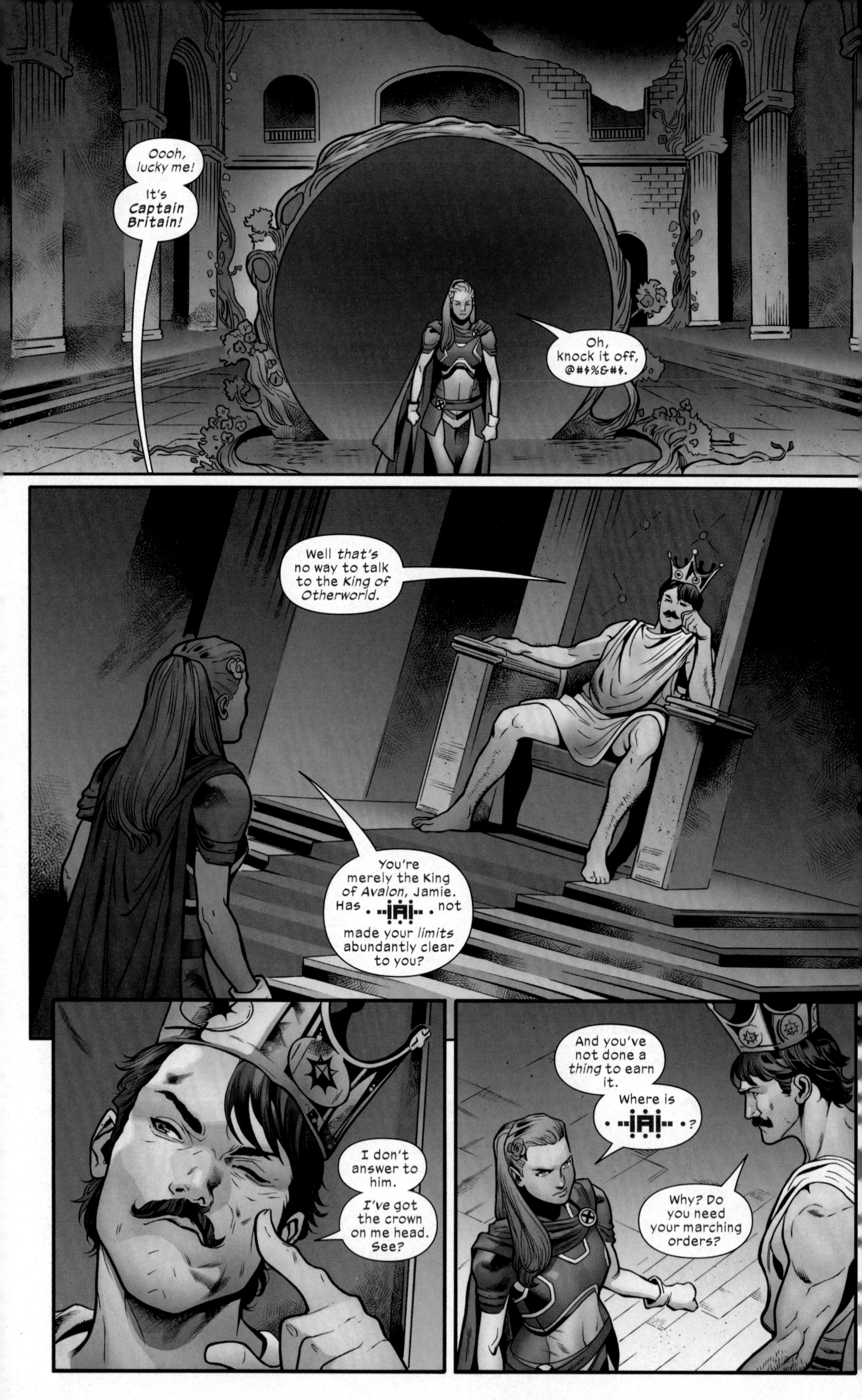

Oooh, lucky me!
It's Captain Britain!
Oh, knock it off, @#$%&#$.
Well that's no way to talk to the King of Otherworld.
You're merely the King of Avalon, Jamie. Has not made your limits abundantly clear to you?
I don't answer to him.
I've got the crown on me head. See?
And you've not done a thing to earn it.
Where is ?
Why? Do you need your marching orders?

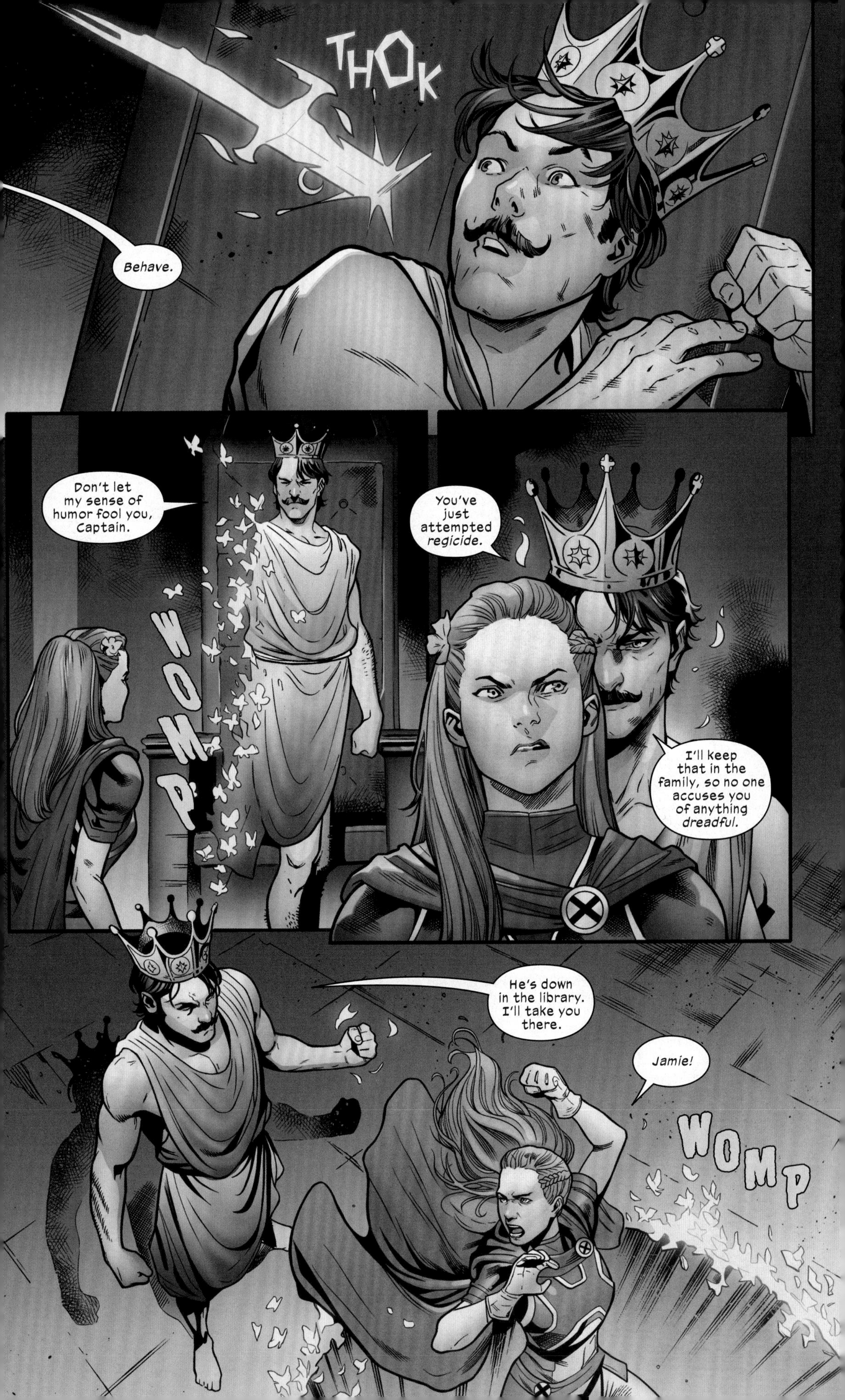
THOK
Behave.
Don't let my sense of humor fool you, Captain.
WOMP
You've just attempted *regicide*.
I'll keep that in the family, so no one accuses you of anything *dreadful*.
He's down in the library. I'll take you there.
Jamie!
WOMP

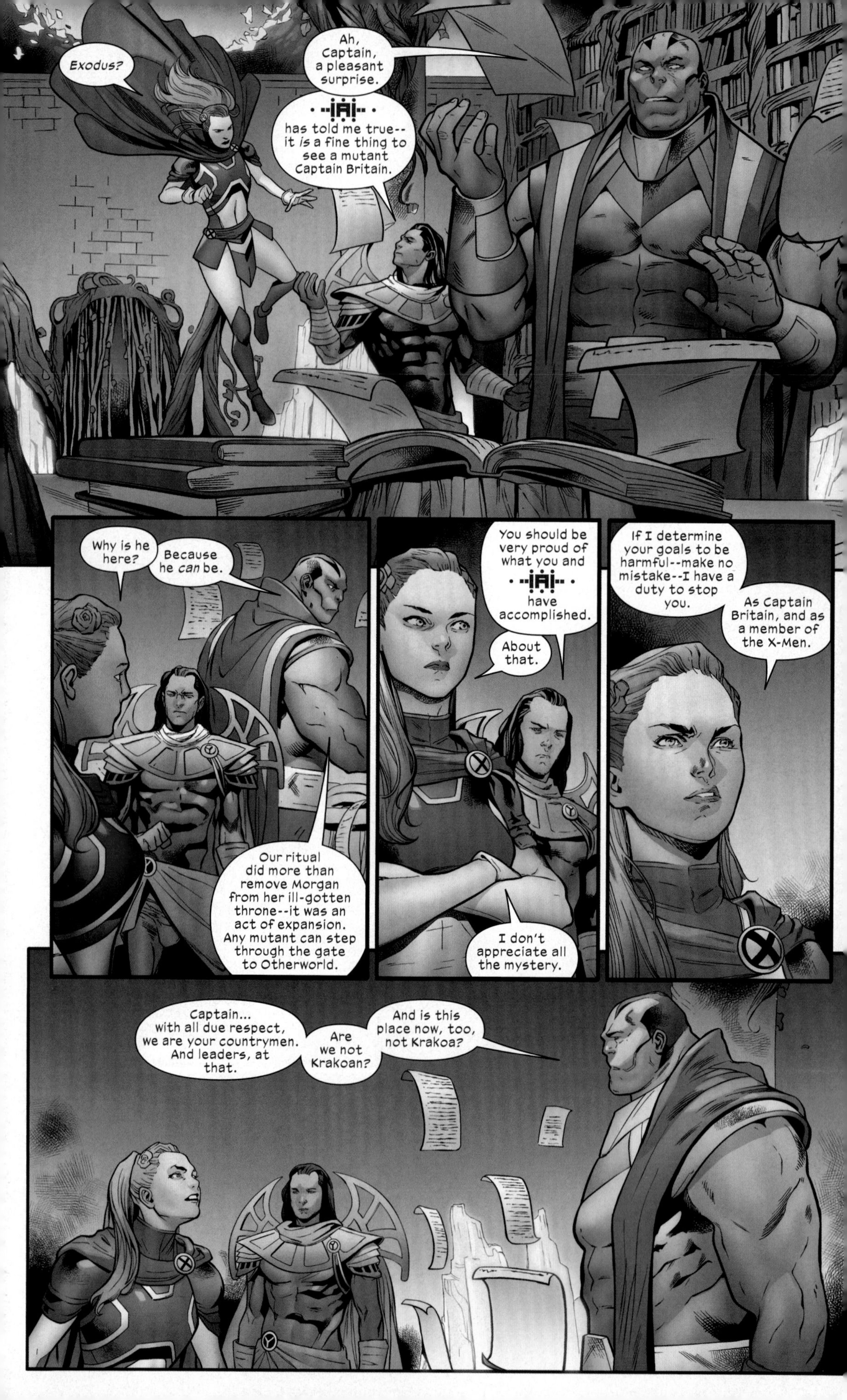
Exodus?
Ah, Captain, a pleasant surprise.
has told me true-- it *is* a fine thing to see a mutant Captain Britain.
Why is he here?
Because he *can* be.
Our ritual did more than remove Morgan from her ill-gotten throne--it was an act of expansion. Any mutant can step through the gate to Otherworld.
You should be very proud of what you and
have accomplished.
About that.
I don't appreciate all the mystery.
If I determine your goals to be harmful--make no mistake--I have a duty to stop you.
As Captain Britain, and as a member of the X-Men.
Captain... with all due respect, we are your countrymen. And leaders, at that.
Are we not Krakoan?
And is this place now, too, not Krakoa?

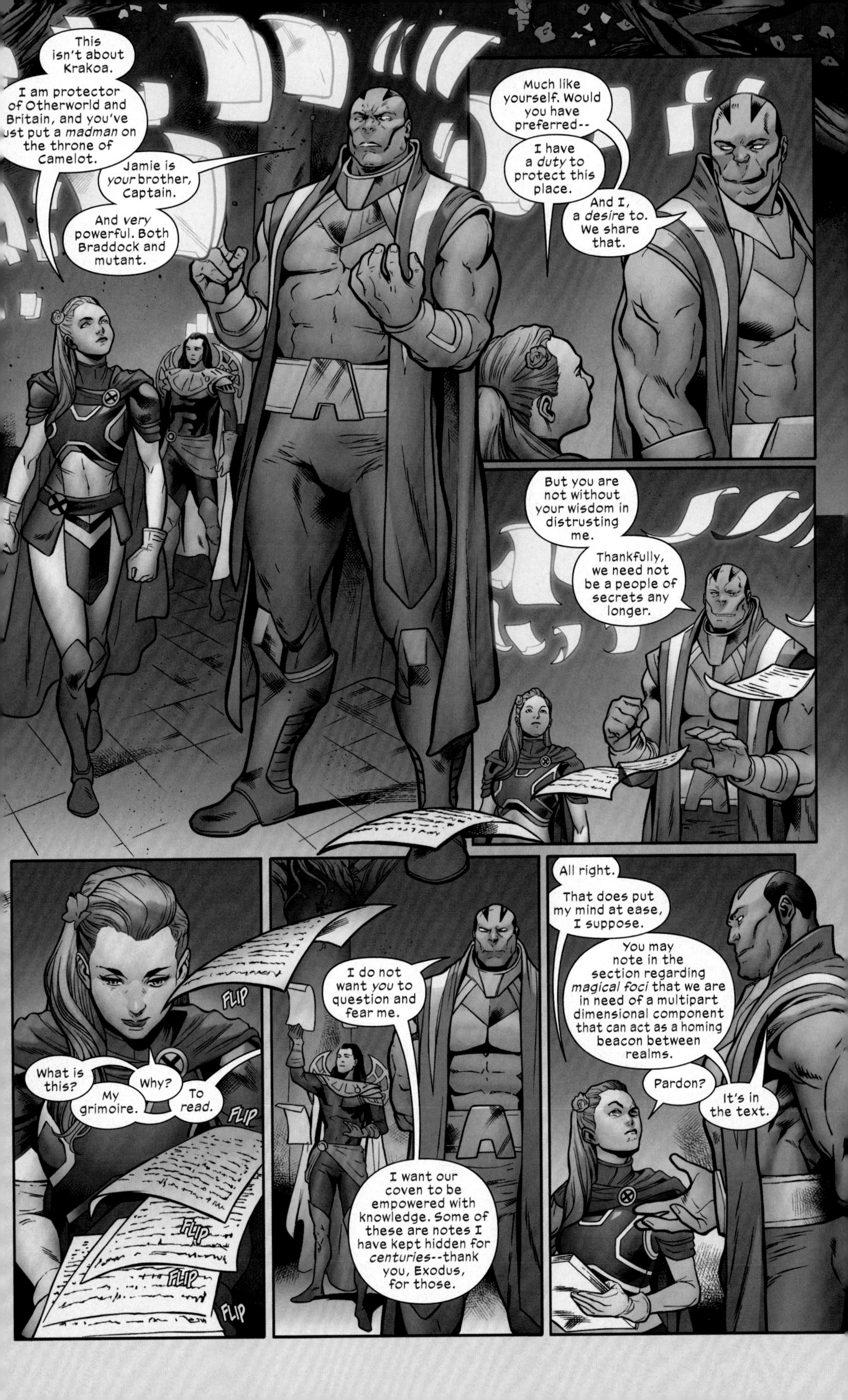
This isn't about Krakoa.
I am protector of Otherworld and Britain, and you've just put a *madman* on the throne of Camelot.
Jamie is *your* brother, Captain.
And *very* powerful. Both Braddock and mutant.
Much like yourself. Would you have preferred--
I have a *duty* to protect this place.
And I, a *desire* to. We share that.
But you are not without your wisdom in distrusting me.
Thankfully, we need not be a people of secrets any longer.
What is this?
Why?
My grimoire.
To read.
FLIP
FLIP
FLIP
FLIP
FLIP
I do not want *you* to question and fear me.
I want our coven to be empowered with knowledge. Some of these are notes I have kept hidden for *centuries*--thank you, Exodus, for those.
All right.
That does put my mind at ease, I suppose.
You may note in the section regarding *magical foci* that we are in need of a multipart dimensional component that can act as a homing beacon between realms.
Pardon?
It's in the text.

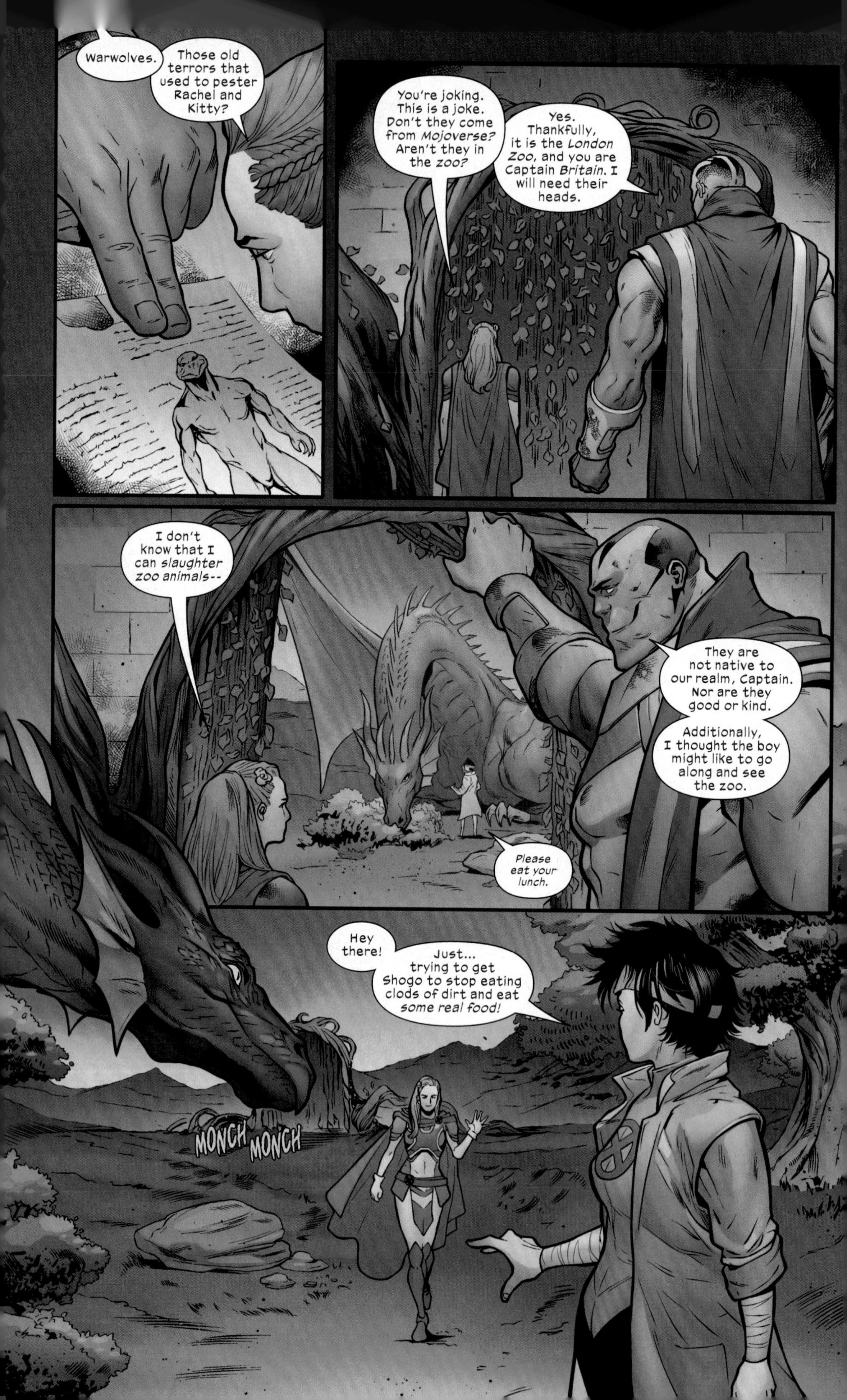
Warwolves.
Those old terrors that used to pester Rachel and Kitty?
You're joking. This is a joke. Don't they come from *Mojoverse?* Aren't they in the *zoo?*
Yes. Thankfully, it is the *London Zoo*, and you are Captain *Britain*. I will need their heads.
I don't know that I can *slaughter zoo animals*--
They are not native to our realm, Captain. Nor are they good or kind.
Additionally, I thought the boy might like to go along and see the zoo.
Please eat your lunch.
Hey there!
Just... trying to get Shogo to stop eating clods of dirt and eat *some real food!*
MONCH MONCH

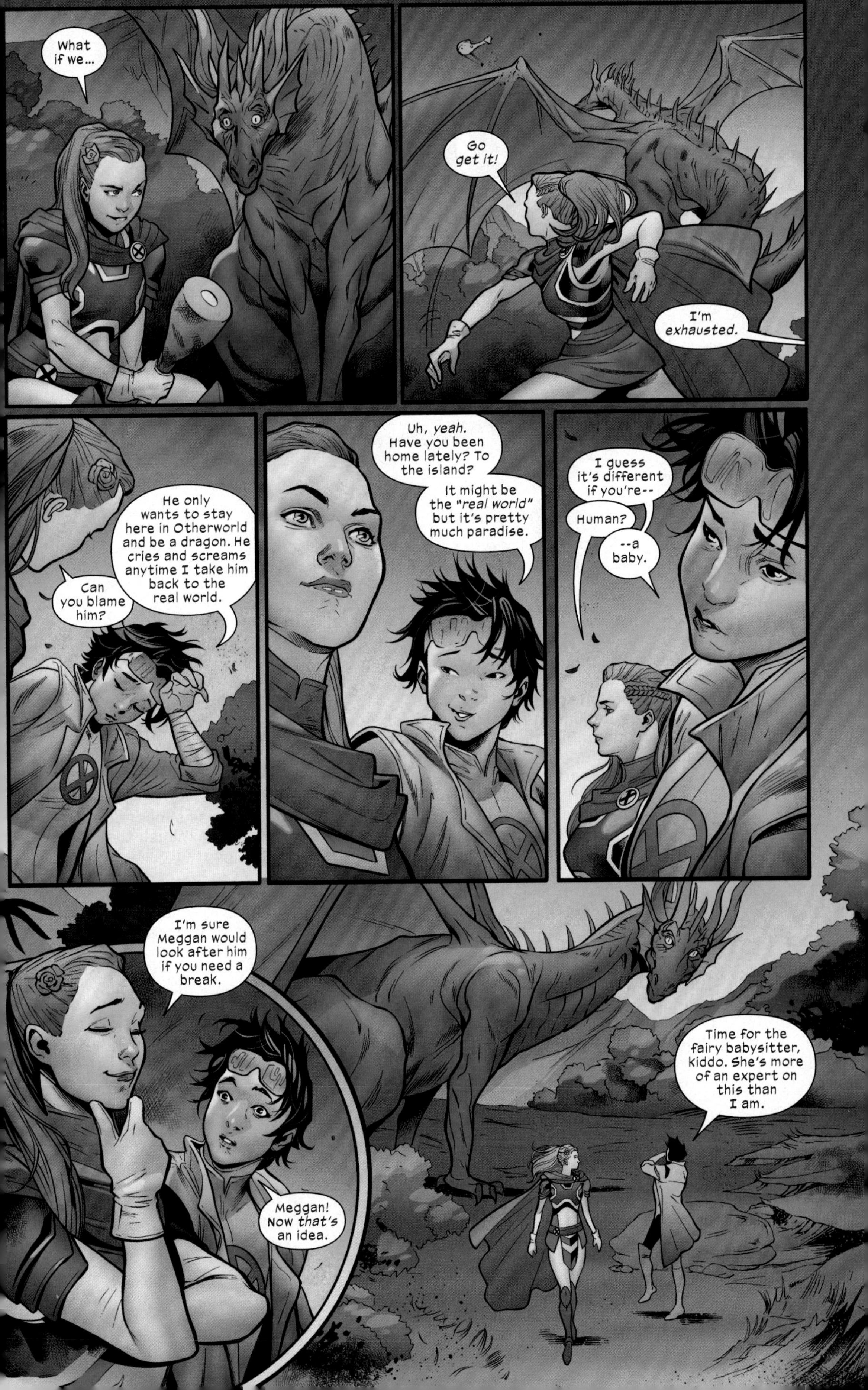
What if we...
Go get it!
I'm *exhausted.*
He only wants to stay here in Otherworld and be a dragon. He cries and screams anytime I take him back to the real world.
Can you blame him?
Uh, *yeah.* Have you been home lately? To the island?
It might be the "*real world*" but it's pretty much paradise.
I guess it's different if you're--
Human?
--a baby.
I'm sure Meggan would look after him if you need a break.
Meggan! Now *that's* an idea.
Time for the fairy babysitter, kiddo. She's more of an expert on this than I am.

FROM THE GRIMOIRE OF

EX MAGICA: BESTIARY (Fig. 23)

WARWOLF - ⫶◌̇◌̇⋔◌⫶⬚⇞⫶

Otherdimensional predator species - Genus unknown.

Once an elevated species hailing from ⬚◌̇◌̇⬚⫶◌̇⊃⇞, recent research suggests a decline in the supernatural faculties of these hybrids. A cross between humanoid and lupine, attempts were made by *Homo sapiens* to socialize and appeal to their more humanoid nature during the beasts' tenure in the London Zoo.

These amateur and somewhat mocking socialization attempts succeeded in a marked regression among the warwolves, appearing to diminish their faculties for shapeshifting, speech, and other signs of higher intelligence to incidental and reactionary at best.

Like most species, they become more violent, animalistic, and harmful under the guidance of *Homo sapiens*, losing the abilities that once made them unique.

The otherdimensional nature of their flesh is a potentially powerful conduit. [see: *EX MAGICA: ALMANAC* fig 1.]

Numbers: 5 (in captivity)

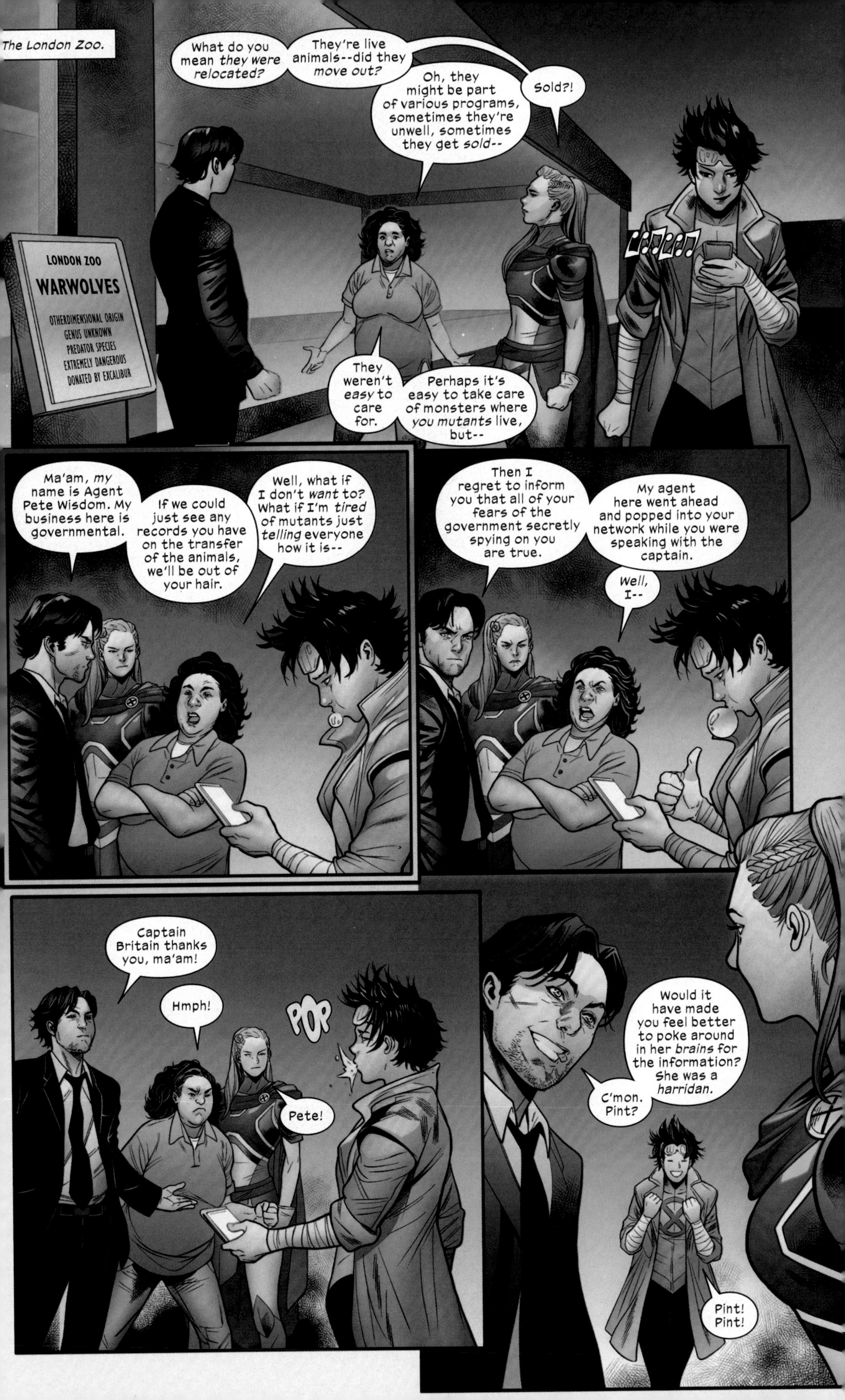
The London Zoo.
What do you mean they were relocated?
They're live animals--did they move out?
Oh, they might be part of various programs, sometimes they're unwell, sometimes they get sold--
Sold?!
LONDON ZOO
WARWOLVES
OTHERDIMENSIONAL ORIGIN
GENUS UNKNOWN
PREDATOR SPECIES
EXTREMELY DANGEROUS
DONATED BY EXCALIBUR
They weren't easy to care for.
Perhaps it's easy to take care of monsters where you mutants live, but--
Ma'am, my name is Agent Pete Wisdom. My business here is governmental.
If we could just see any records you have on the transfer of the animals, we'll be out of your hair.
Well, what if I don't want to? What if I'm tired of mutants just telling everyone how it is--
Then I regret to inform you that all of your fears of the government secretly spying on you are true.
My agent here went ahead and popped into your network while you were speaking with the captain.
Well, I--
Captain Britain thanks you, ma'am!
Hmph!
POP
Pete!
Would it have made you feel better to poke around in her brains for the information? She was a harridan.
C'mon. Pint?
Pint! Pint!

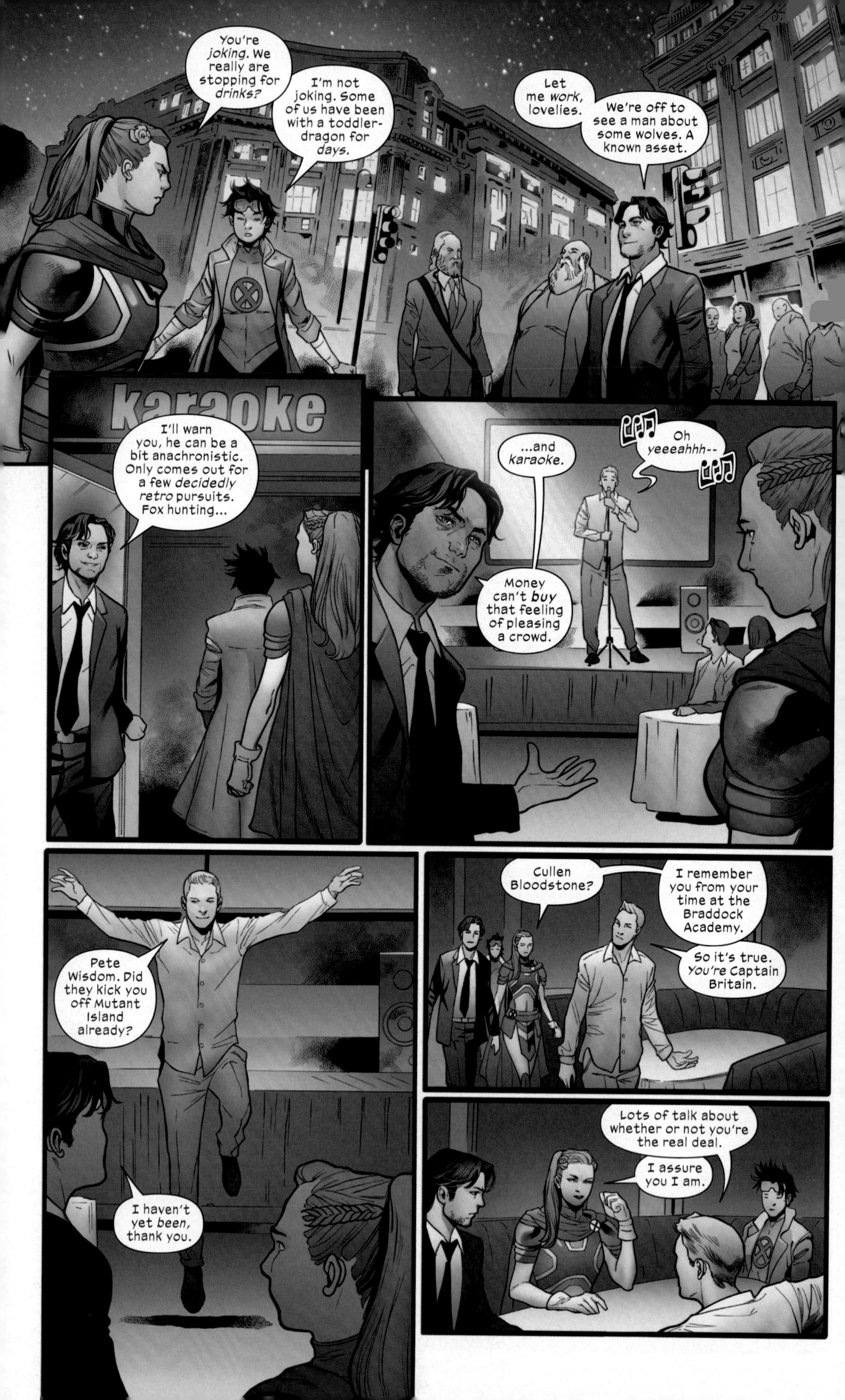
You're *joking*. We really are stopping for *drinks?*
I'm not joking. Some of us have been with a toddler-dragon for *days*.
Let me *work*, lovelies.
We're off to see a man about some wolves. A known asset.
karaoke
I'll warn you, he can be a bit anachronistic. Only comes out for a few *decidedly retro* pursuits. Fox hunting...
...and *karaoke.*
Oh *yeeeahhh--*
Money can't ***buy*** that feeling of pleasing a crowd.
Pete Wisdom. Did they kick you off Mutant Island already?
I haven't yet *been*, thank you.
Cullen Bloodstone?
I remember you from your time at the Braddock Academy.
So it's true. *You're* Captain Britain.
Lots of talk about whether or not you're the real deal.
I assure you I am.

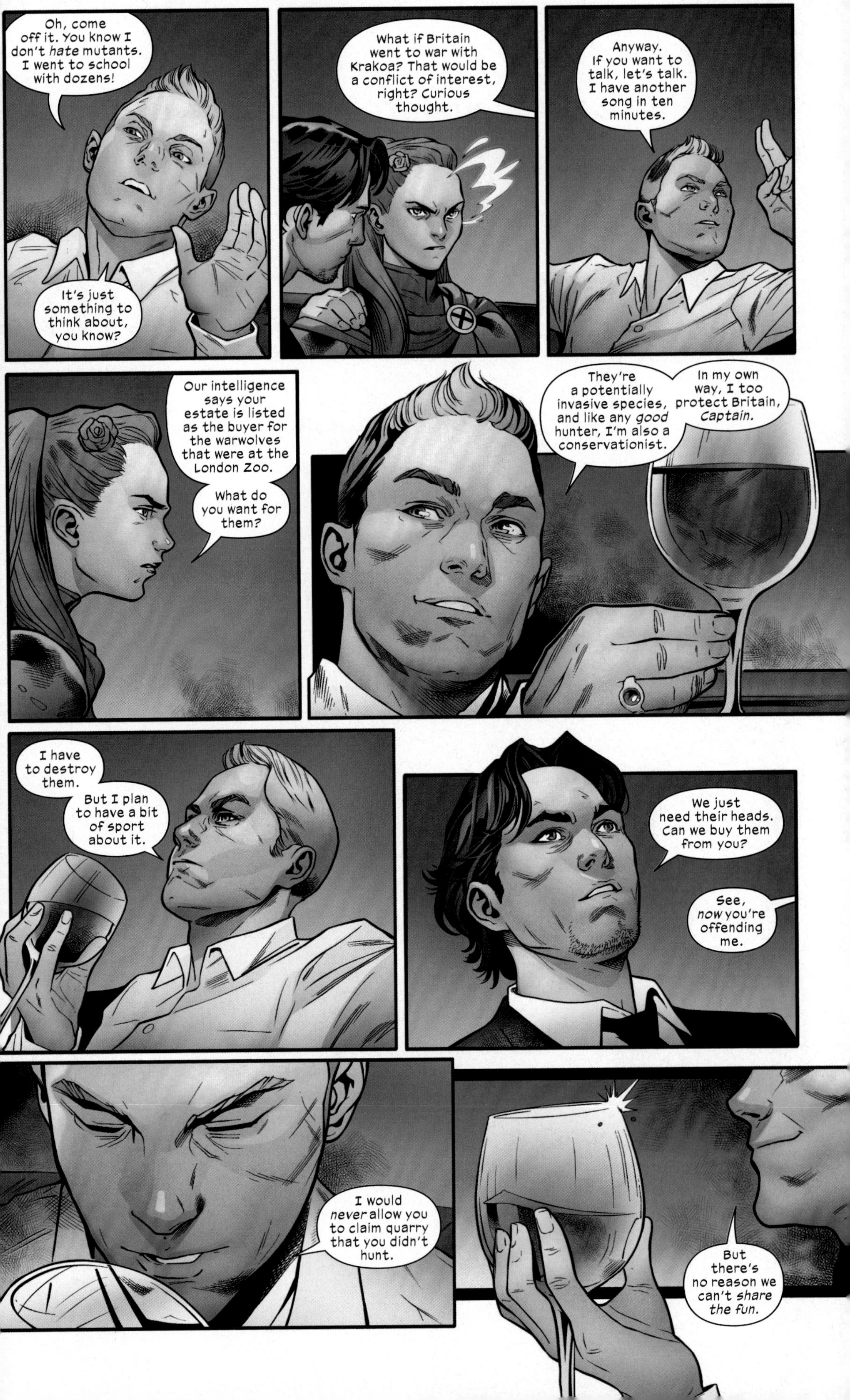
Oh, come off it. You know I don't *hate* mutants. I went to school with dozens!
It's just something to think about, you know?
What if Britain went to war with Krakoa? That would be a conflict of interest, right? Curious thought.
Anyway. If you want to talk, let's talk. I have another song in ten minutes.
Our intelligence says your estate is listed as the buyer for the warwolves that were at the London Zoo.
What do you want for them?
They're a potentially invasive species, and like any *good* hunter, I'm also a conservationist.
In my own way, I too protect Britain, *Captain.*
I have to destroy them.
But I plan to have a bit of sport about it.
We just need their heads. Can we buy them from you?
See, *now* you're offending me.
I would *never* allow you to claim quarry that you didn't hunt.
But there's no reason we can't *share* the fun.

The **Bloodstone Summer Lodge and Preserve**
cordially requests the pleasure of your company at

A Warwolf Hunt

Rules of Engagement:

· NO GATES OR KRAKOAN FLORA OF ANY
KIND ARE PERMITTED ON THE
BLOODSTONE PRESERVE

· SPORTSMANSHIP IS REQUIRED

· YOUR HOST DOES NOT TAKE KINDLY
TO UNFAIR GAMES

Champagne reception at sundown following
the first evening's activities.

Attire: Cape Casual

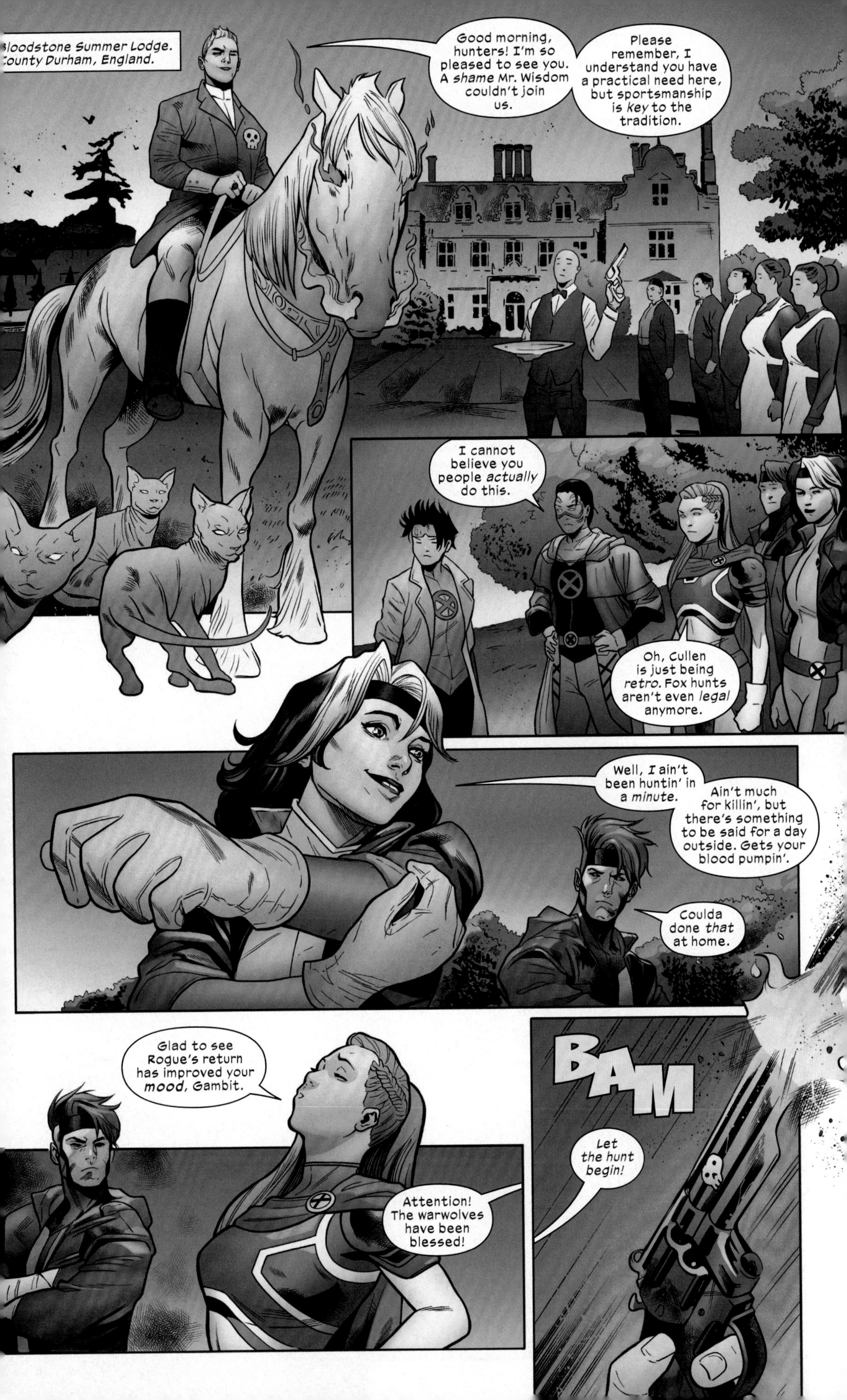
Bloodstone Summer Lodge. County Durham, England.
Good morning, hunters! I'm so pleased to see you. A shame Mr. Wisdom couldn't join us.
Please remember, I understand you have a practical need here, but sportsmanship is key to the tradition.
I cannot believe you people actually do this.
Oh, Cullen is just being retro. Fox hunts aren't even legal anymore.
Well, I ain't been huntin' in a minute.
Ain't much for killin', but there's something to be said for a day outside. Gets your blood pumpin'.
Coulda done that at home.
Glad to see Rogue's return has improved your mood, Gambit.
Attention! The warwolves have been blessed!
BAM
Let the hunt begin!

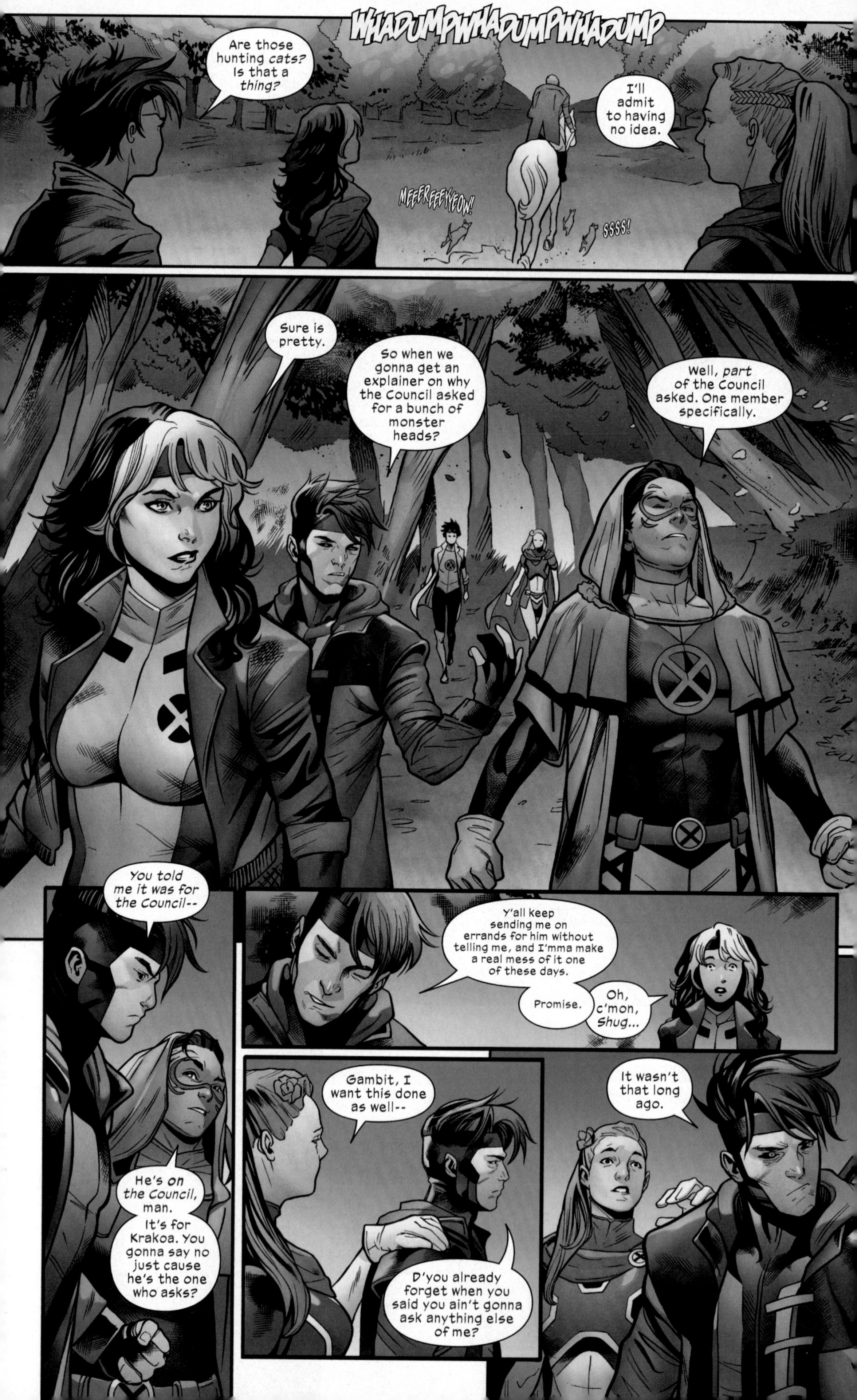
WHADUMPWHADUMPWHADUMP
Are those hunting cats? Is that a thing?
I'll admit to having no idea.
MEEERREEEYYEOW!
SSSS!
Sure is pretty.
So when we gonna get an explainer on why the Council asked for a bunch of monster heads?
Well, part of the Council asked. One member specifically.
You told me it was for the Council--
He's on the Council, man.
It's for Krakoa. You gonna say no just cause he's the one who asks?
Y'all keep sending me on errands for him without telling me, and I'mma make a real mess of it one of these days.
Promise.
Oh, c'mon, Shug...
Gambit, I want this done as well--
D'you already forget when you said you ain't gonna ask anything else of me?
It wasn't that long ago.

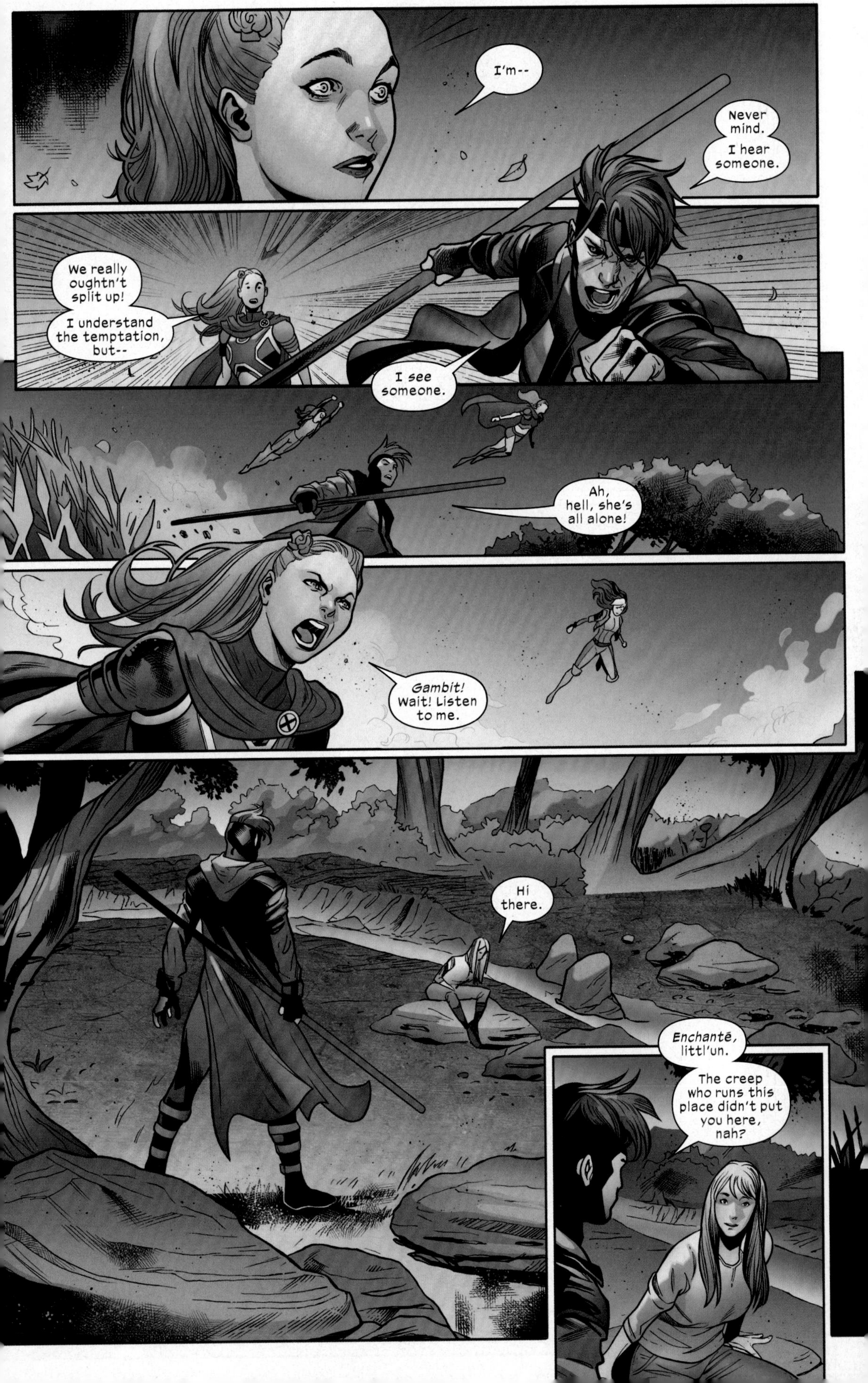
I'm--
Never mind.
I hear someone.
We really oughtn't split up!
I understand the temptation, but--
I see someone.
Ah, hell, she's all alone!
Gambit! Wait! Listen to me.
Hi there.
Enchanté, littl'un.
The creep who runs this place didn't put you here, nah?

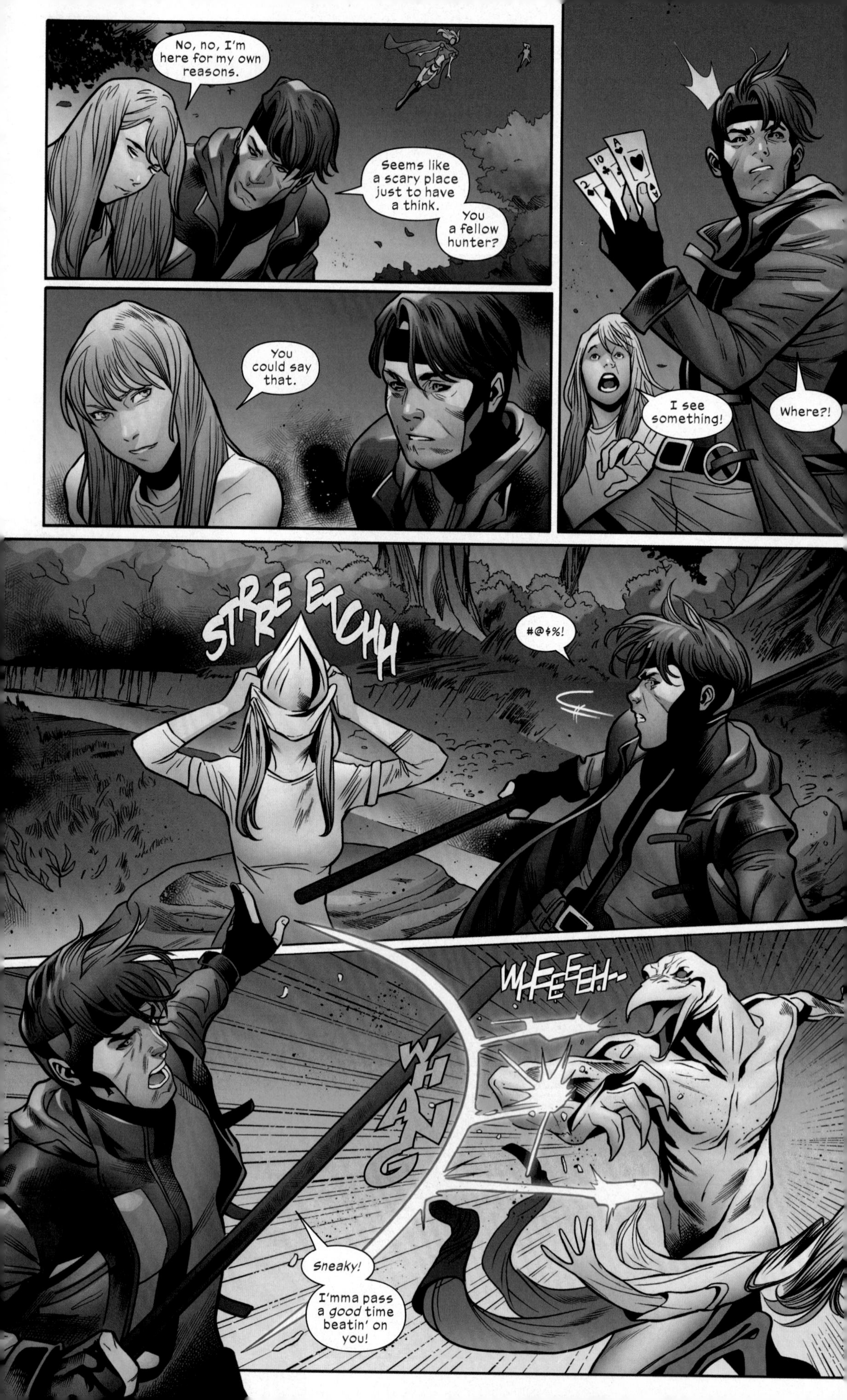

No, no, I'm here for my own reasons.
Seems like a scary place just to have a think.
You a fellow hunter?
You could say that.
I see something!
Where?!
STRREEETCHH
#@$%!
WHEEEH--
WHANG
Sneaky!
I'mma pass a *good* time beatin' on you!

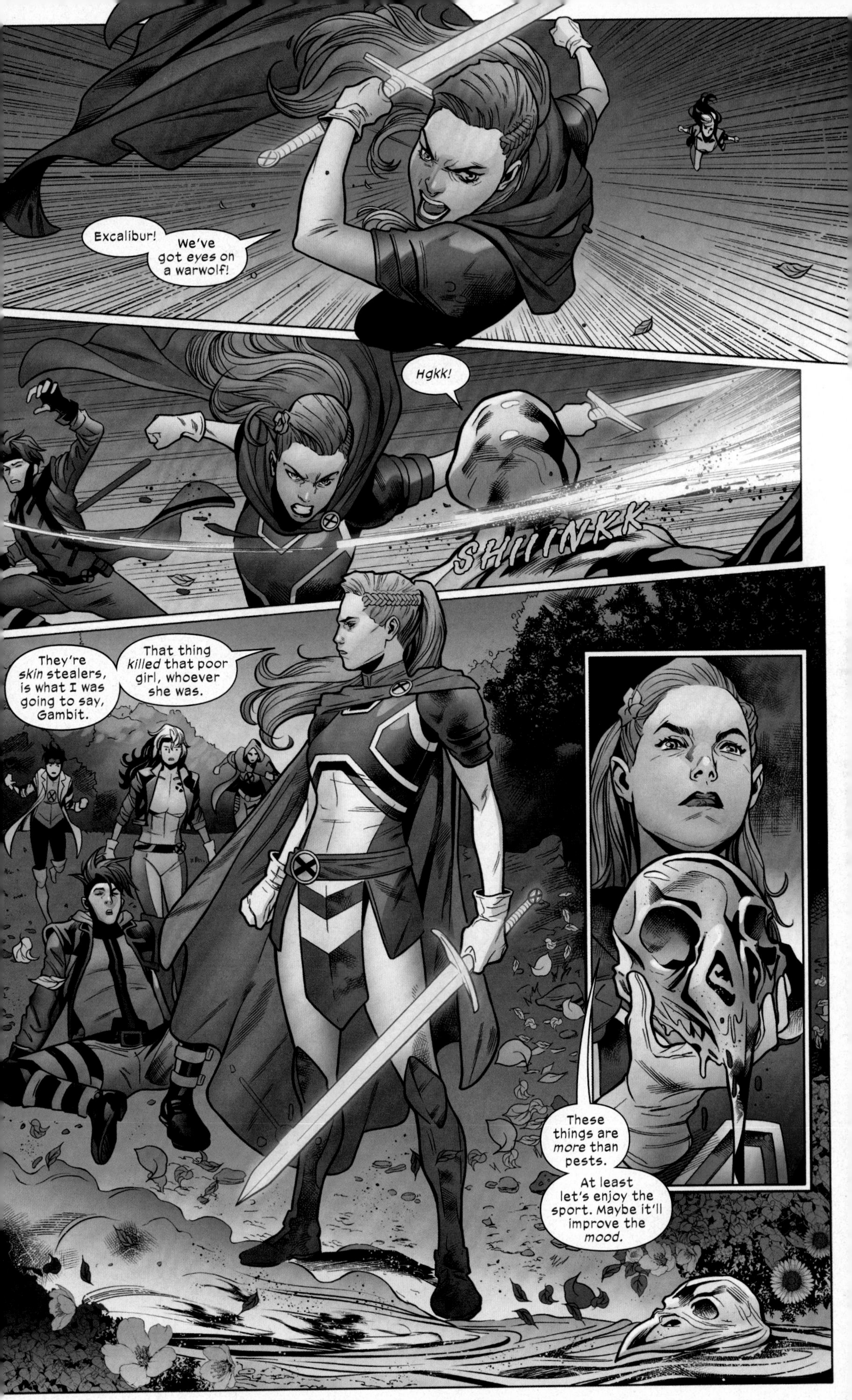
Excalibur! We've got eyes on a warwolf!
Hgkk!
SHIIINKK
They're skin stealers, is what I was going to say, Gambit.
That thing killed that poor girl, whoever she was.
These things are more than pests.
At least let's enjoy the sport. Maybe it'll improve the mood.

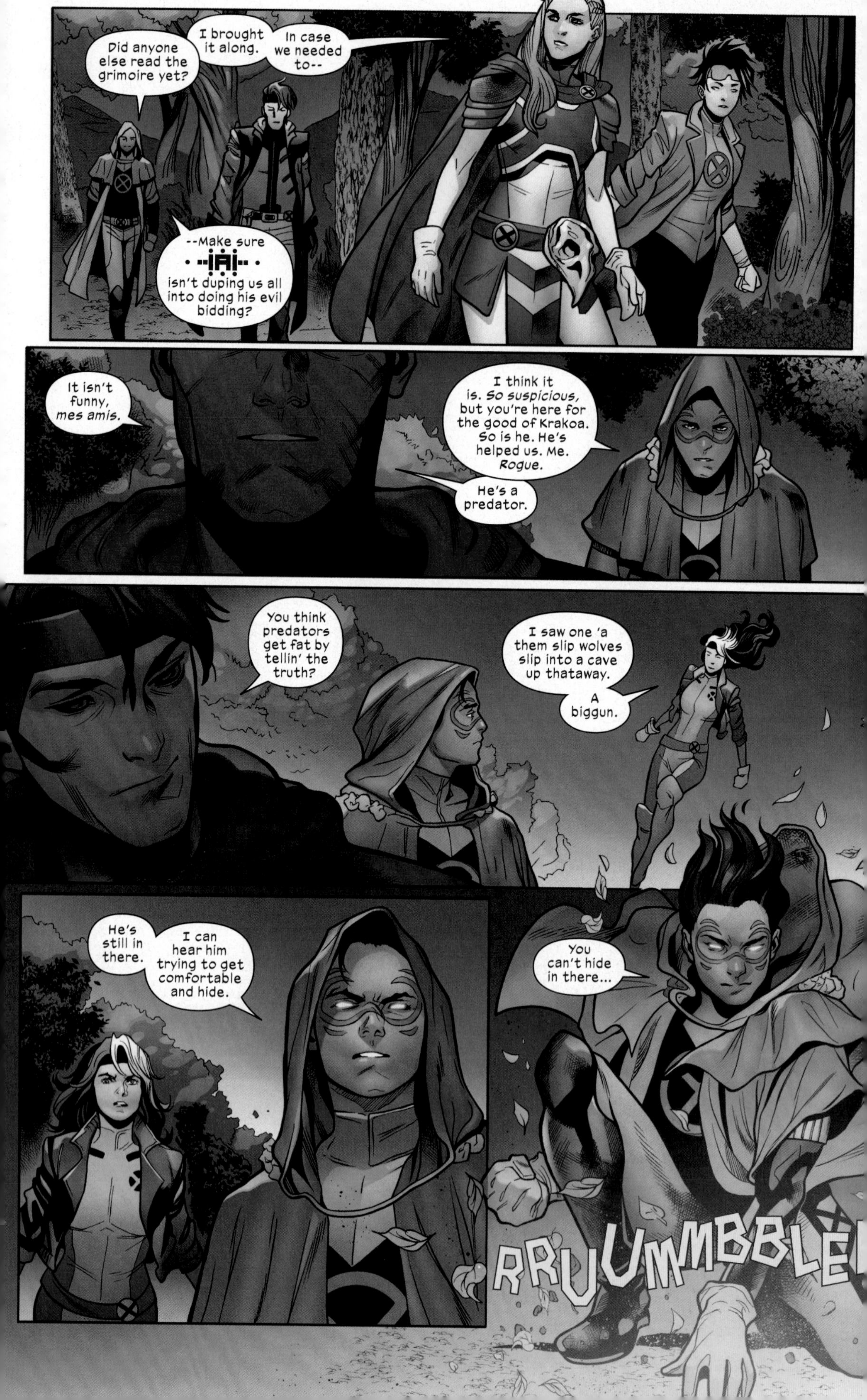
Did anyone else read the grimoire yet?
I brought it along.
In case we needed to--
--Make sure
isn't duping us all into doing his evil bidding?
It isn't funny, mes amis.
I think it is. So suspicious, but you're here for the good of Krakoa. So is he. He's helped us. Me. Rogue.
He's a predator.
You think predators get fat by tellin' the truth?
I saw one 'a them slip wolves slip into a cave up thataway.
A biggun.
He's still in there.
I can hear him trying to get comfortable and hide.
You can't hide in there...
RRUUMMBBLE

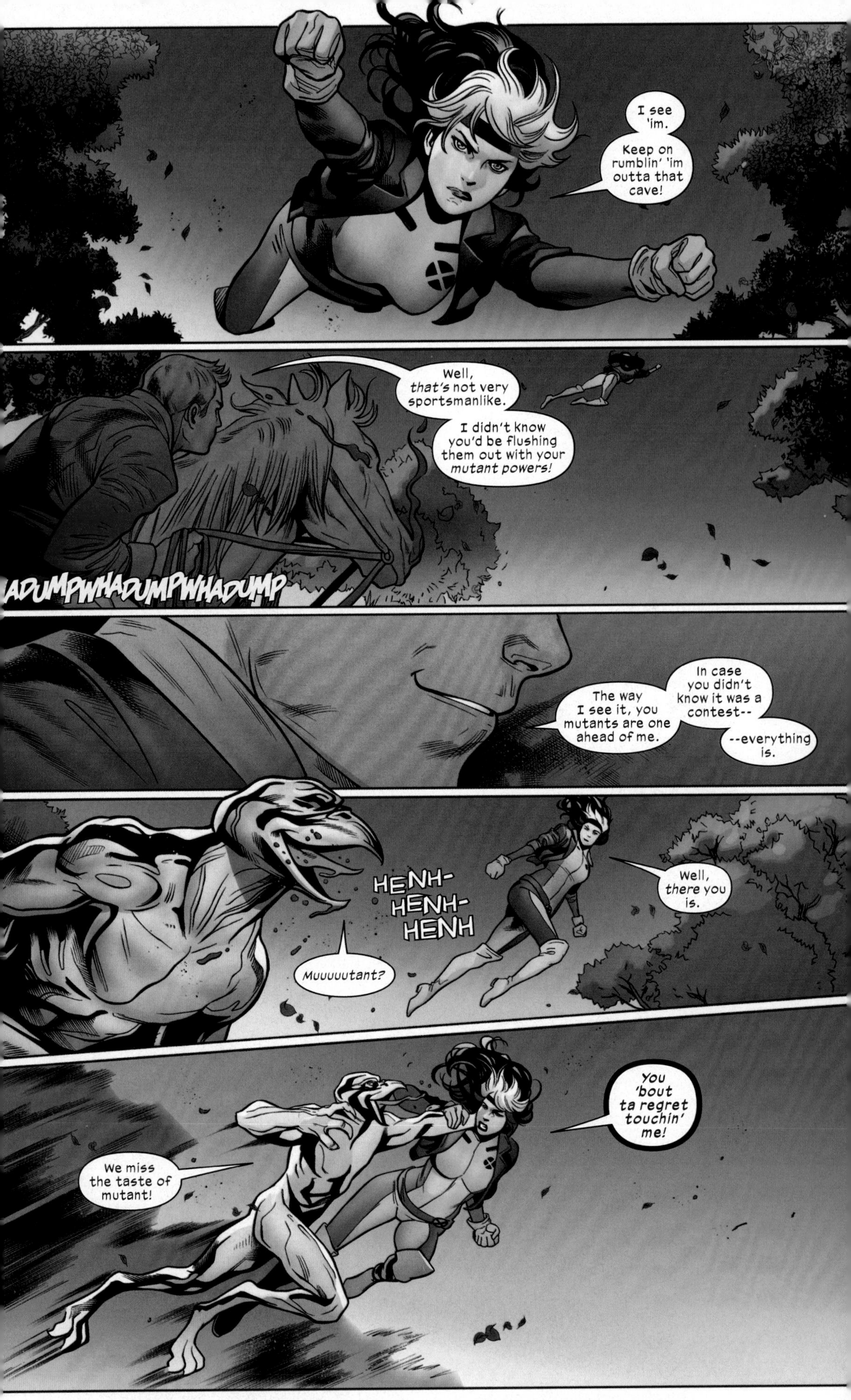

I see 'im.
Keep on rumblin' 'im outta that cave!
Well, *that's* not very sportsmanlike.
I didn't know you'd be flushing them out with your *mutant powers!*
ADUMPWHADUMPWHADUMP
The way I see it, you mutants are one ahead of me.
In case you didn't know it was a contest--
--everything is.
HENH-HENH-HENH
Well, *there* you is.
Muuuuutant?
You 'bout ta regret touchin' me!
We miss the taste of mutant!

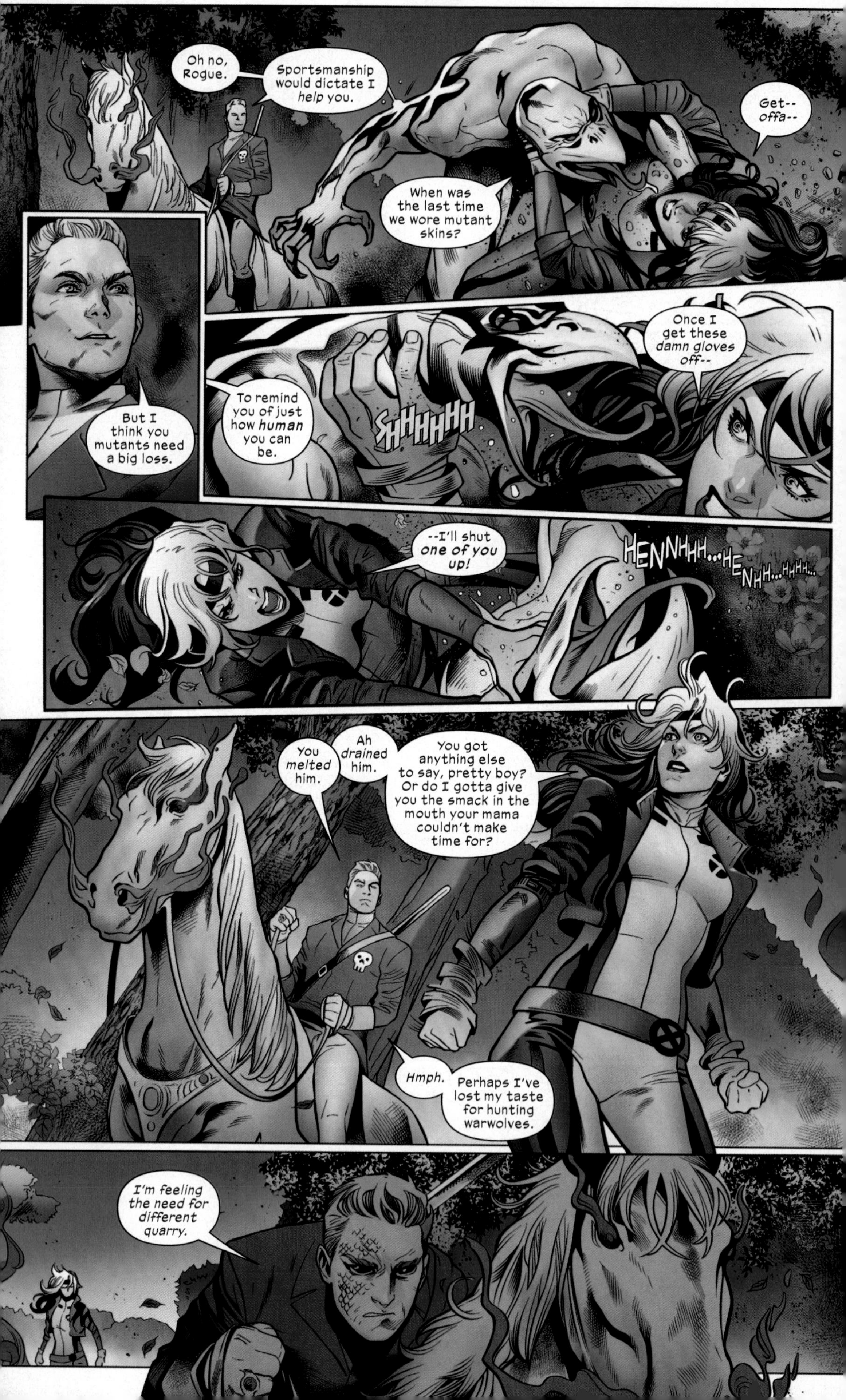

Oh no, Rogue.
Sportsmanship would dictate I *help* you.
Get-- offa--
When was the last time we wore mutant skins?
But I think you mutants need a big loss.
To remind you of just how *human* you can be.
Once I get these damn gloves off--
SHHHHHH
--I'll shut *one of you* up!
HENNHHH...HENHH...HHHH...
You melted him.
Ah *drained* him.
You got anything else to say, pretty boy? Or do I gotta give you the smack in the mouth your mama couldn't make time for?
Hmph.
Perhaps I've lost my taste for hunting warwolves.
I'm feeling the need for different quarry.

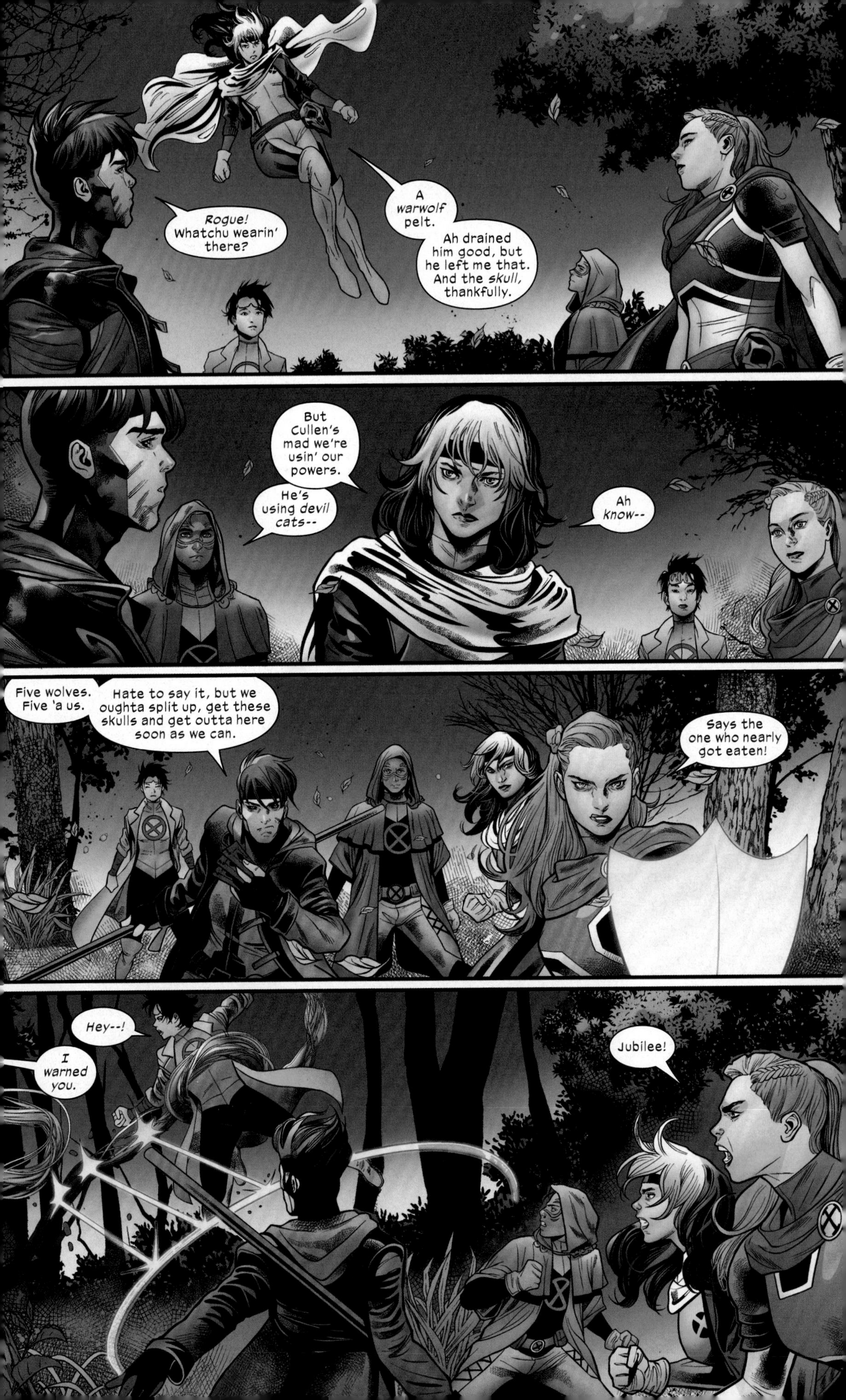
Rogue! Whatchu wearin' there?
A warwolf pelt.
Ah drained him good, but he left me that. And the skull, thankfully.
But Cullen's mad we're usin' our powers.
He's using devil cats--
Ah know--
Five wolves. Five 'a us.
Hate to say it, but we oughta split up, get these skulls and get outta here soon as we can.
Says the one who nearly got eaten!
Hey--!
I warned you.
Jubilee!

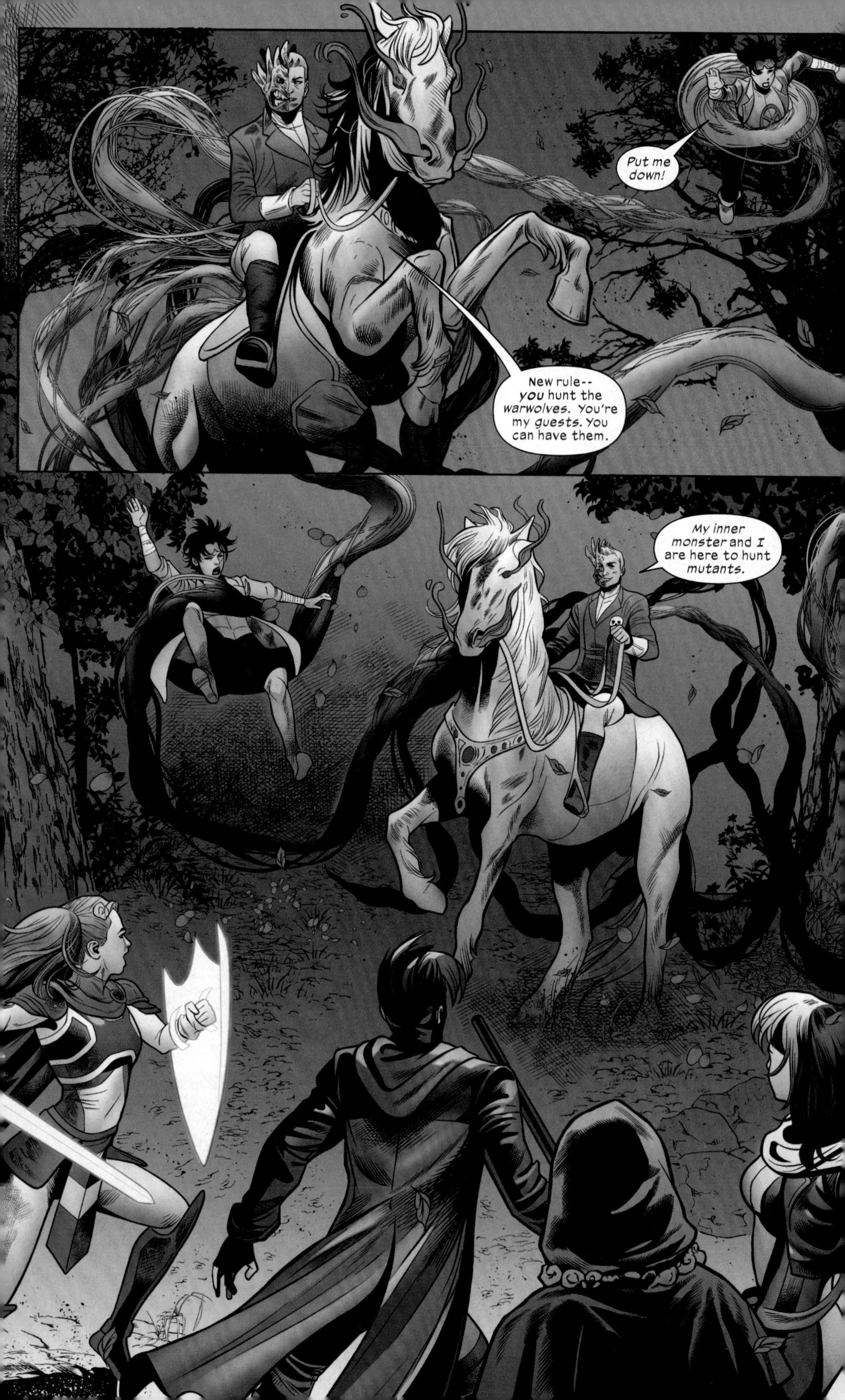
Put me down!
New rule-- you hunt the warwolves. You're my guests. You can have them.
My inner monster and I are here to hunt mutants.

[dawn_of_x]

[kra_]
[koa_]

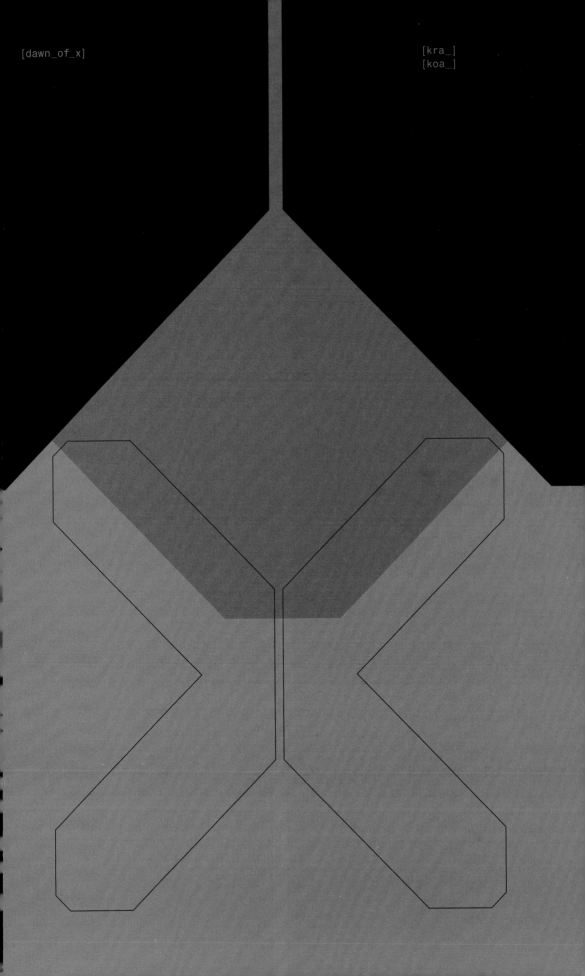

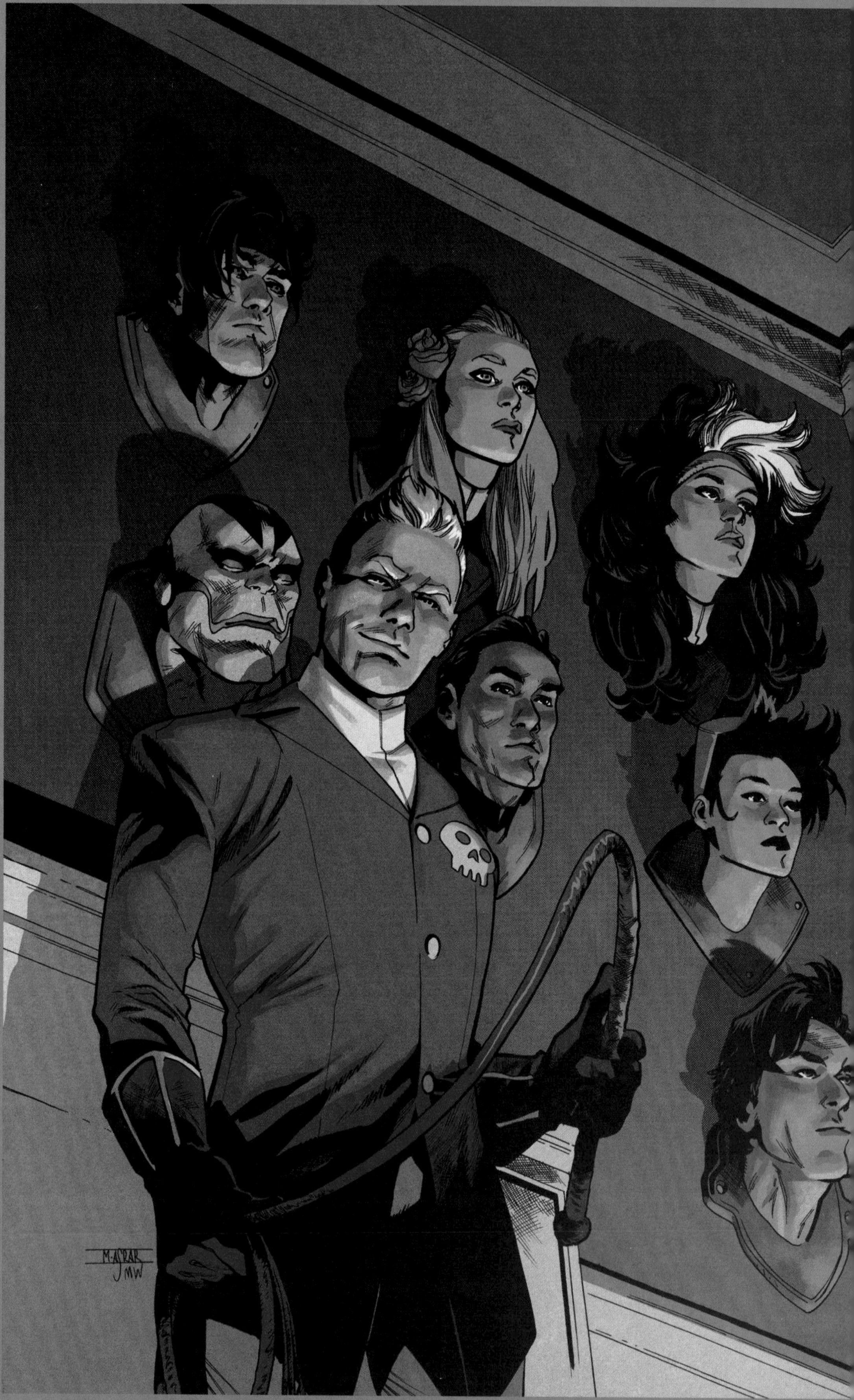
M-ASRAR
MW

The Unspeakable
and the Uneatable II

[dawn_of_x]

[kra_]
[koa_]

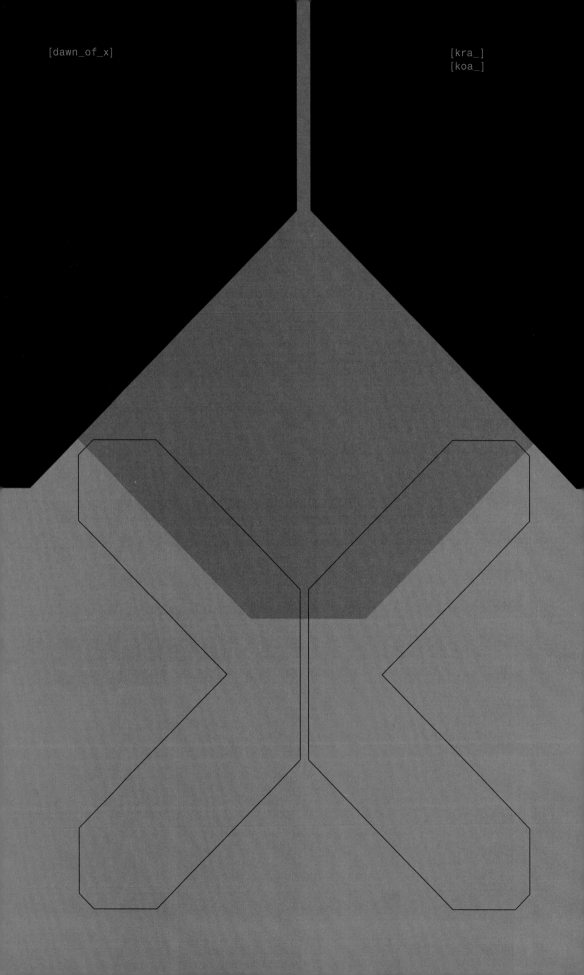

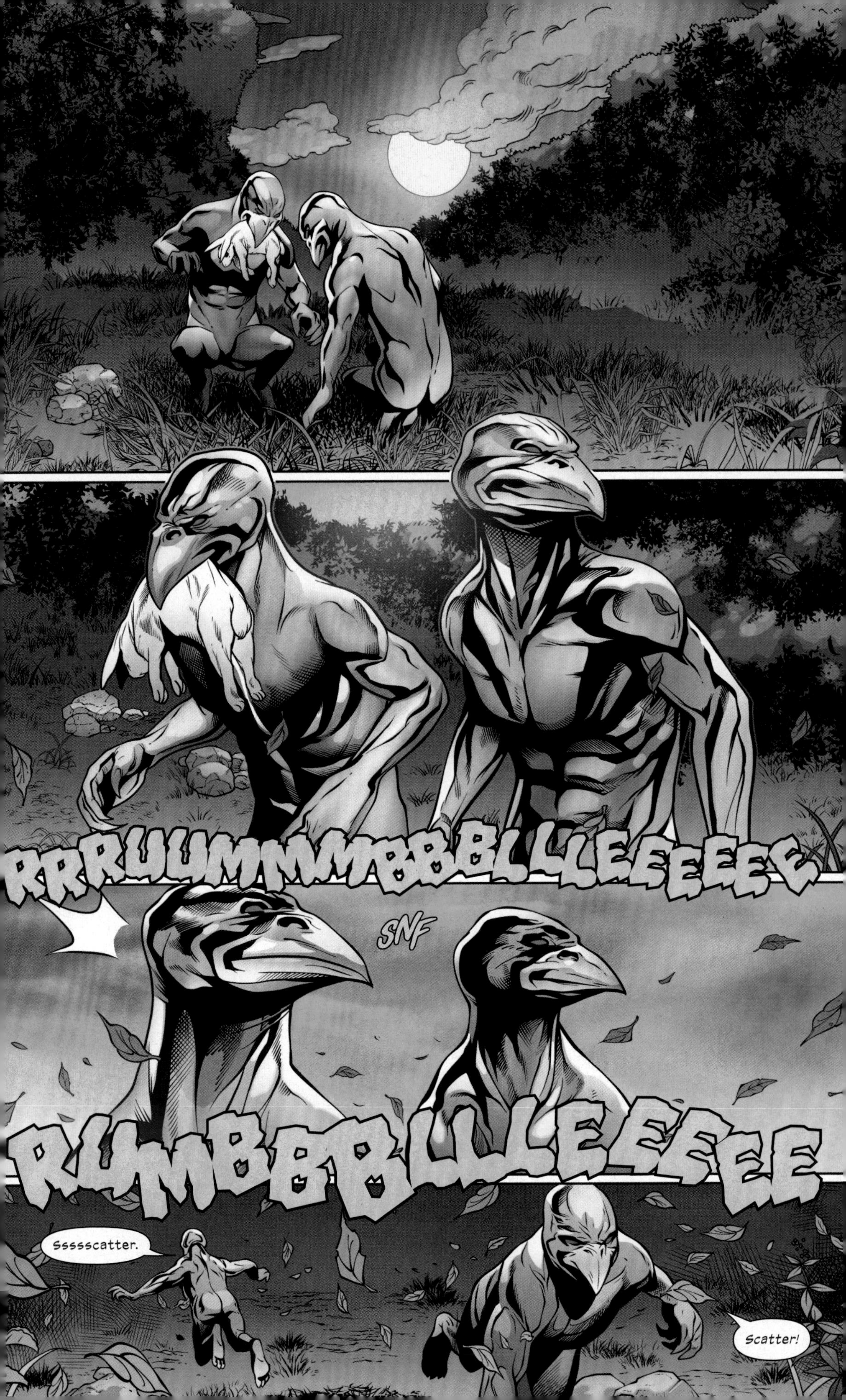
RRRUUMMMBBBLLEEEEEE
SNF
RUMBBBLLLEEEEE
Ssssscatter.
Scatter!

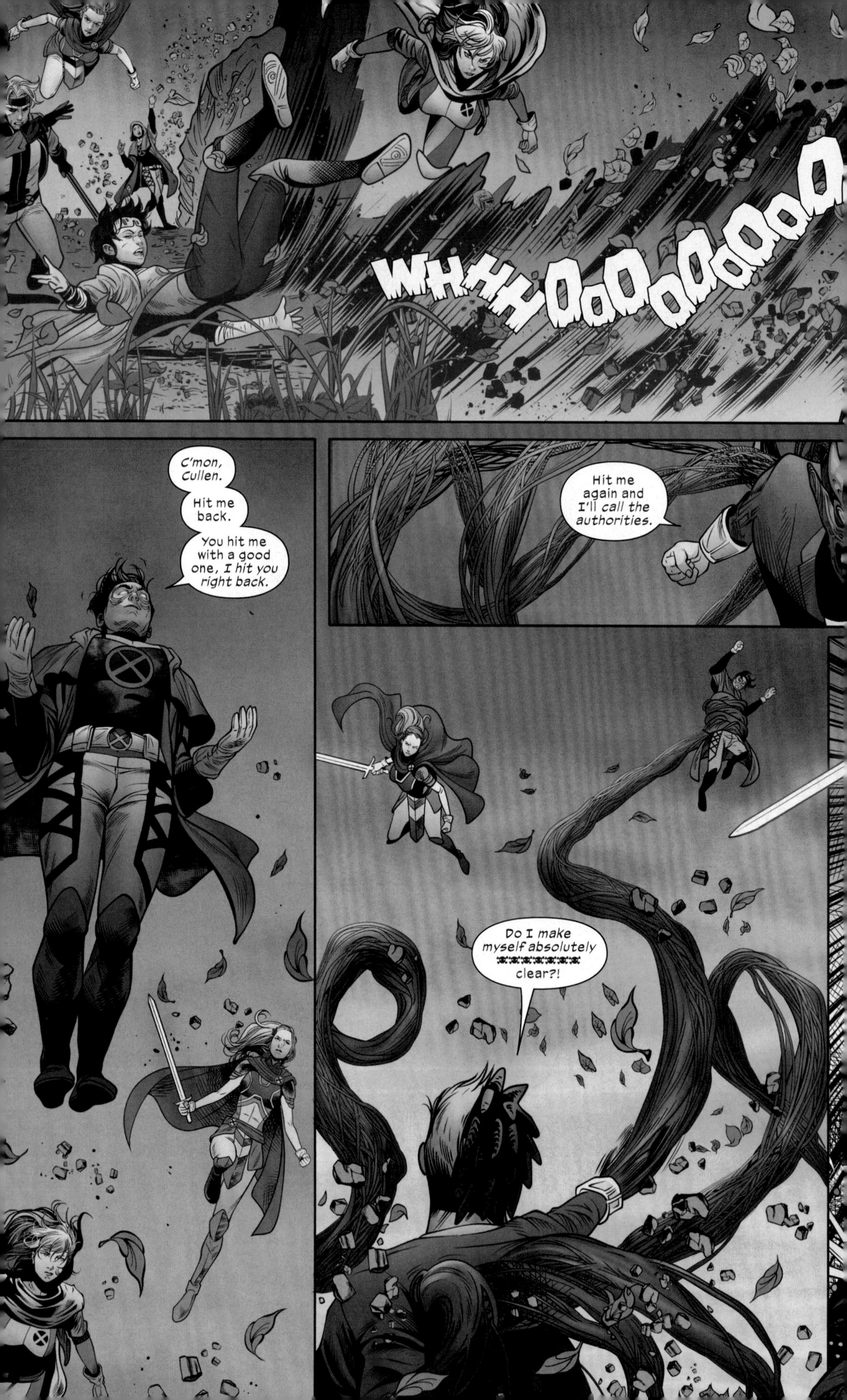
WHHHOOOOOOOOOOO
C'mon, Cullen.
Hit me back.
You hit me with a good one, I hit you right back.
Hit me again and I'll call the authorities.
Do I make myself absolutely ☠☠☠☠☠☠☠ clear?!

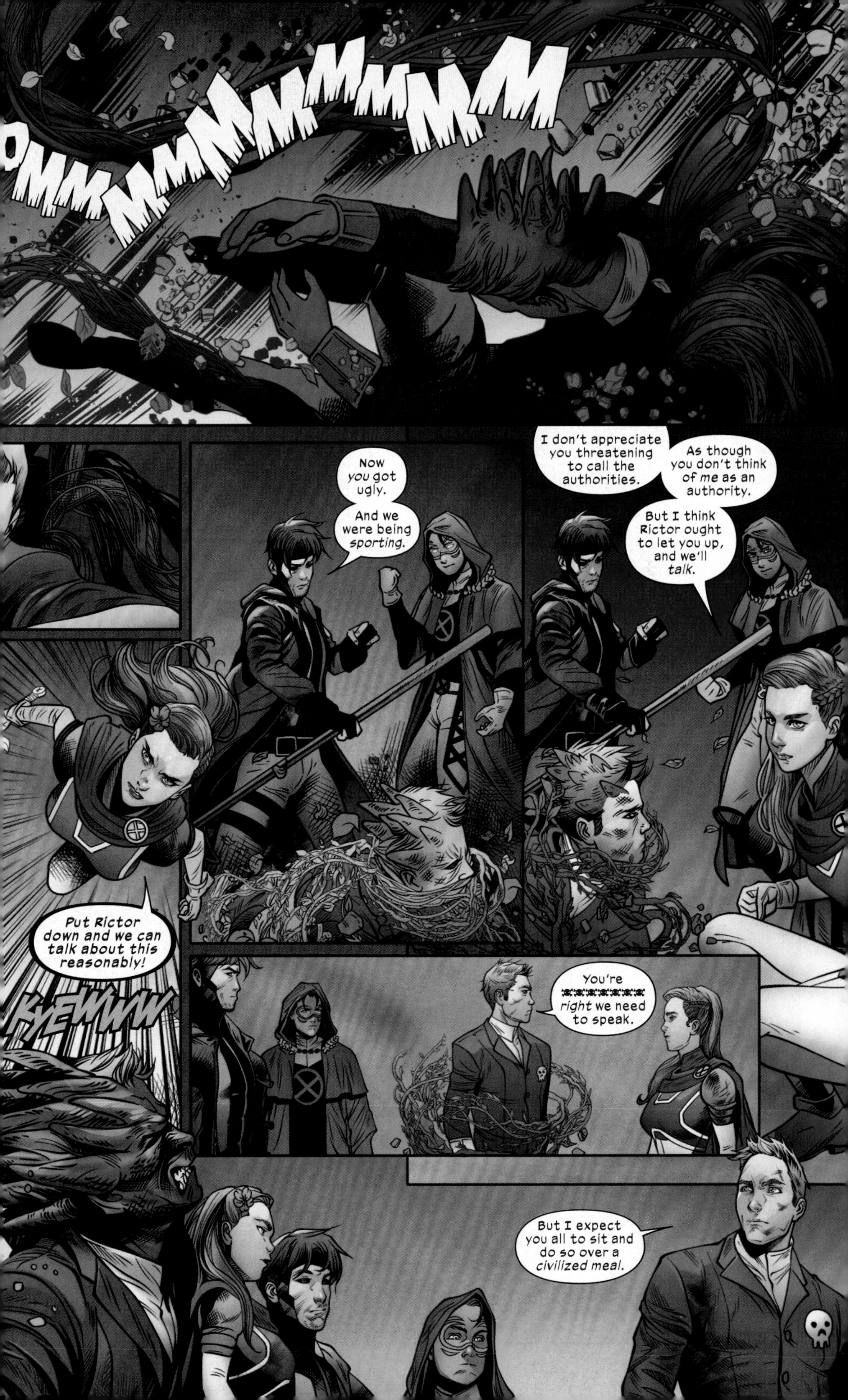
Now you got ugly.
And we were being sporting.
I don't appreciate you threatening to call the authorities.
As though you don't think of me as an authority.
But I think Rictor ought to let you up, and we'll talk.
Put Rictor down and we can talk about this reasonably!
You're
right we need to speak.
But I expect you all to sit and do so over a civilized meal.

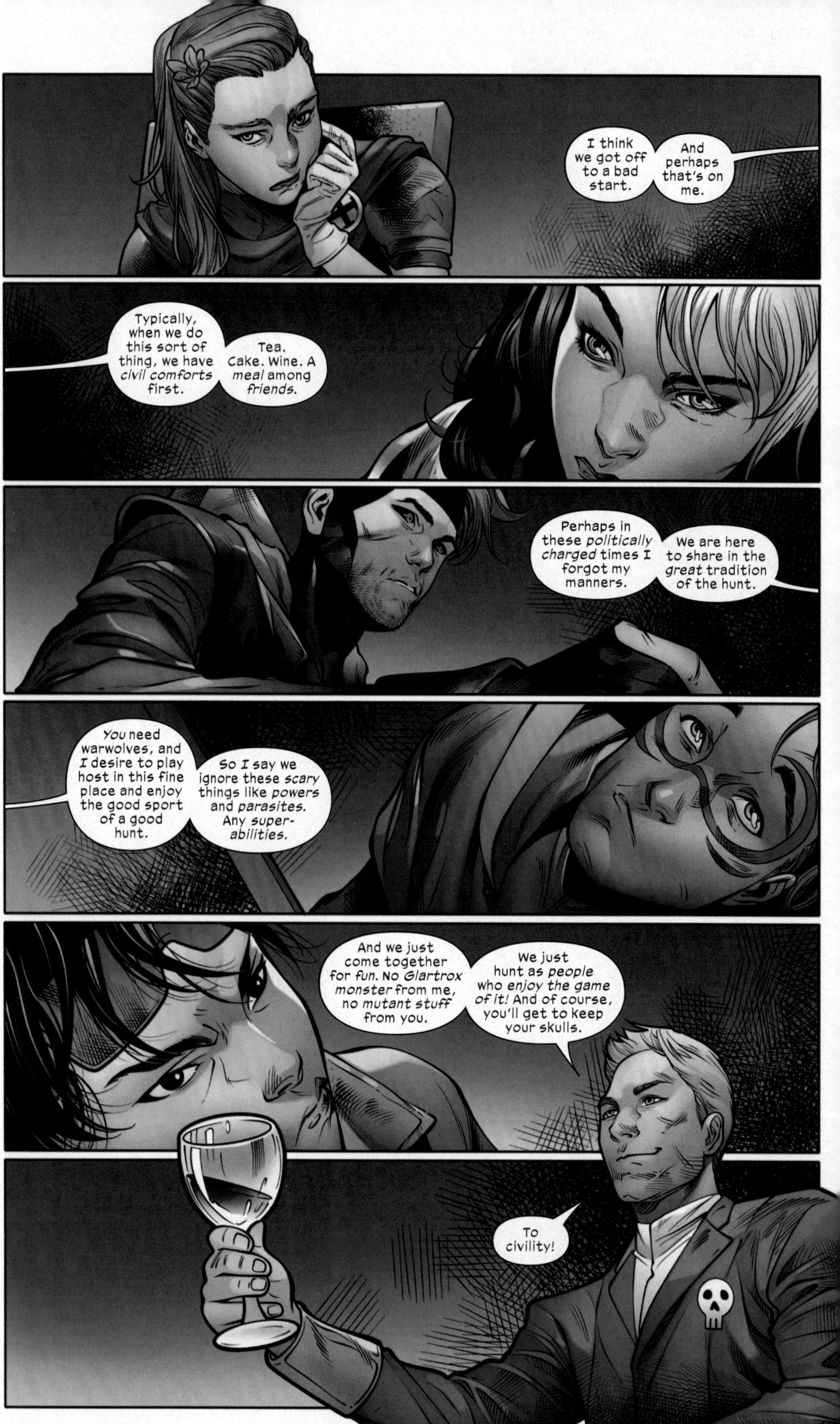

I think we got off to a bad start.
And perhaps that's on me.
Typically, when we do this sort of thing, we have *civil comforts* first.
Tea. Cake. Wine. A *meal* among *friends*.
Perhaps in these *politically charged* times I forgot my manners.
We are here to share in the *great* tradition of the hunt.
You need warwolves, and *I* desire to play host in this fine place and enjoy the good sport of a good hunt.
So *I* say we ignore these *scary* things like *powers* and *parasites*. Any *super-abilities*.
And we just come together for *fun*. No *Glartrox monster* from me, no *mutant stuff* from you.
We just hunt as *people* who *enjoy the game of it!* And of course, you'll get to keep your skulls.
To civility!

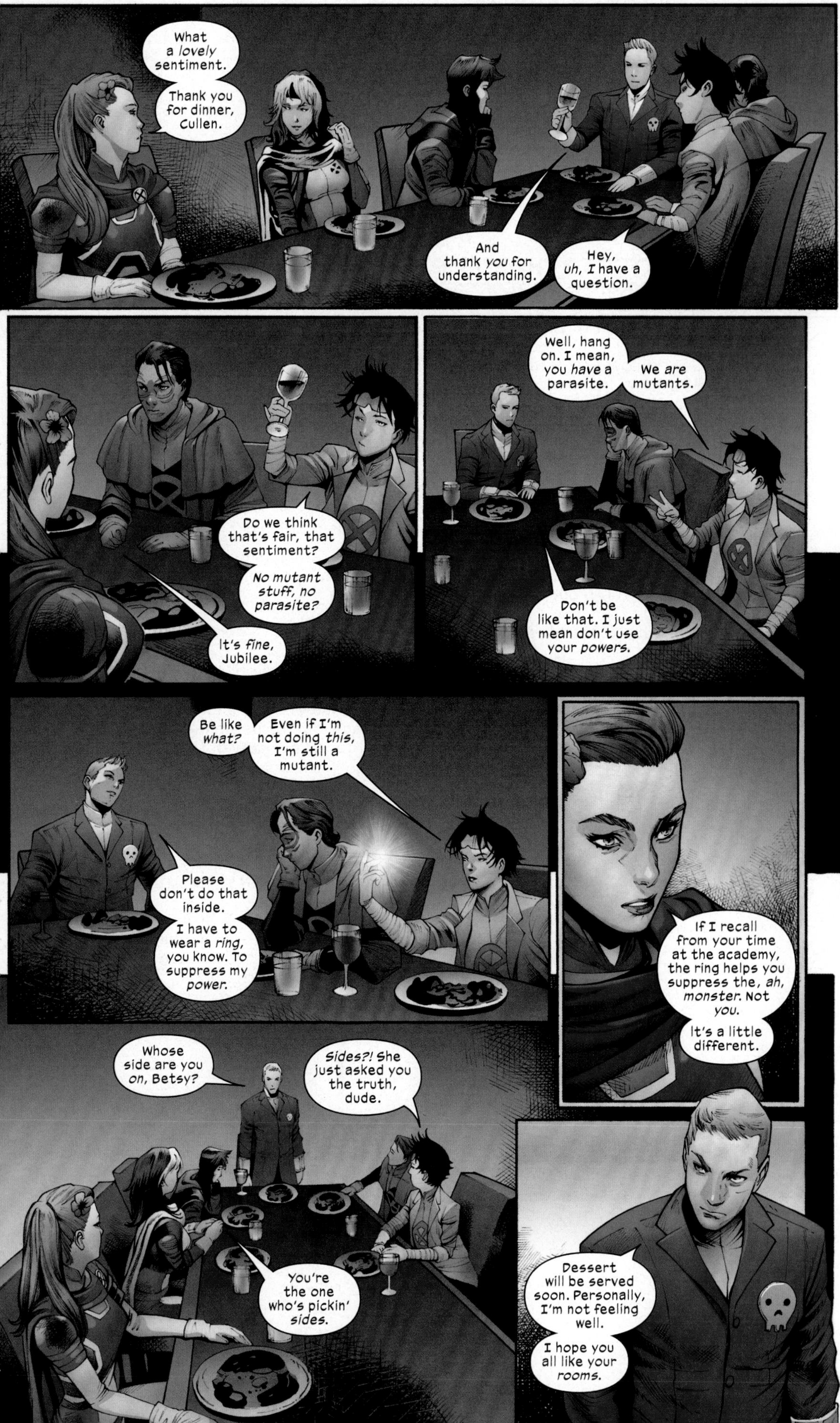
What a *lovely* sentiment.
Thank you for dinner, Cullen.
And thank *you* for understanding.
Hey, *uh, I* have a question.
Do we think that's fair, that sentiment?
No mutant stuff, no parasite?
It's *fine,* Jubilee.
Well, hang on. I mean, you *have* a parasite.
We *are* mutants.
Don't be like that. I just mean don't use your *powers.*
Be like *what?*
Even if I'm not doing *this,* I'm still a mutant.
Please don't do that inside.
I have to wear a *ring,* you know. To suppress my *power.*
If I recall from your time at the academy, the ring helps you suppress the, *ah, monster.* Not *you.*
It's a little different.
Whose side are you *on,* Betsy?
Sides?! She just asked you the truth, dude.
You're the one who's pickin' *sides.*
Dessert will be served soon. Personally, I'm not feeling well.
I hope you all like your *rooms.*

A LETTER TO THE NOBLE *HOMO SAPIENS* OF BRITAIN
THE BLOODSTONE ESTATE OR EXECUTOR THEREOF;

Attn: Master of the House

Dear fellow protector of the Commonwealth:

Greetings. I wish I could come to you with better tidings.

As you well know, the recent establishment of the nation of Krakoa has been seen by some as an act of terrorist isolation. Those who call themselves "superior" dangle lifesaving drugs over the heads of our brave nation, patronizing the powerful abilities of our own countrymen.

Protection from and mastery of the supernatural has long been part of our national fabric. The power inherent in our connection to the land is vital to our culture and our defense.

These Krakoans have put us on the defensive.

We reach out to you today not only to ask for your support as one of Britain's most vital supernatural families, but also to offer our own. Should the presence of Krakoans in Britain make you uncomfortable or threatened, we encourage you to reach out to us immediately. As an alternative to MI-13, we are not burdened by many of the same concerns of diversity.

Merry part,

R. Brousseau

Reuben Brousseau
Coven Akkaba
London

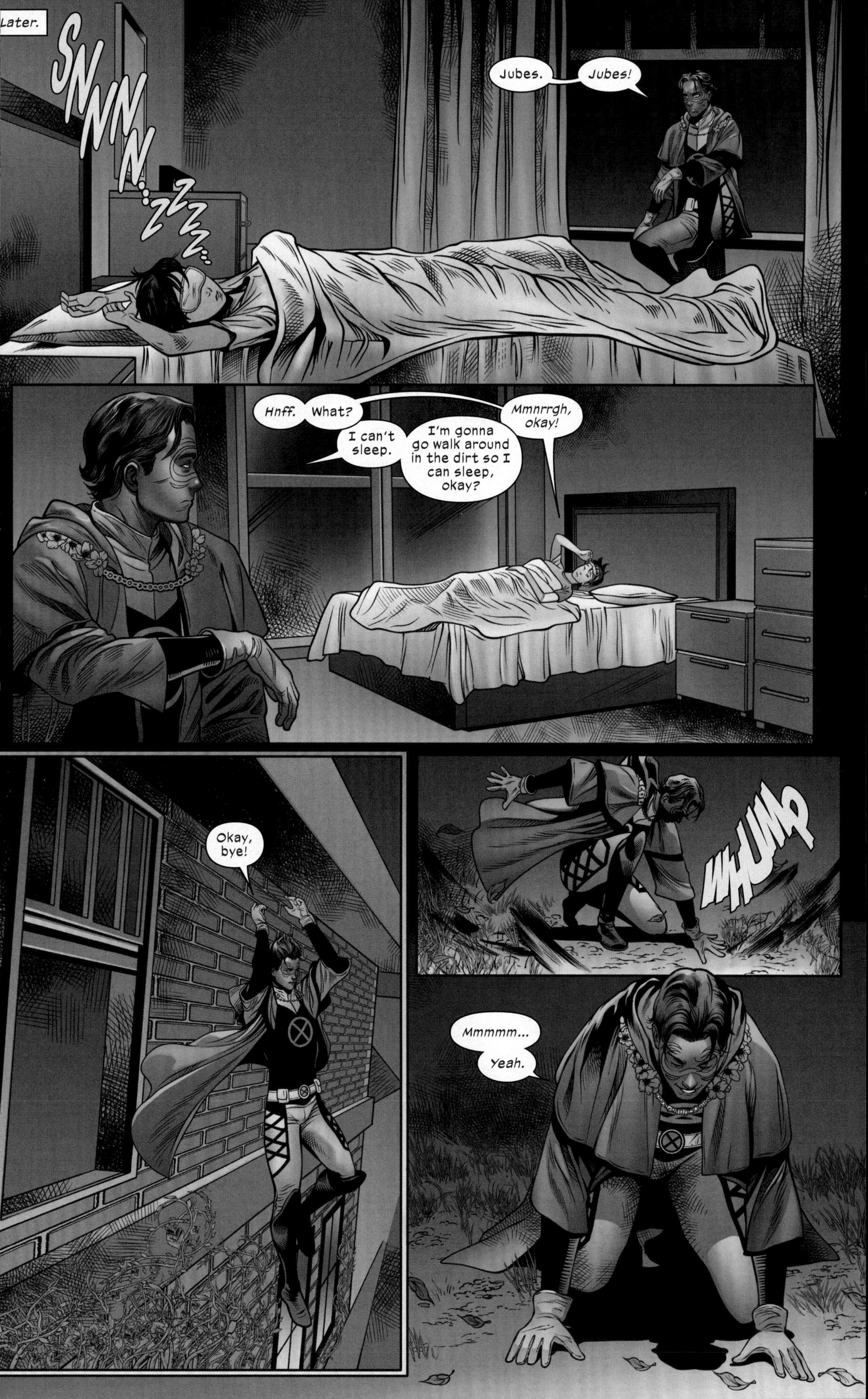
Later.
SNNNN...ZZZZ...
Jubes.
Jubes!
Hnff.
What?
I can't sleep.
I'm gonna go walk around in the dirt so I can sleep, okay?
Mmnrrgh, okay!
Okay, bye!
WHUMP
Mmmmm...
Yeah.

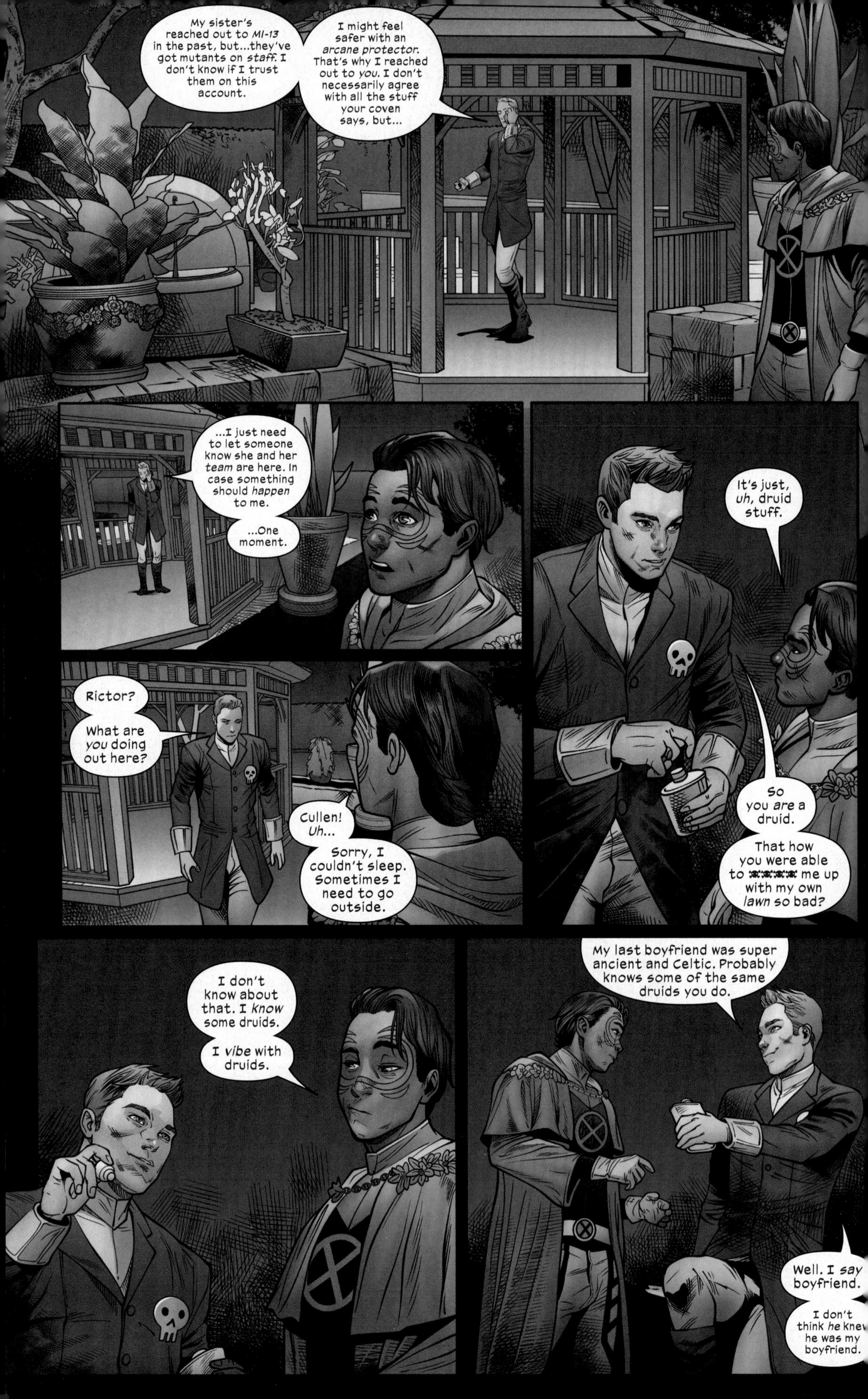
My sister's reached out to *MI-13* in the past, but...they've got mutants on *staff.* I don't know if I trust them on this account.
I might feel safer with an *arcane protector.* That's why I reached out to *you.* I don't necessarily agree with all the stuff your coven says, but...
...I just need to let someone know she and her *team* are here. In case something should *happen* to me.
...One moment.
It's just, *uh,* druid stuff.
Rictor?
What are *you* doing out here?
Cullen! *Uh...*
Sorry, I couldn't sleep. Sometimes I need to go outside.
So you *are* a druid.
That how you were able to ☠☠☠☠ me up with my own *lawn* so bad?
I don't know about that. I *know* some druids.
I *vibe* with druids.
My last boyfriend was super ancient and Celtic. Probably knows some of the same druids you do.
Well. I *say* boyfriend.
I don't think *he* knew he was my boyfriend.

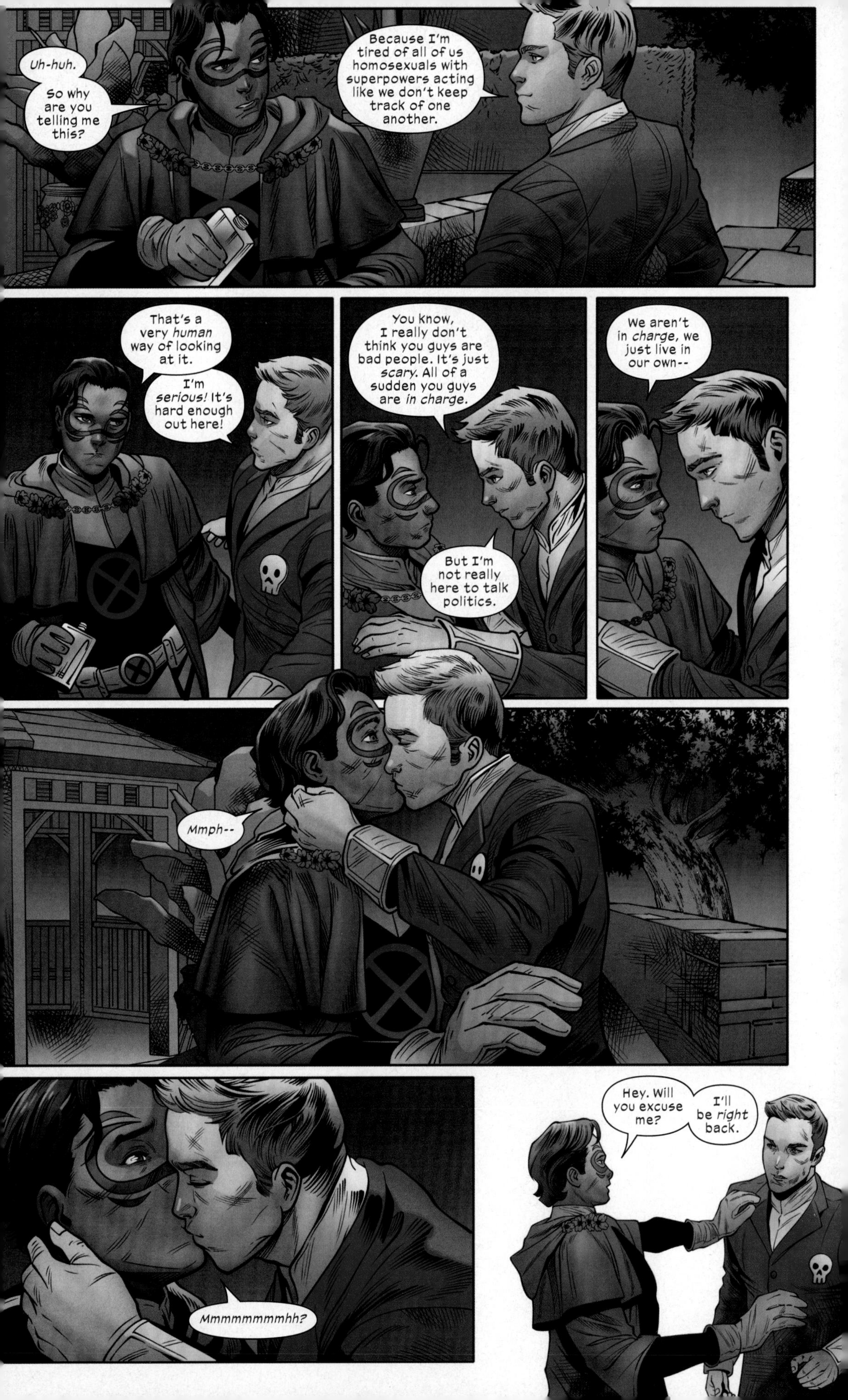
Uh-huh.
So why are you telling me this?
Because I'm tired of all of us homosexuals with superpowers acting like we don't keep track of one another.
That's a very *human* way of looking at it.
I'm *serious!* It's hard enough out here!
You know, I really don't think you guys are bad people. It's just *scary.* All of a sudden you guys are *in charge.*
But I'm not really here to talk politics.
We aren't in *charge,* we just live in our own--
Mmph--
Mmmmmmmmhh?
Hey. Will you excuse me?
I'll be *right* back.

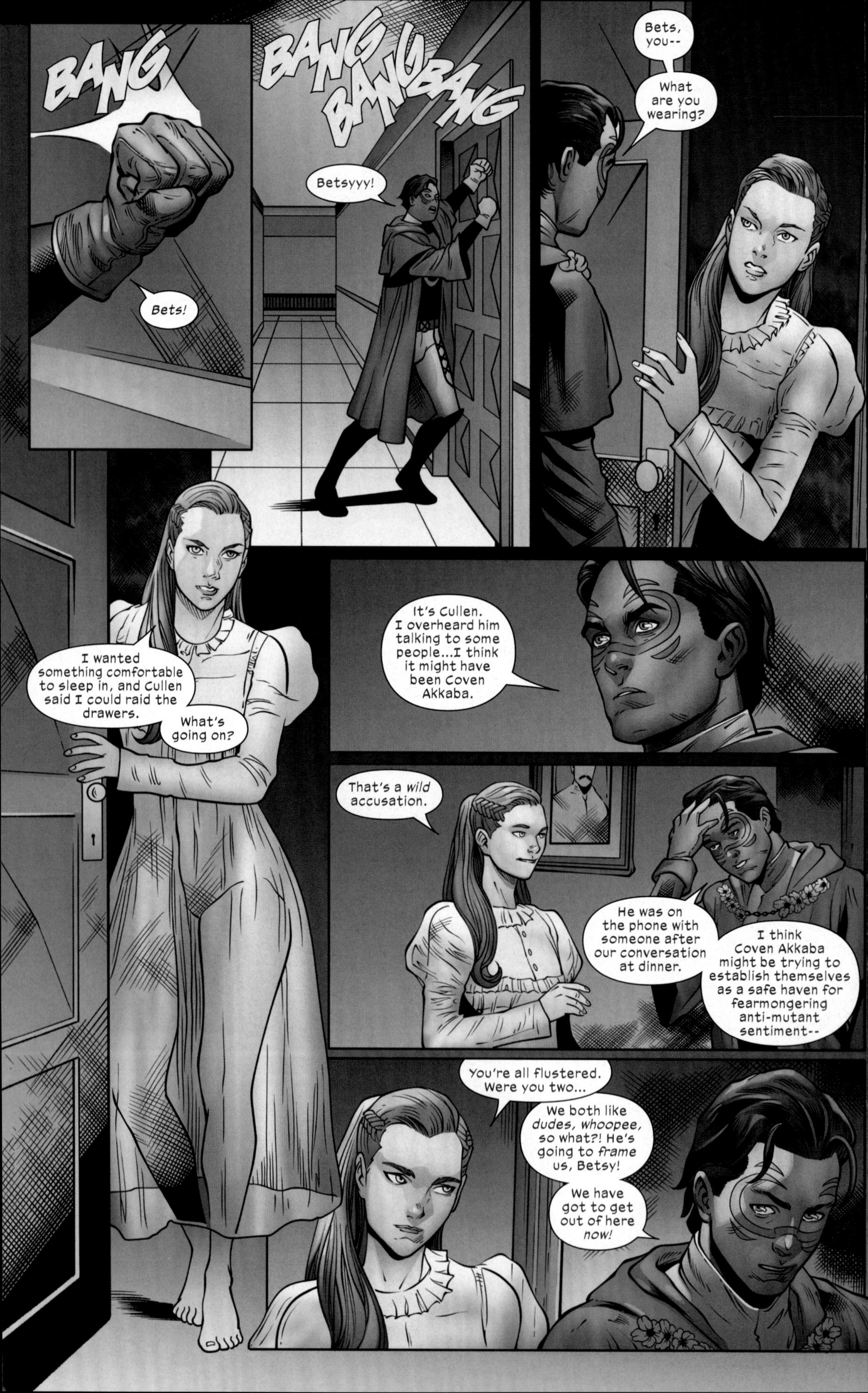
BANG
Bets!
BANG BANG BANG
Betsyyy!
Bets, you--
What are you wearing?
I wanted something comfortable to sleep in, and Cullen said I could raid the drawers.
What's going on?
It's Cullen. I overheard him talking to some people...I think it might have been Coven Akkaba.
That's a *wild* accusation.
He was on the phone with someone after our conversation at dinner.
I think Coven Akkaba might be trying to establish themselves as a safe haven for fearmongering anti-mutant sentiment--
You're all flustered. Were you two...
We both like *dudes, whoopee,* so what?! He's going to *frame* us, Betsy!
We have got to get out of here *now!*

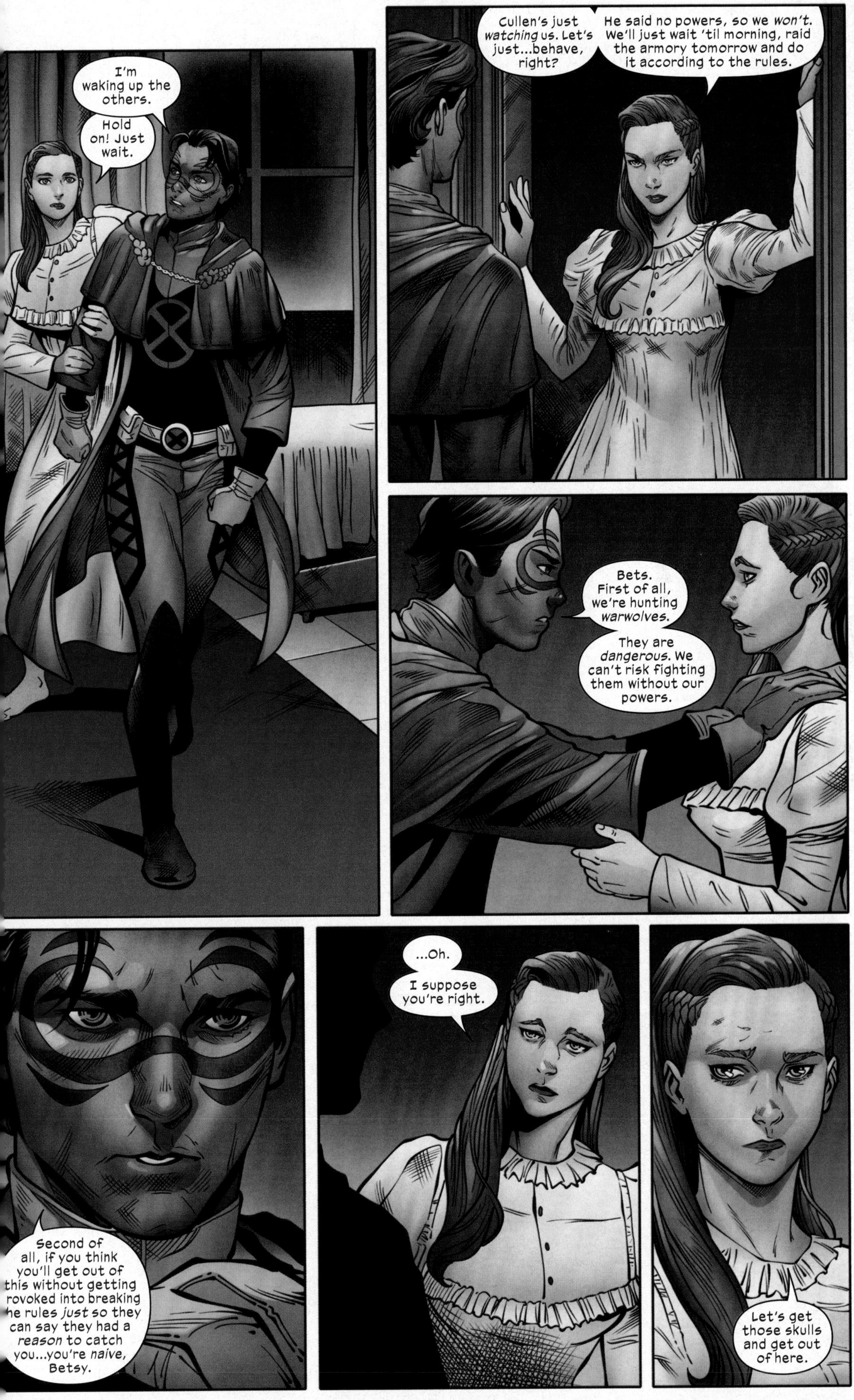
I'm waking up the others.
Hold on! Just wait.
Cullen's just *watching* us. Let's just...behave, right?
He said no powers, so we *won't*. We'll just wait 'til morning, raid the armory tomorrow and do it according to the rules.
Bets. First of all, we're hunting *warwolves*.
They are *dangerous*. We can't risk fighting them without our powers.
Second of all, if you think you'll get out of this without getting rovoked into breaking he rules *just* so they can say they had a *reason* to catch you...you're *naive*, Betsy.
...Oh.
I suppose you're right.
Let's get those skulls and get out of here.

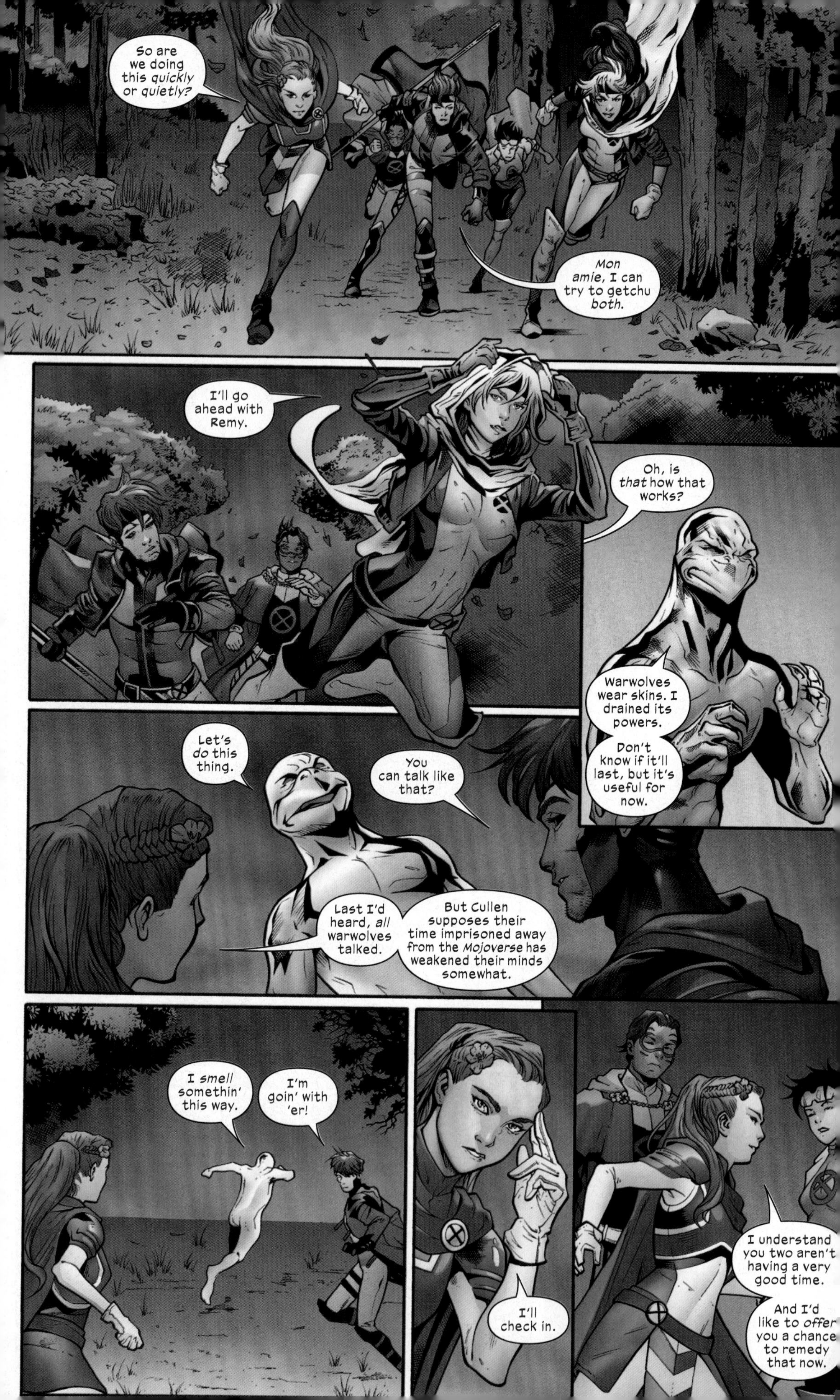
So are we doing this *quickly* or *quietly?*
Mon amie, I can try to getchu *both.*
I'll go ahead with Remy.
Oh, is *that* how that works?
Warwolves wear skins. I drained its powers.
Don't know if it'll last, but it's useful for now.
Let's *do* this thing.
You can talk like that?
Last I'd heard, *all* warwolves talked.
But Cullen supposes their time imprisoned away from the *Mojoverse* has weakened their minds somewhat.
I *smell* somethin' this way.
I'm goin' with 'er!
I'll check in.
I understand you two aren't having a very good time.
And I'd like to *offer* you a chance to remedy that now.

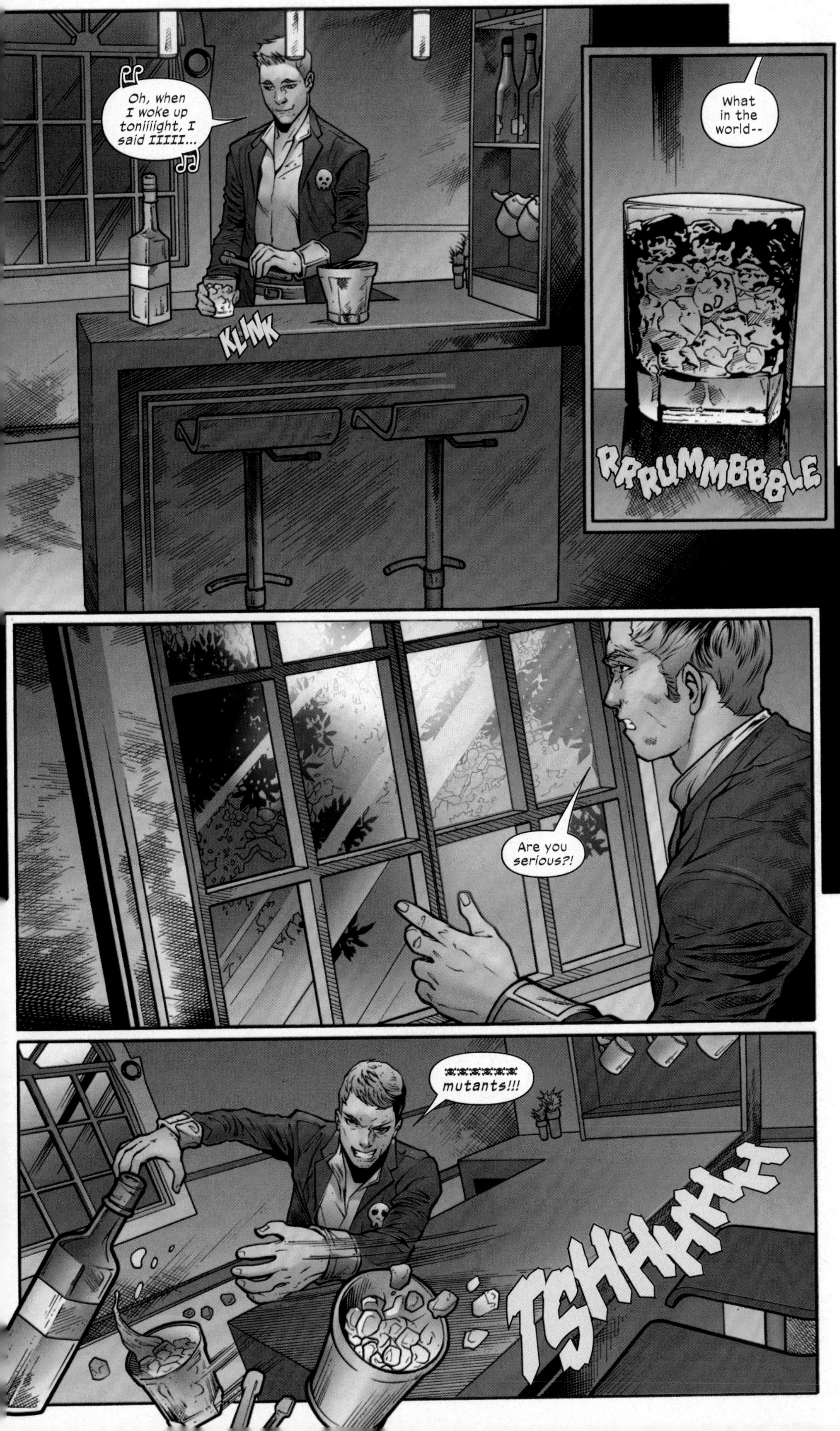
Oh, when I woke up toniiiight, I said IIIII...
KLINK
What in the world--
RRRUMMBBBLE
Are you serious?!
mutants!!!
TSHHHH

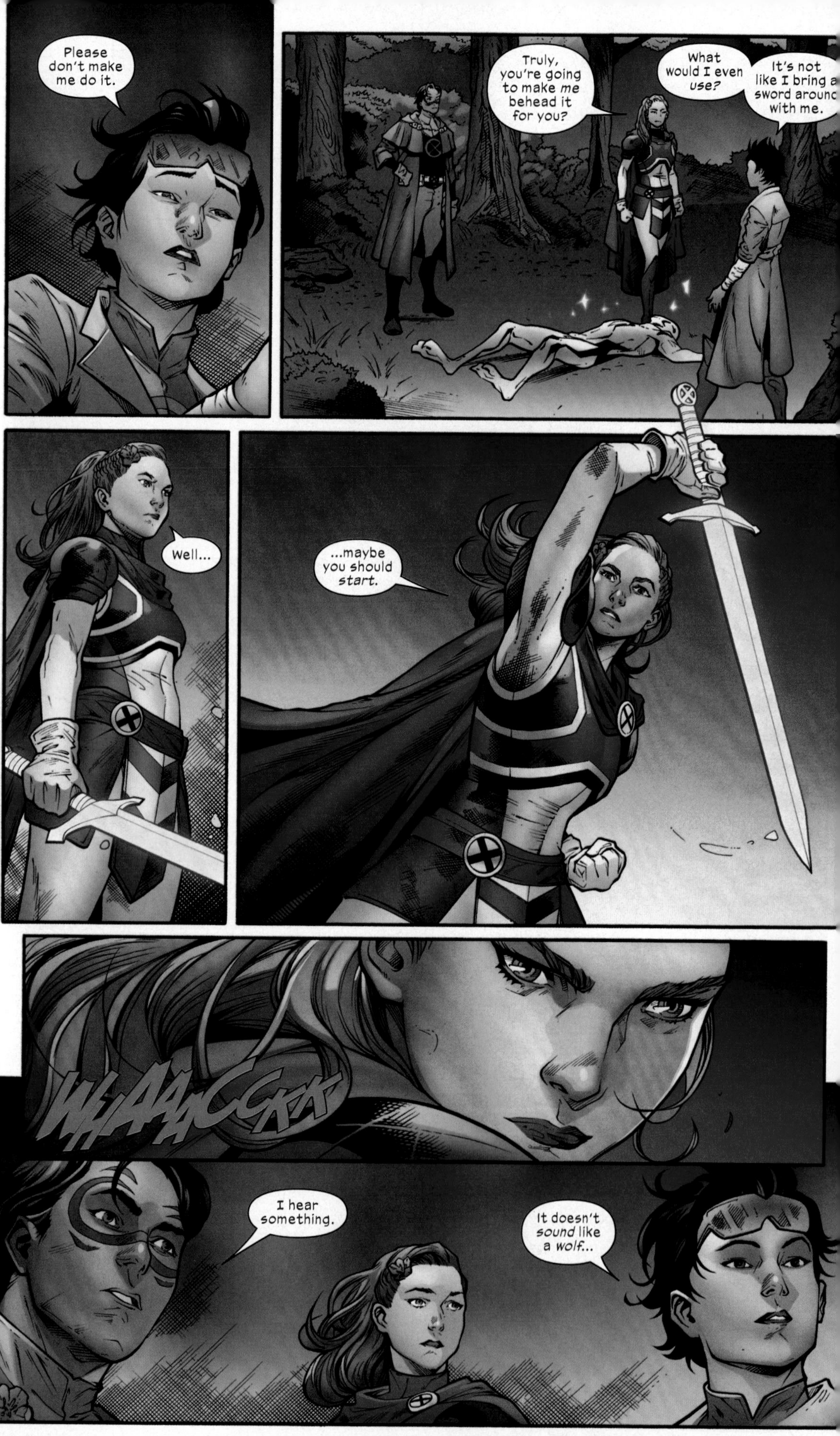
Please don't make me do it.
Truly, you're going to make me behead it for you?
What would I even use?
It's not like I bring a sword around with me.
Well...
...maybe you should start.
WHAAACCKK
I hear something.
It doesn't sound like a wolf...

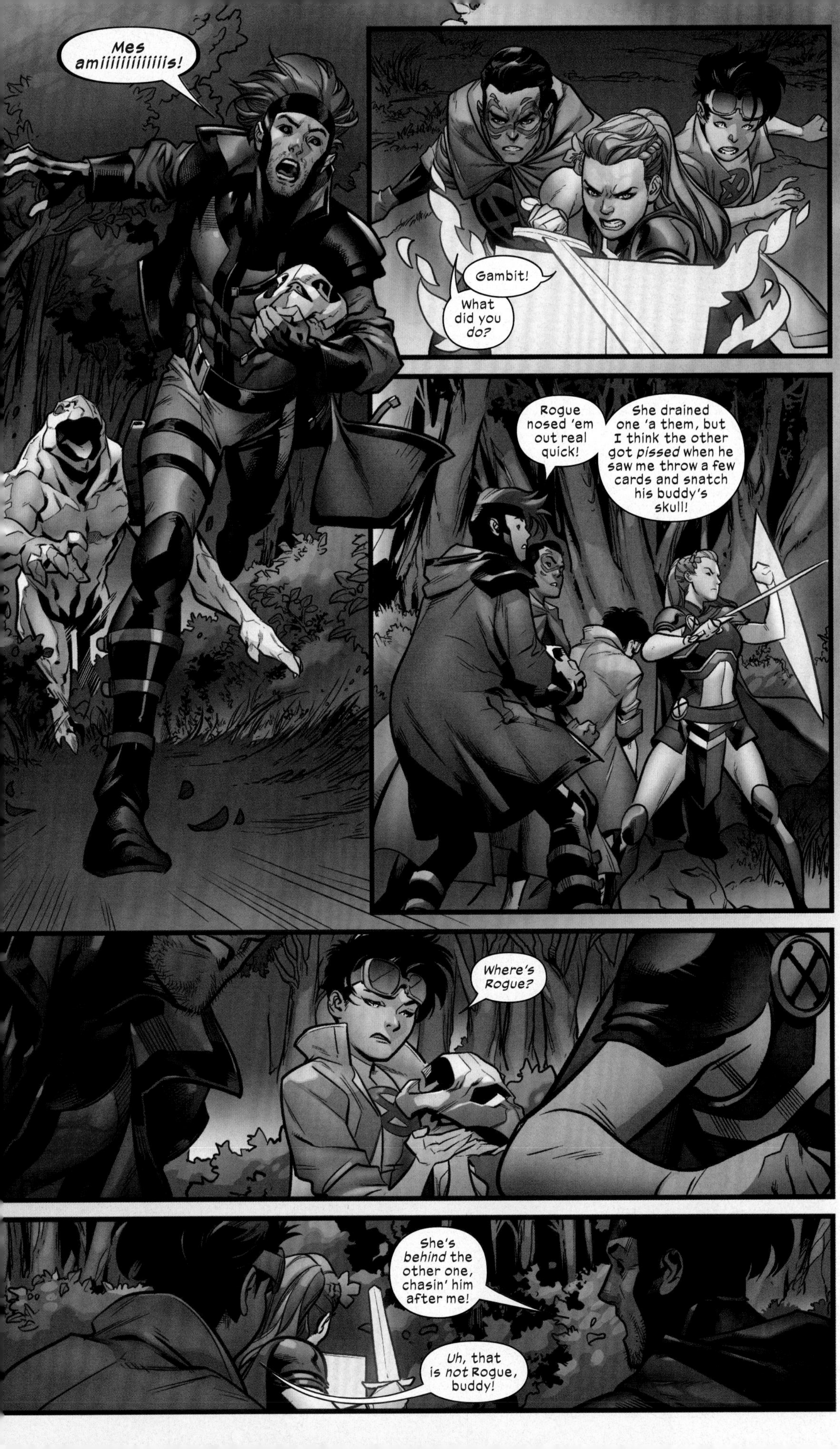
Mes amiiiiiiiiiiiiis!
Gambit!
What did you do?
Rogue nosed 'em out real quick!
She drained one 'a them, but I think the other got *pissed* when he saw me throw a few cards and snatch his buddy's skull!
Where's Rogue?
She's *behind* the other one, chasin' him after me!
Uh, that is *not* Rogue, buddy!

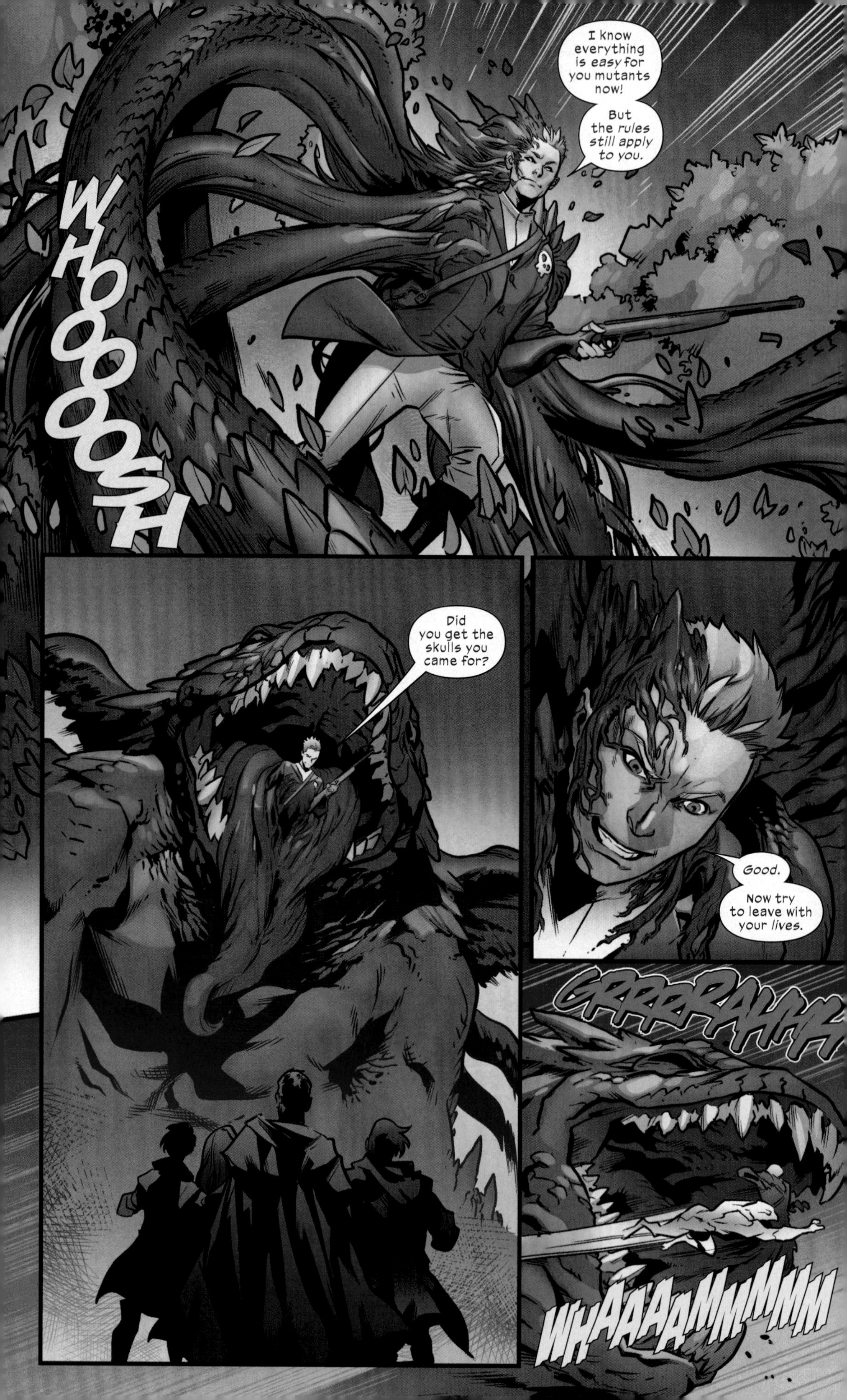
I know everything is easy for you mutants now!
But the rules still apply to you.
WHOOOOOOSH
Did you get the skulls you came for?
Good.
Now try to leave with your lives.
GRRRRAHHH
WHAAAAMMMMM

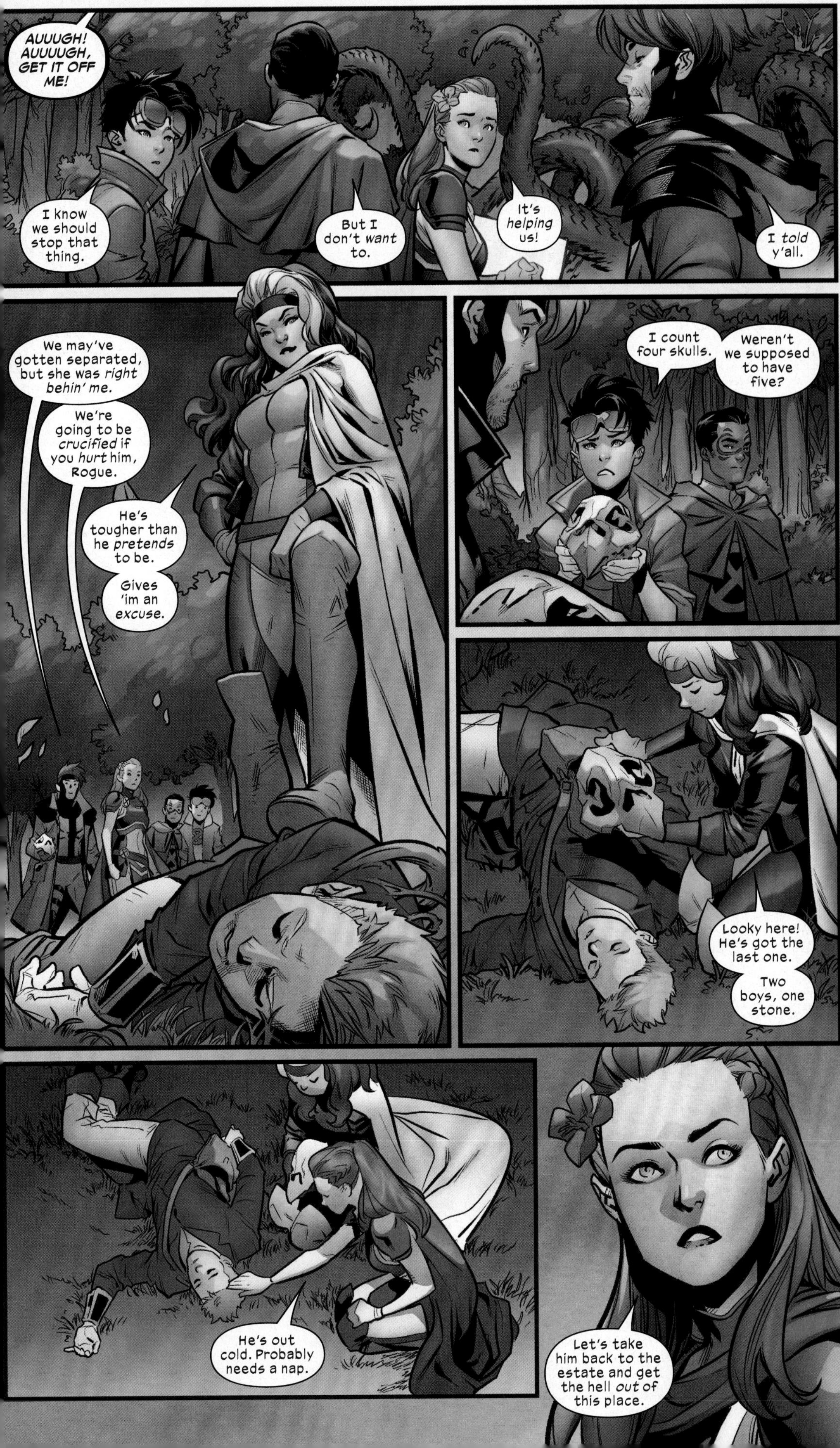
AUUUGH! AUUUUGH, GET IT OFF ME!
I know we should stop that thing.
But I don't *want* to.
It's *helping* us!
I *told* y'all.
We may've gotten separated, but she was *right behin' me.*
We're going to be *crucified* if you *hurt* him, Rogue.
He's tougher than he *pretends* to be.
Gives 'im an *excuse.*
I count four skulls.
Weren't we supposed to have five?
Looky here! He's got the last one.
Two boys, one stone.
He's out cold. Probably needs a nap.
Let's take him back to the estate and get the hell *out* of this place.

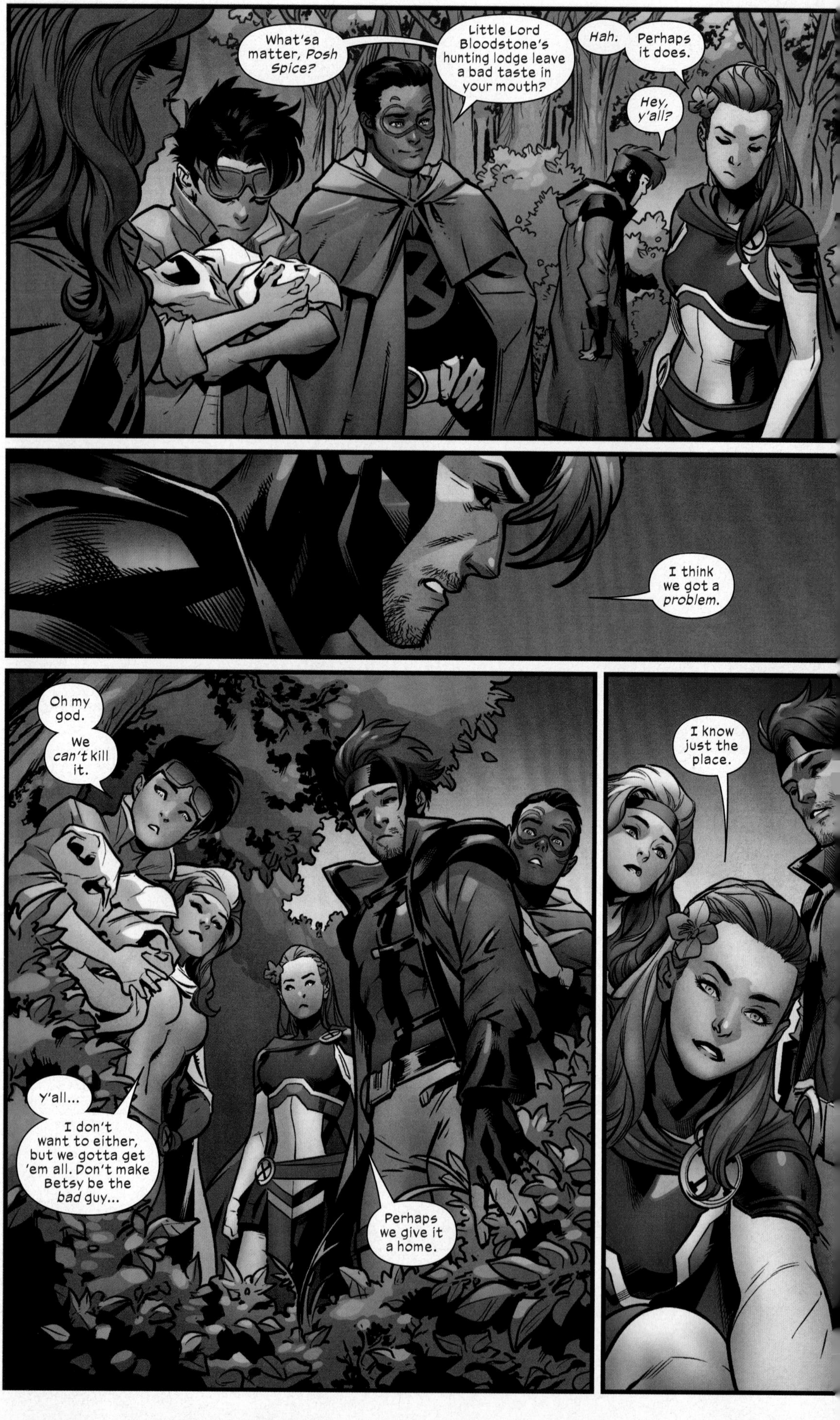
What'sa matter, Posh Spice?
Little Lord Bloodstone's hunting lodge leave a bad taste in your mouth?
Hah.
Perhaps it does.
Hey, y'all?
I think we got a problem.
Oh my god.
We can't kill it.
Y'all...
I don't want to either, but we gotta get 'em all. Don't make Betsy be the bad guy...
Perhaps we give it a home.
I know just the place.

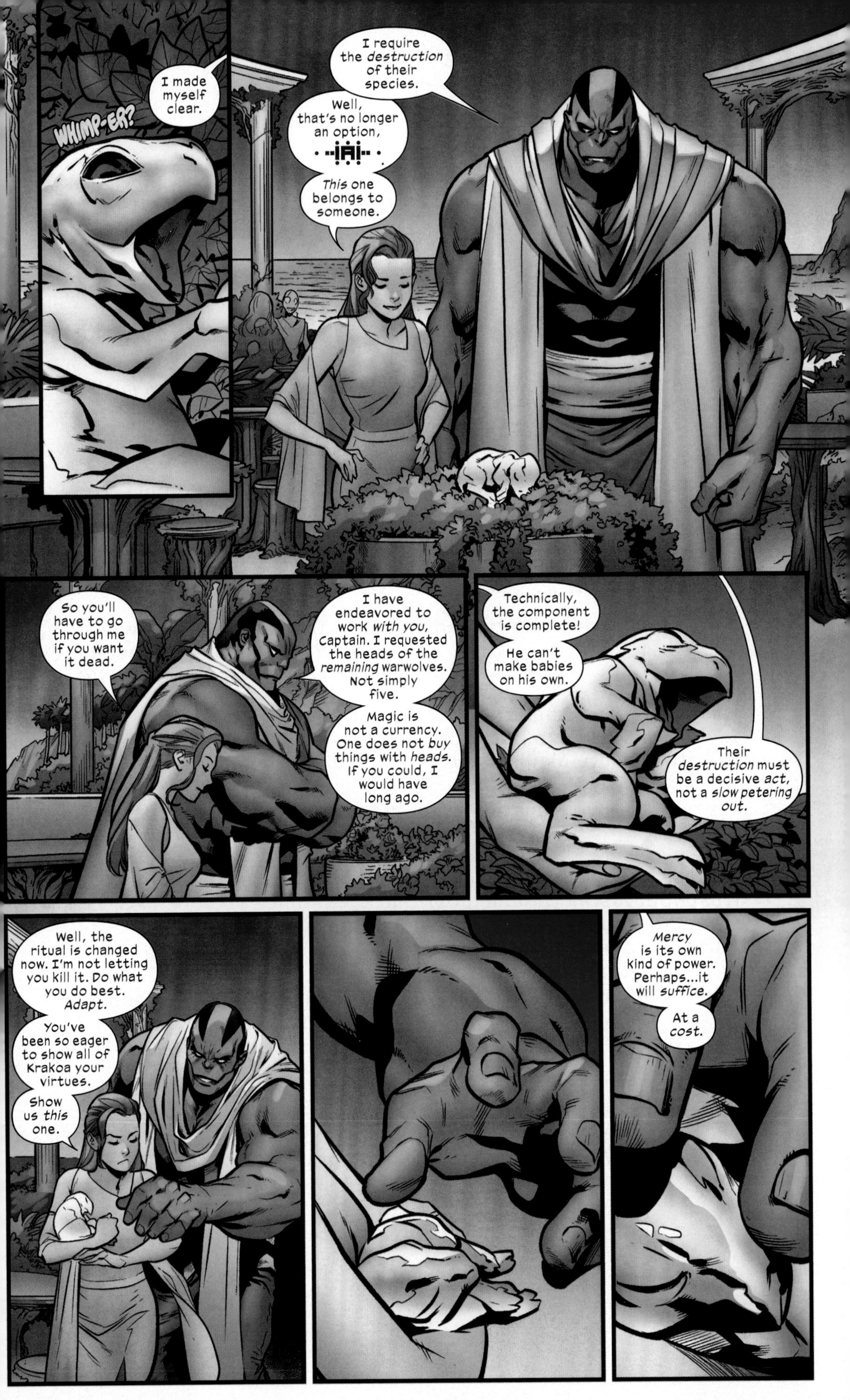
I made myself clear.
WHIMP-ER?
I require the *destruction* of their species.
Well, that's no longer an option,
This one belongs to someone.
So you'll have to go through me if you want it dead.
I have endeavored to work *with you*, Captain. I requested the heads of the *remaining* warwolves. Not simply five.
Magic is not a currency. One does not *buy* things with *heads*. If you could, I would have long ago.
Technically, the component is complete!
He can't make babies on his own.
Their *destruction* must be a decisive *act*, not a *slow petering out*.
Well, the ritual is changed now. I'm not letting you kill it. Do what you do best. *Adapt*.
You've been so eager to show all of Krakoa your virtues.
Show us *this* one.
Mercy is its own kind of power. Perhaps...it will *suffice*.
At a *cost*.

★TO THE STARS, FROM THE STARS★

Out here, the sky is silent. Harmonious pulses of binary stars in time with Krakoa's heart are heard in the quiet refuge of the flowers.

These messages come from the stars outside to the stars within us.

We share them, interpreted from startongue, with our brothers and sisters below.

- 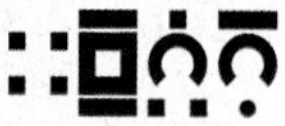

"A sword with two edges is not the same as two swords with a single edge each."

- the pulsar known as RX J0806.4-4123

It is a very bad week to procrastinate. If you sleep facing westward to put your back to the dawn, you will stay up late digging your own grave.

Have you a song that is haunting you? Turn it off. It is drowning out your truth.

A message for those who were born at sunrise -- trust your instinct. Remember that sometimes your instinct is louder than your ego. Dim the lights if you must in order to confront the self.

"If you hunt a beast you do not wish to eat, you become the hand of the cook."

- the Methuselah star, HD 140283

Though it pains us to say, it is an inauspicious era for twins.

We invite you to join us to pray for luck.

★★

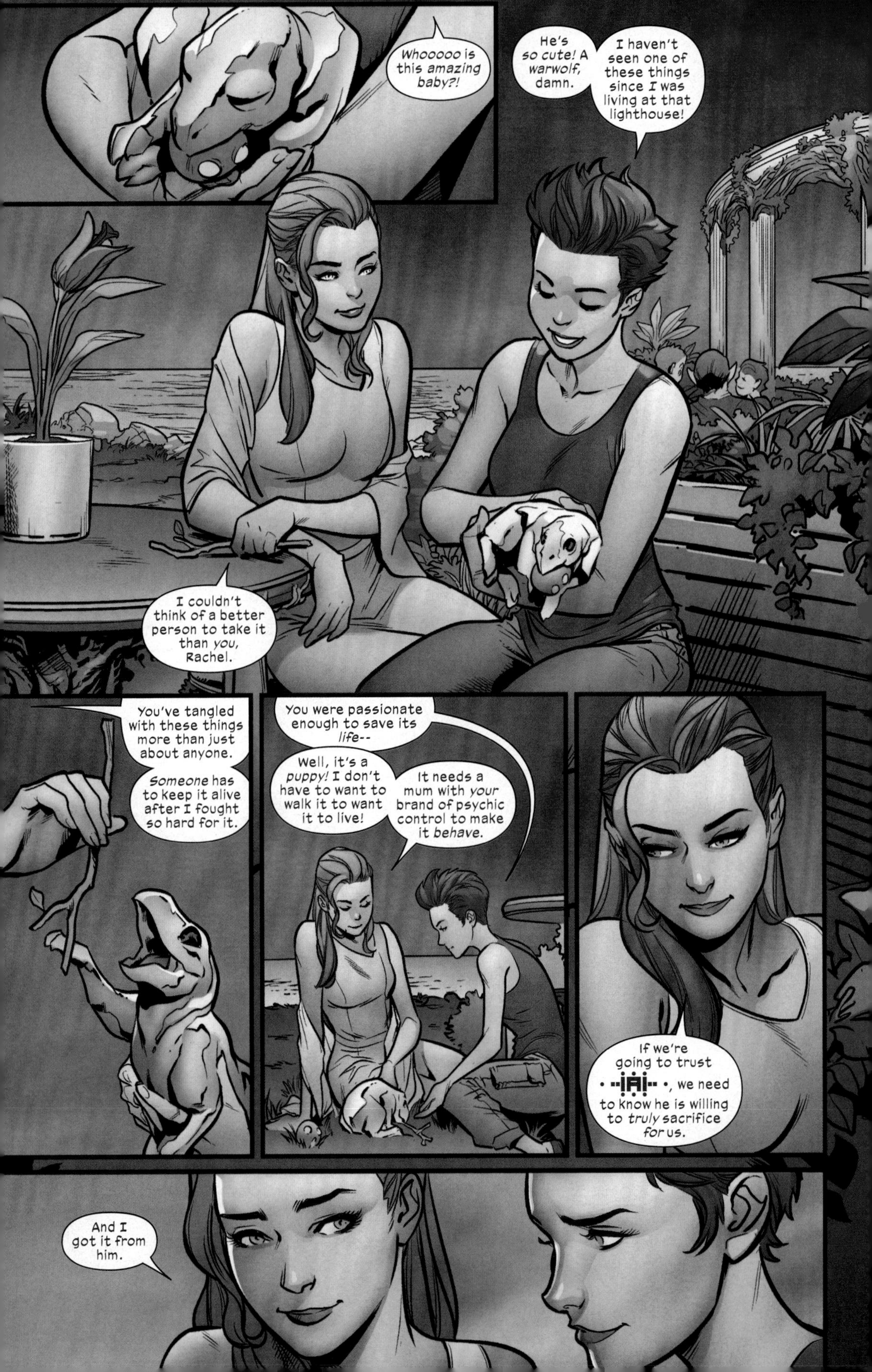

Whoooooo is this amazing baby?!
He's so cute! A warwolf, damn.
I haven't seen one of these things since I was living at that lighthouse!
I couldn't think of a better person to take it than you, Rachel.
You've tangled with these things more than just about anyone.
Someone has to keep it alive after I fought so hard for it.
You were passionate enough to save its life--
Well, it's a puppy! I don't have to want to walk it to want it to live!
It needs a mum with your brand of psychic control to make it behave.
If we're going to trust , we need to know he is willing to truly sacrifice for us.
And I got it from him.

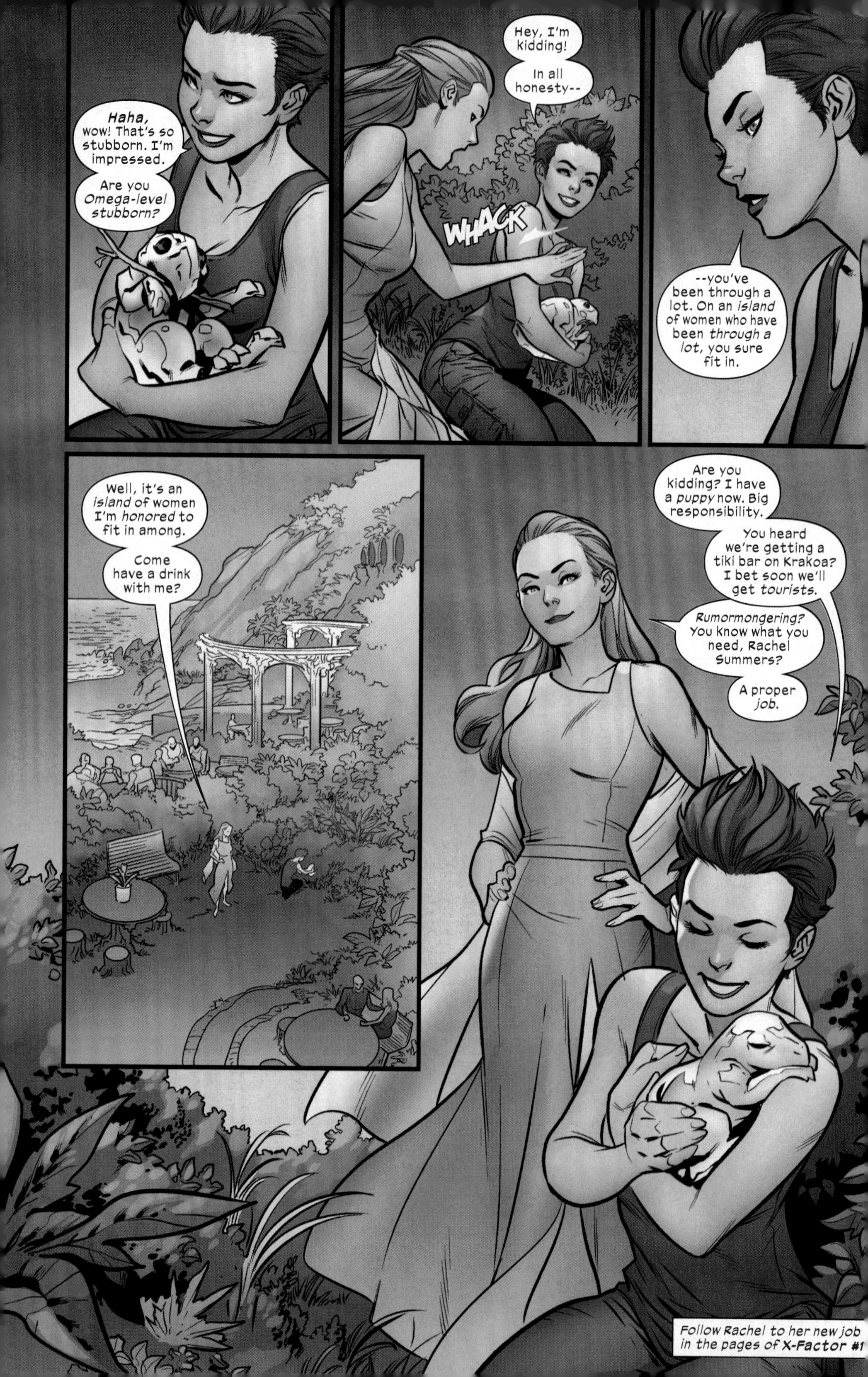

Haha, wow! That's so stubborn. I'm impressed.
Are you *Omega-level* stubborn?
Hey, I'm kidding!
In all honesty--
WHACK
--you've been through a lot. On an *island* of women who have been *through a lot,* you sure fit in.
Well, it's an *island* of women I'm *honored* to fit in among.
Come have a drink with me?
Are you kidding? I have a *puppy* now. Big responsibility.
You heard we're getting a tiki bar on Krakoa? I bet soon we'll get *tourists.*
Rumormongering? You know what you need, Rachel Summers?
A proper *job.*
Follow Rachel to her new job in the pages of **X-Factor #1**

[dawn_of_x]

[kra_]
[koa_]

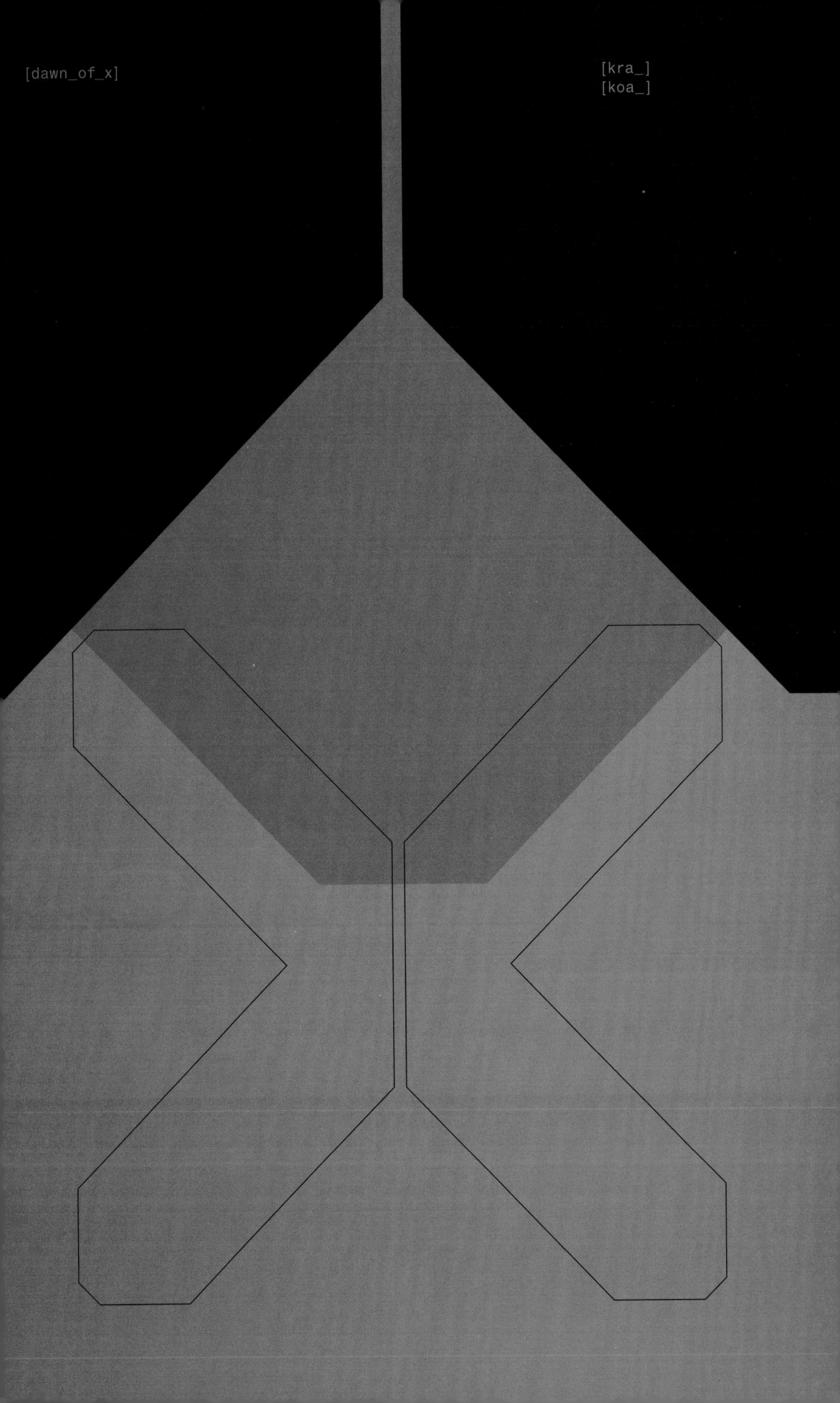

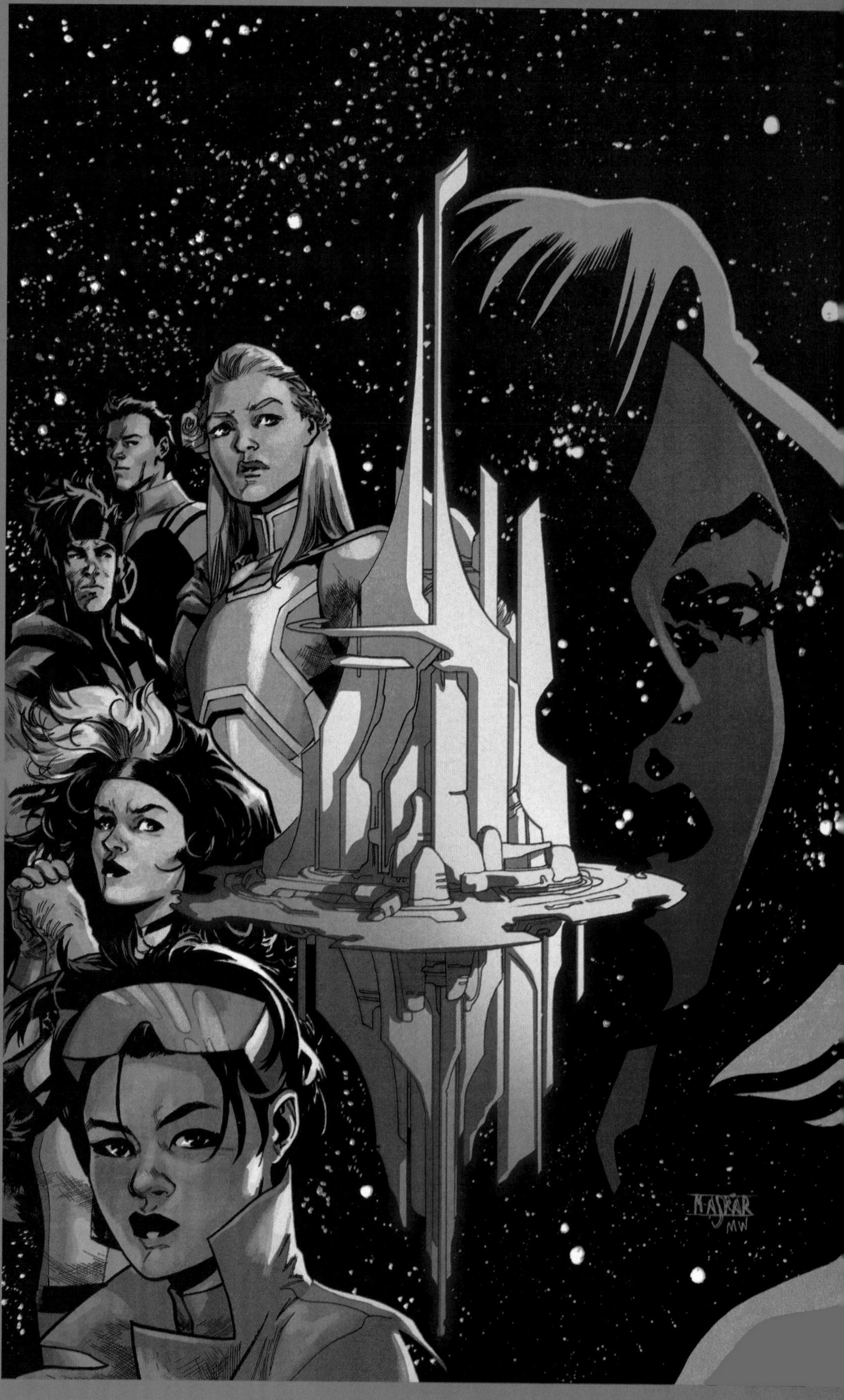

Schools of Magic

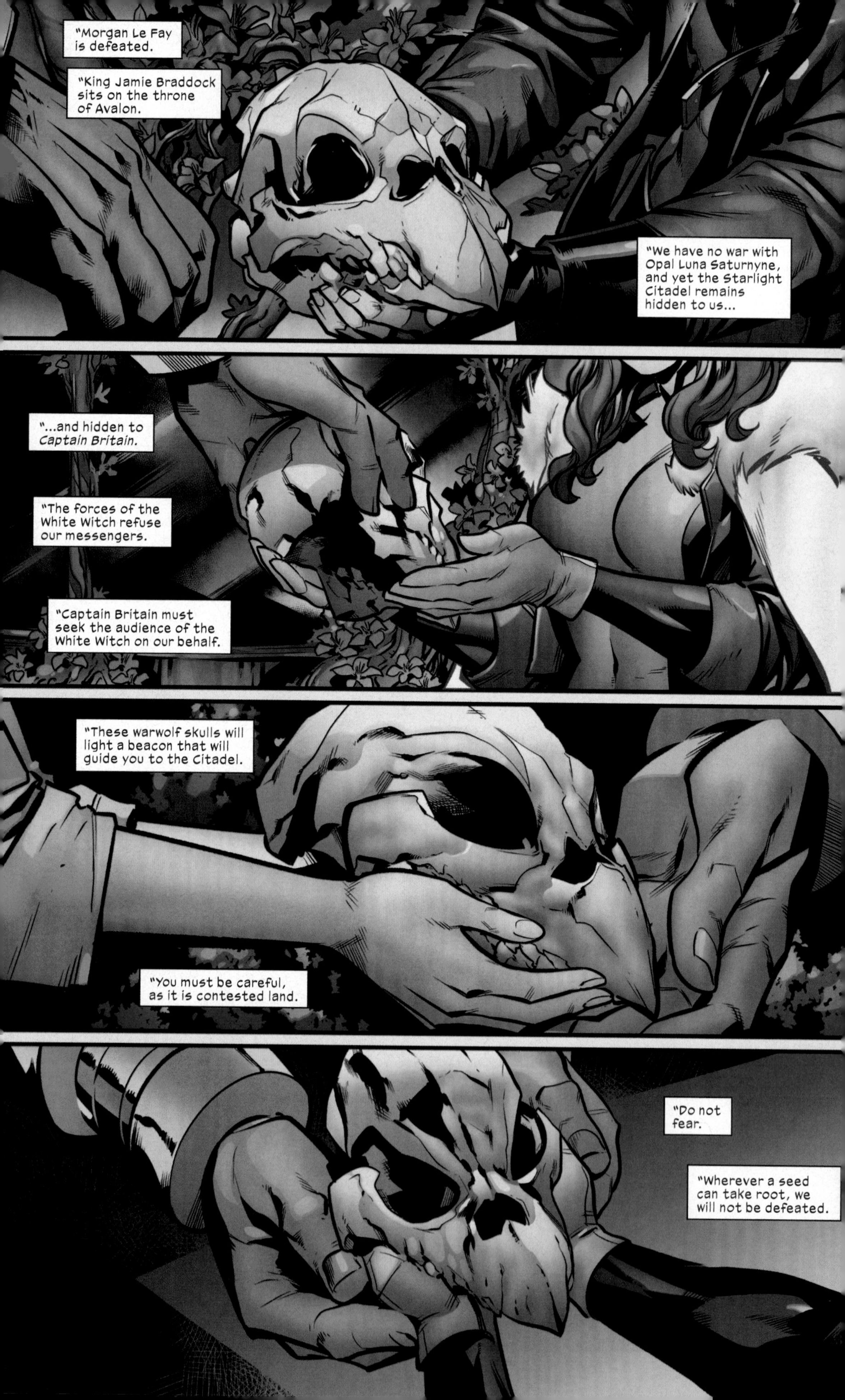
"Morgan Le Fay is defeated.
"King Jamie Braddock sits on the throne of Avalon.
"We have no war with Opal Luna Saturnyne, and yet the Starlight Citadel remains hidden to us...
"...and hidden to *Captain Britain.*
"The forces of the White Witch refuse our messengers.
"Captain Britain must seek the audience of the White Witch on our behalf.
"These warwolf skulls will light a beacon that will guide you to the Citadel.
"You must be careful, as it is contested land.
"Do not fear.
"Wherever a seed can take root, we will not be defeated.

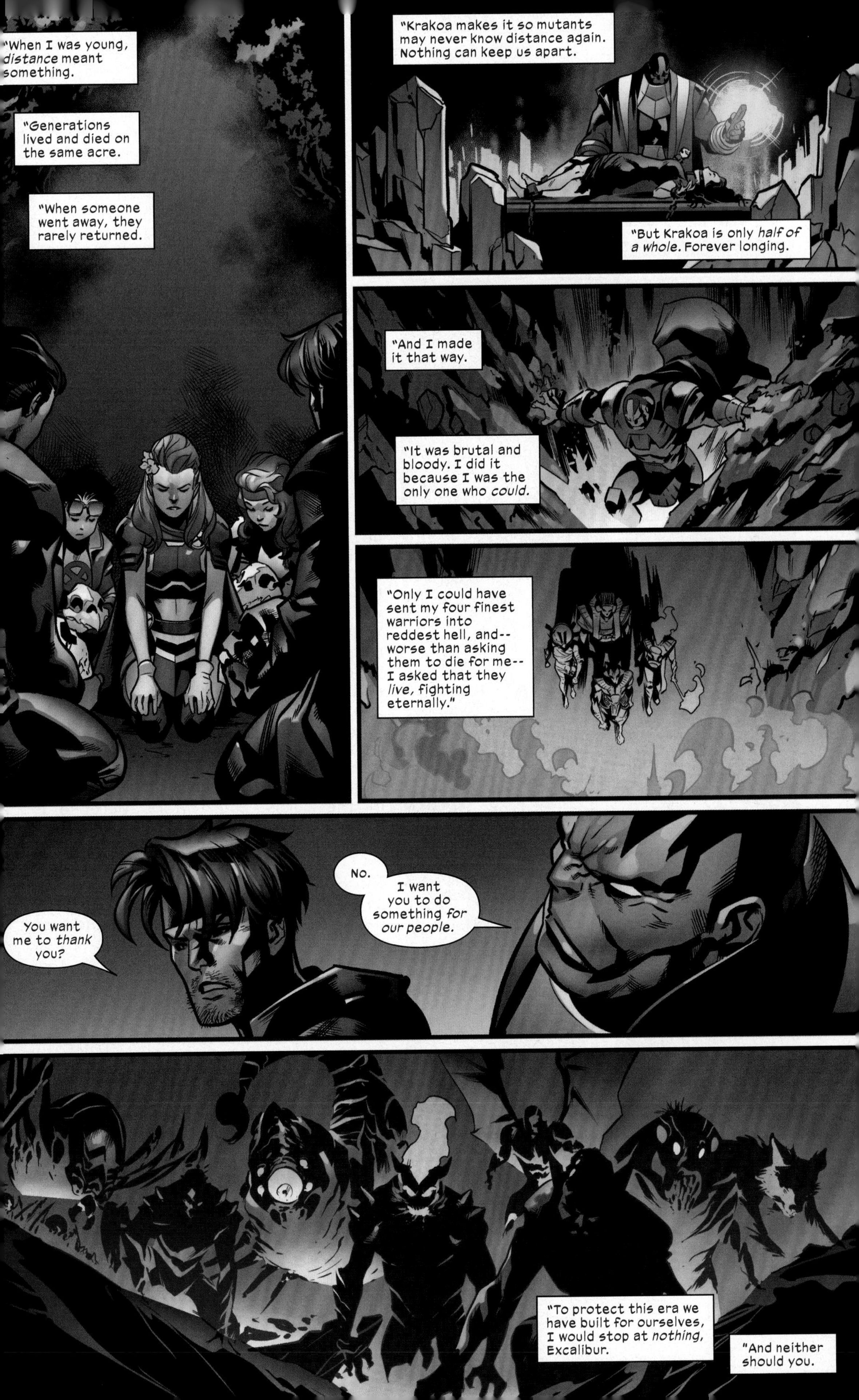
"When I was young, distance meant something.
"Generations lived and died on the same acre.
"When someone went away, they rarely returned.
"Krakoa makes it so mutants may never know distance again. Nothing can keep us apart.
"But Krakoa is only half of a whole. Forever longing.
"And I made it that way.
"It was brutal and bloody. I did it because I was the only one who could.
"Only I could have sent my four finest warriors into reddest hell, and-- worse than asking them to die for me-- I asked that they live, fighting eternally."
You want me to thank you?
No.
I want you to do something for our people.
"To protect this era we have built for ourselves, I would stop at nothing, Excalibur.
"And neither should you.

THE STARLIGHT CITADEL

The exact origins of the Starlight Citadel are unknown. By all accounts it has existed as long as Otherworld itself and serves as a meeting place and administrative nexus for all realities. Earliest writings from the Otherworld claim the tower was named for its visibility -- due to its height and lumination, it can be seen at night from any point in Otherworld.

In the past, the Citadel has been host to various residents -- the mysterious Merlyn, his daughter Roma and the now destroyed **Captain Britain Corps.** Currently, it serves as the central fortress of Otherworldly guardian and Omniversal Majestrix **Opal Luna Saturnyne**.

The tower (and Otherworld itself) are unique in that they served as a hub for the various realities in which Captain Britain existed and protected the people of Britain and the Otherworld. During the time of the Captain Britain Corps, the Citadel's unique location between various realities enabled it to serve as a place for trials, weddings and other gatherings. Now, in the absence of the corps, the tower's purpose is unknown, and Saturnyne's motivations are known only to herself.

The Starlight Citadel has been closed to outsiders since the destruction of the Captain Britain Corps. Following the first volley of Morgan Le Fay's attack, it was cloaked from view for safety during wartime and has remained hidden since.

Lady Saturnyne is known for her ambition and she makes clear that she was not born to her position but acquired it through hard work and careful planning. She has since replaced Merlyn as Omniversal Guardian and rewards the similarly ambitious with a devoted school of priestesses who serve her as her hand.

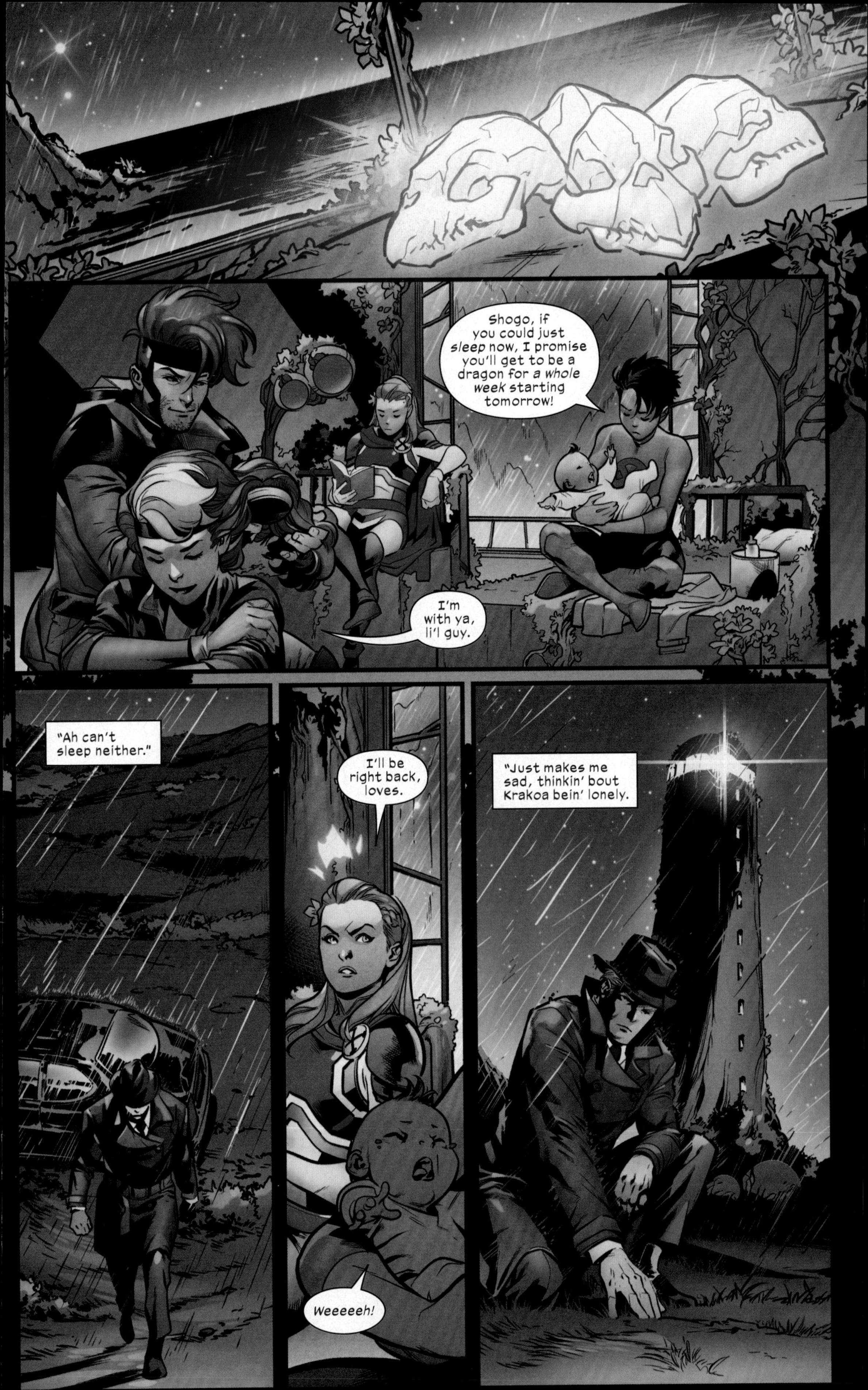
Shogo, if you could just *sleep* now, I promise you'll get to be a dragon for *a whole week* starting tomorrow!
I'm with ya, li'l guy.
"Ah can't sleep neither."
I'll be right back, loves.
Weeeeeh!
"Just makes me sad, thinkin' bout Krakoa bein' lonely.

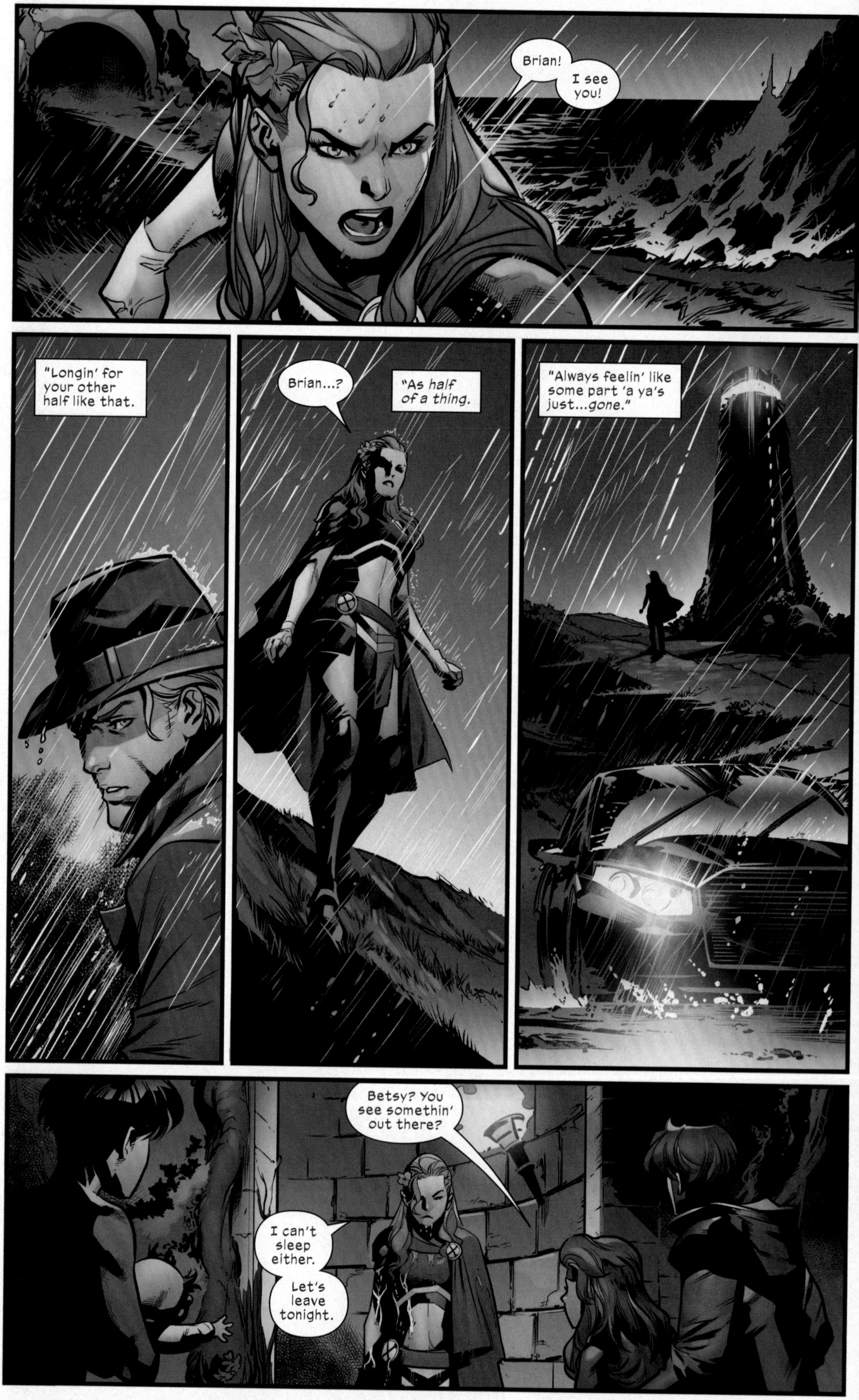

Brian! I see you!
"Longin' for your other half like that.
Brian...?
"As *half* of a thing.
"Always feelin' like some part 'a ya's just...*gone*."
Betsy? You see somethin' out there?
I can't sleep either.
Let's leave tonight.

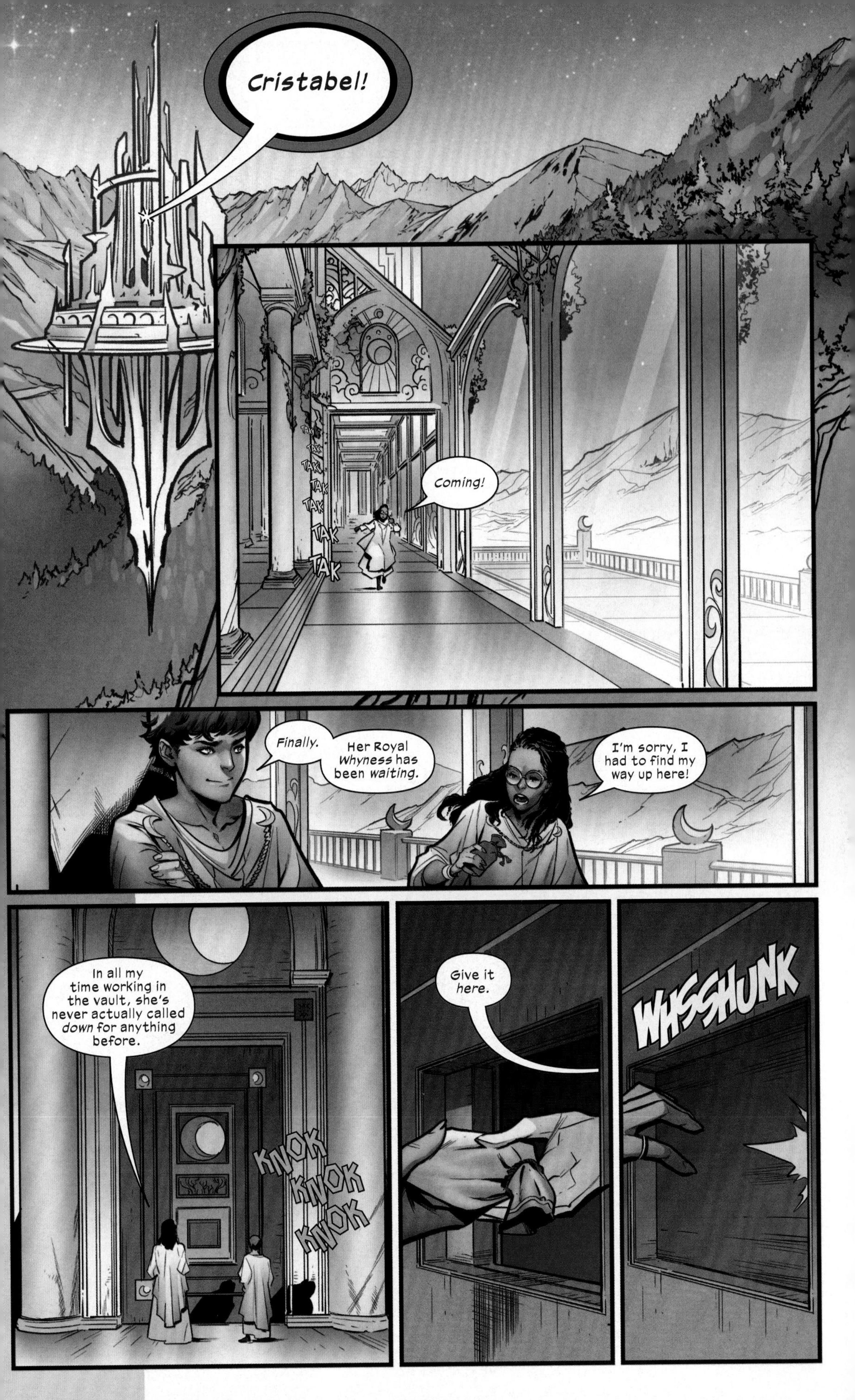
Cristabel!
TAK TAK TAK TAK TAK TAK TAK
Coming!
Finally.
Her Royal Whyness has been waiting.
I'm sorry, I had to find my way up here!
In all my time working in the vault, she's never actually called down for anything before.
KNOK KNOK KNOK
Give it here.
WHSSHUNK

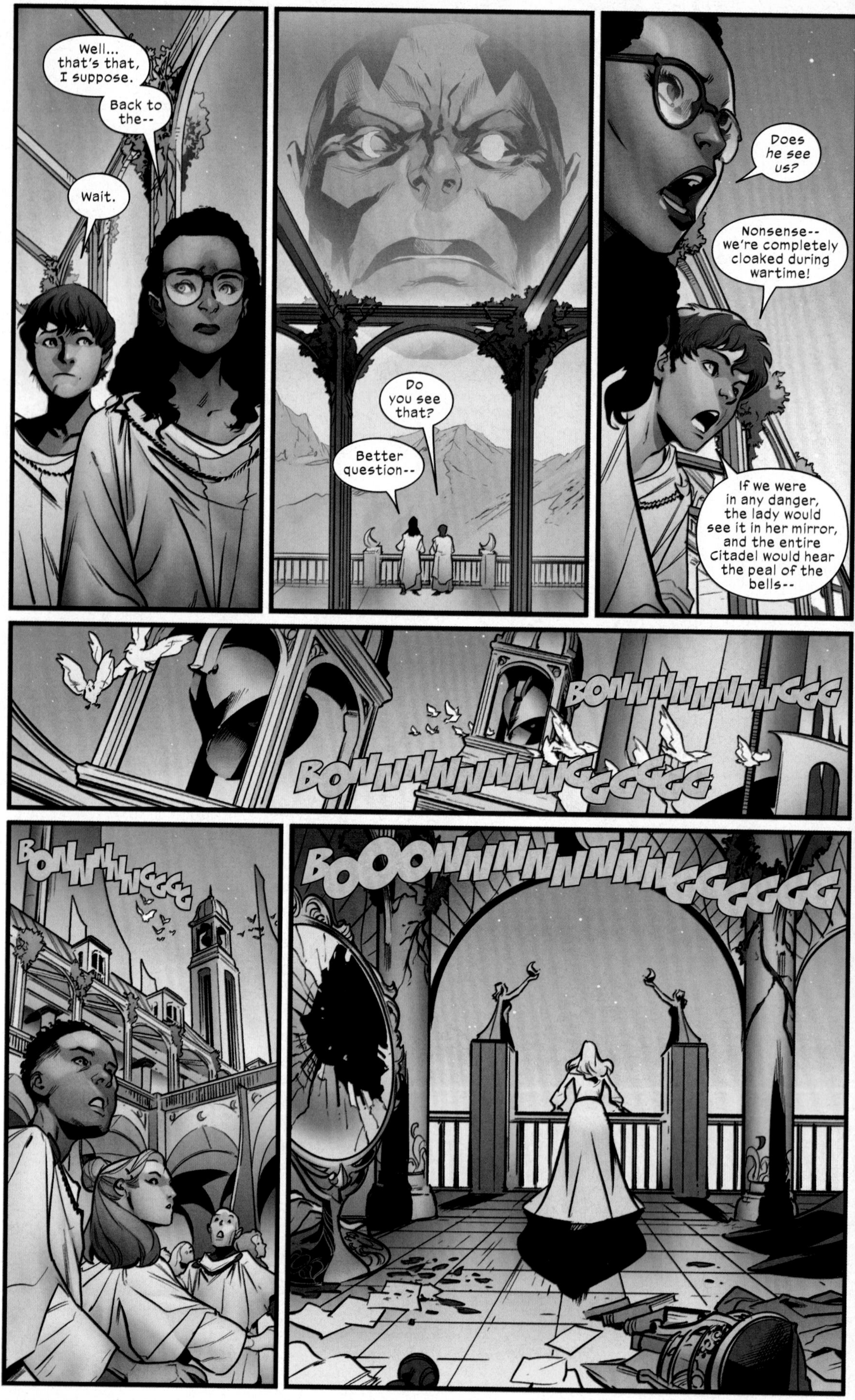
Well... that's that, I suppose.
Back to the--
Wait.
Do you see that?
Better question--
Does he see us?
Nonsense-- we're completely cloaked during wartime!
If we were in any danger, the lady would see it in her mirror, and the entire Citadel would hear the peal of the bells--
BONNNNNNNNGGG
BONNNNNNNNNGGGGG
BONNNNGGGG
BOOONNNNNNNNNNGGGGGG

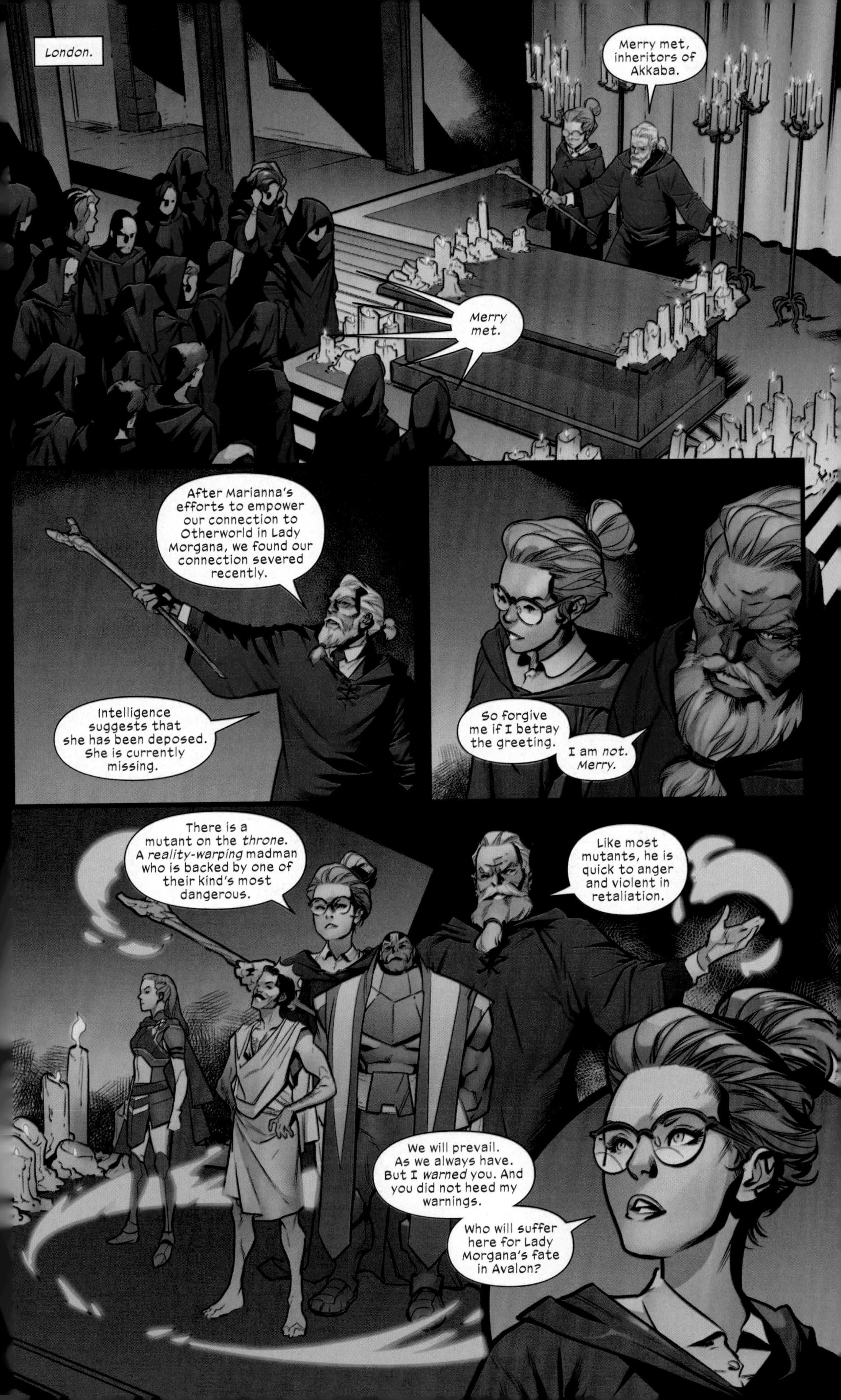
London.
Merry met, inheritors of Akkaba.
Merry met.
After Marianna's efforts to empower our connection to Otherworld in Lady Morgana, we found our connection severed recently.
Intelligence suggests that she has been deposed. She is currently missing.
So forgive me if I betray the greeting.
I am *not*. Merry.
There is a mutant on the *throne*. A *reality-warping* madman who is backed by one of their kind's most dangerous.
Like most mutants, he is quick to anger and violent in retaliation.
We will prevail. As we always have. But I *warned* you. And you did not heed my warnings.
Who will suffer here for Lady Morgana's fate in Avalon?

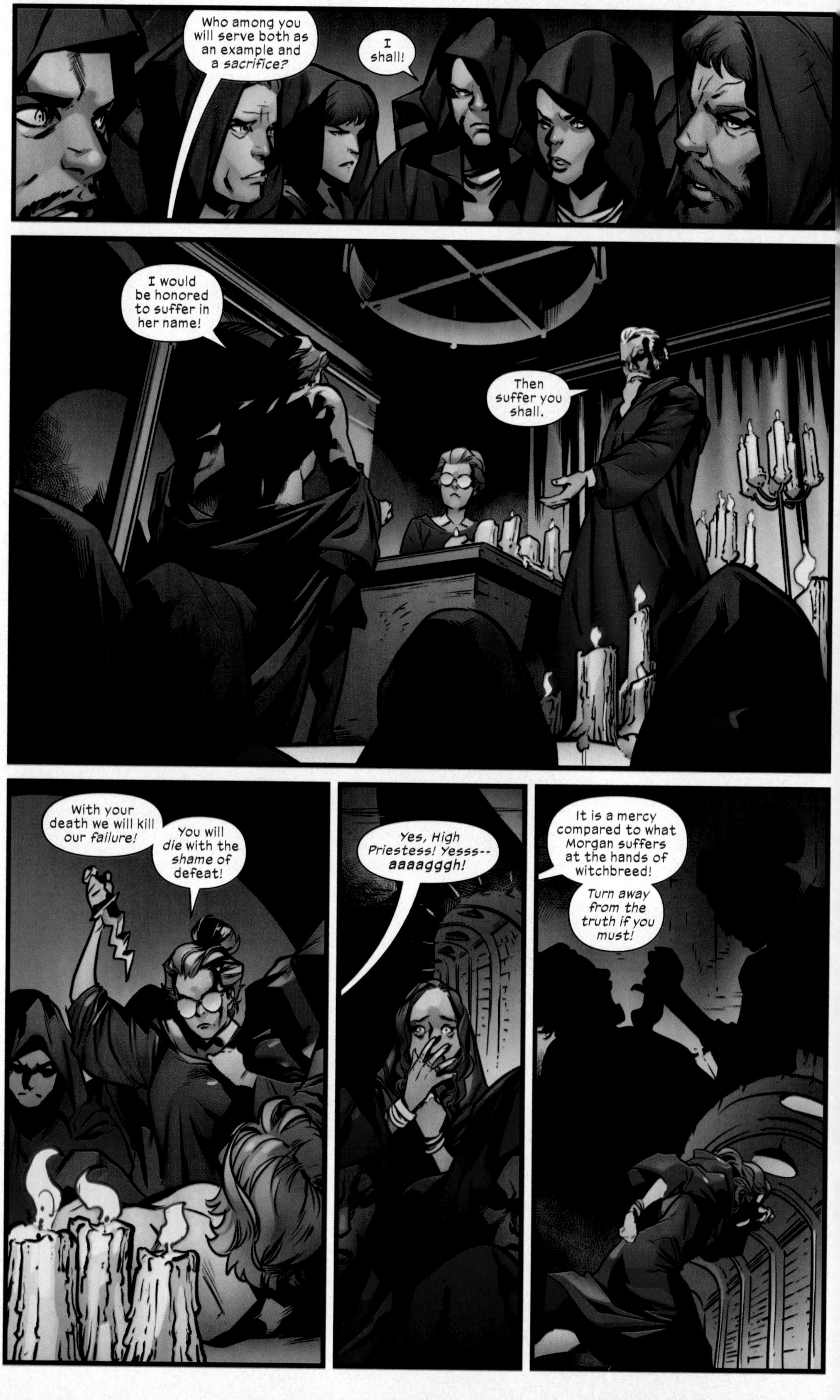

Who among you will serve both as an example and a *sacrifice?*
I shall!
I would be honored to suffer in her name!
Then suffer you shall.
With your death we will kill our *failure!*
You will die with the *shame* of defeat!
Yes, High Priestess! Yesss-- ***aaaagggh!***
It is a mercy compared to what Morgan suffers at the hands of witchbreed!
Turn away from the truth if you must!

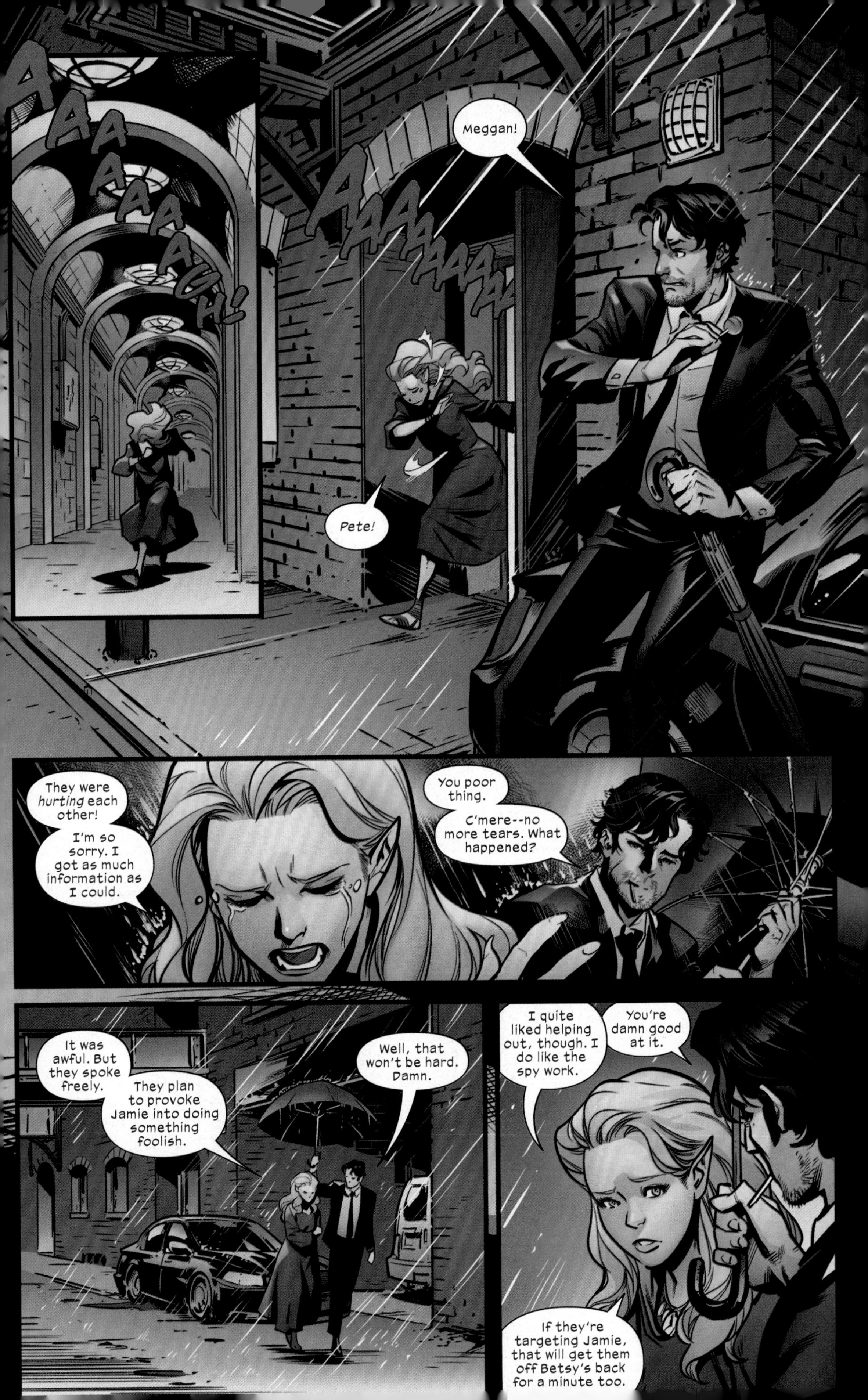
AAAAAAAAUGH!
Meggan!
AAAAAAAAA
Pete!
They were *hurting* each other!
I'm so sorry. I got as much information as I could.
You poor thing.
C'mere--no more tears. What happened?
It was awful. But they spoke freely.
They plan to provoke Jamie into doing something foolish.
Well, that won't be hard. Damn.
I quite liked helping out, though. I do like the spy work.
You're damn good at it.
If they're targeting Jamie, that will get them off Betsy's back for a minute too.

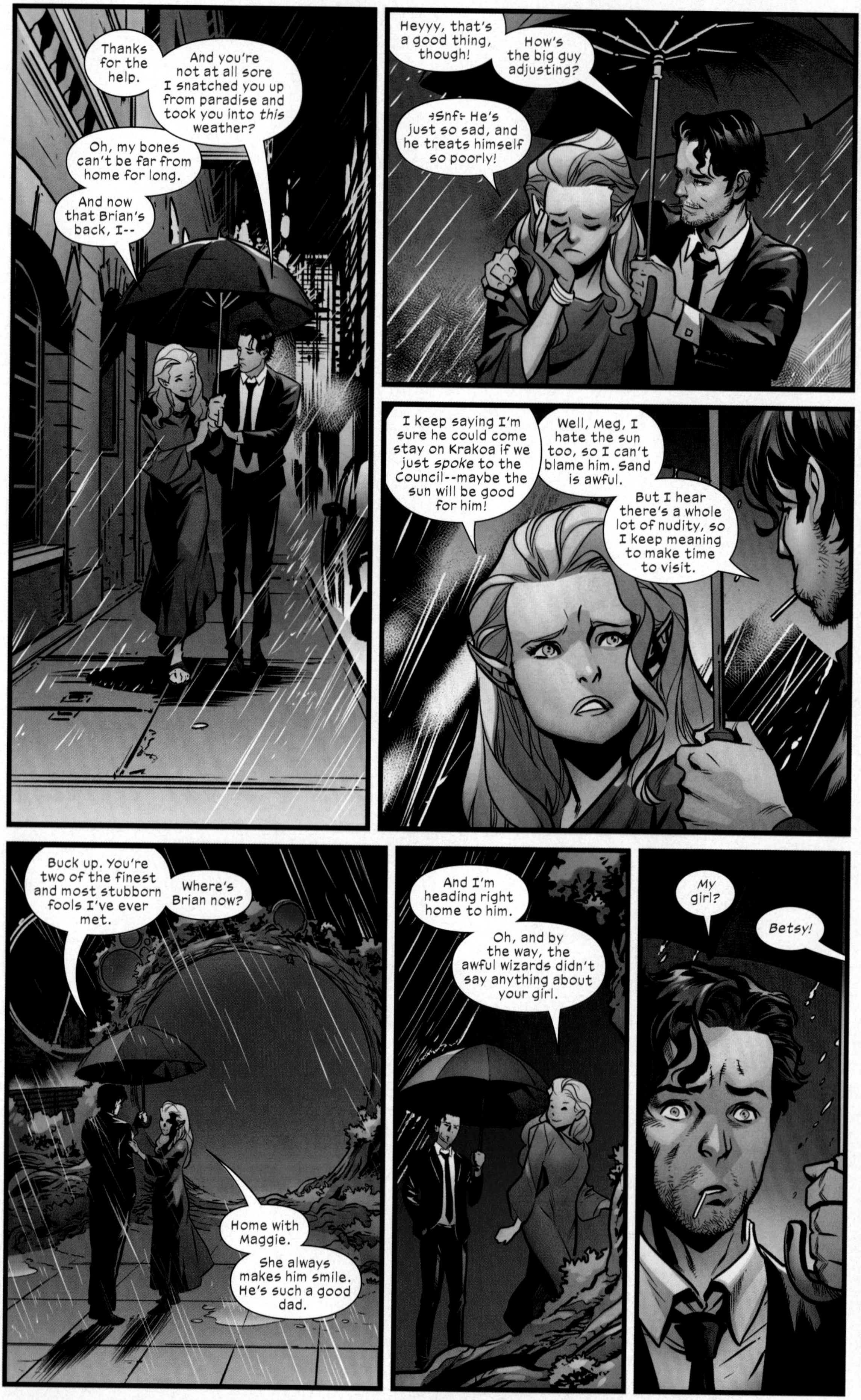
Thanks for the help.
And you're not at all sore I snatched you up from paradise and took you into *this* weather?
Oh, my bones can't be far from home for long.
And now that Brian's back, I--
Heyyy, that's a good thing, though!
How's the big guy adjusting?
+Snf+ He's just so sad, and he treats himself so poorly!
I keep saying I'm sure he could come stay on Krakoa if we just *spoke* to the Council--maybe the sun will be good for him!
Well, Meg, I hate the sun too, so I can't blame him. Sand is awful.
But I hear there's a whole lot of nudity, so I keep meaning to make time to visit.
Buck up. You're two of the finest and most stubborn fools I've ever met.
Where's Brian now?
Home with Maggie.
She always makes him smile. He's such a good dad.
And I'm heading right home to him.
Oh, and by the way, the awful wizards didn't say anything about your girl.
My girl?
Betsy!

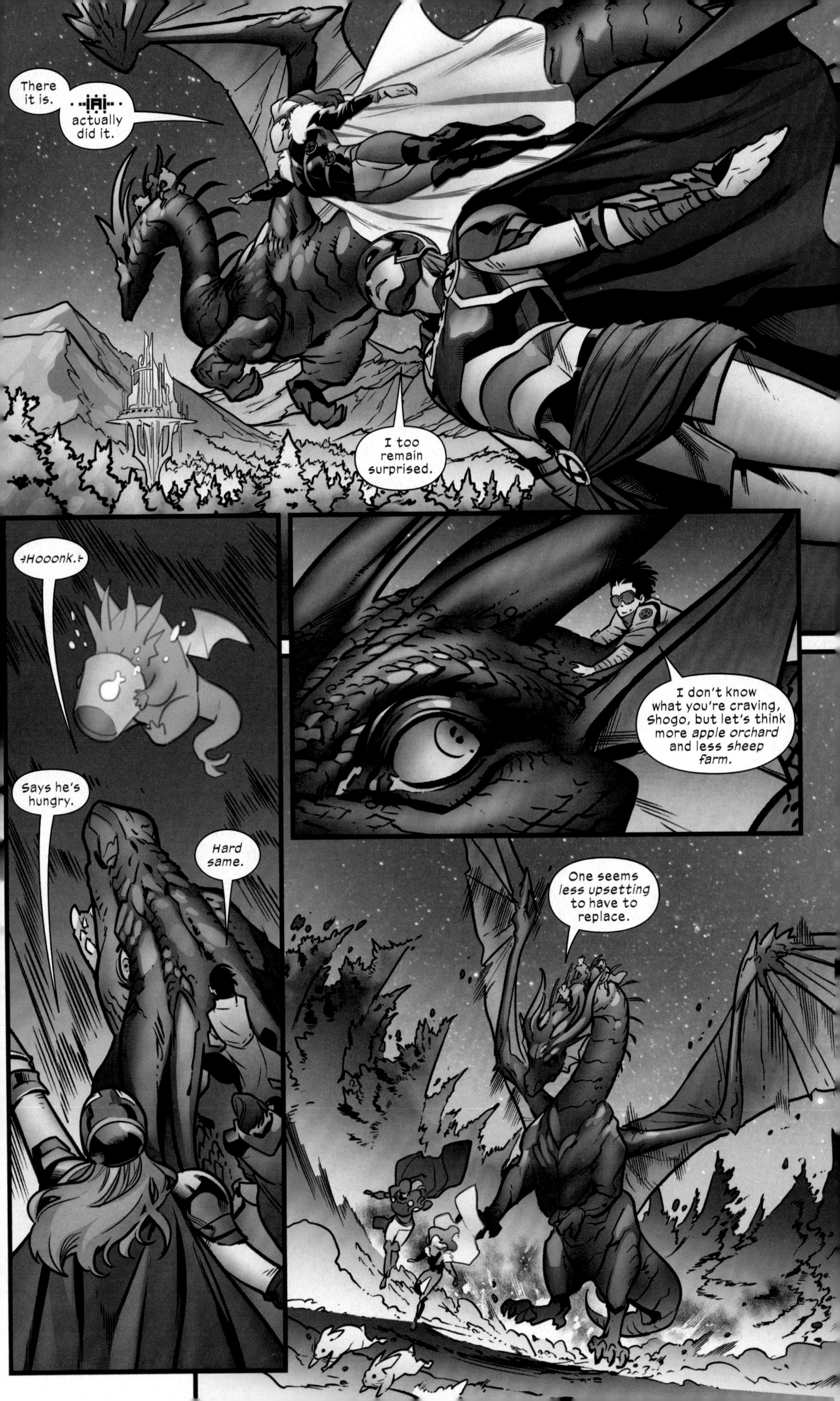
There it is.
..iAi.. actually did it.
I too remain surprised.
Hooonk.
Says he's hungry.
Hard same.
I don't know what you're craving, Shogo, but let's think more *apple orchard* and less *sheep farm*.
One seems *less upsetting* to have to replace.

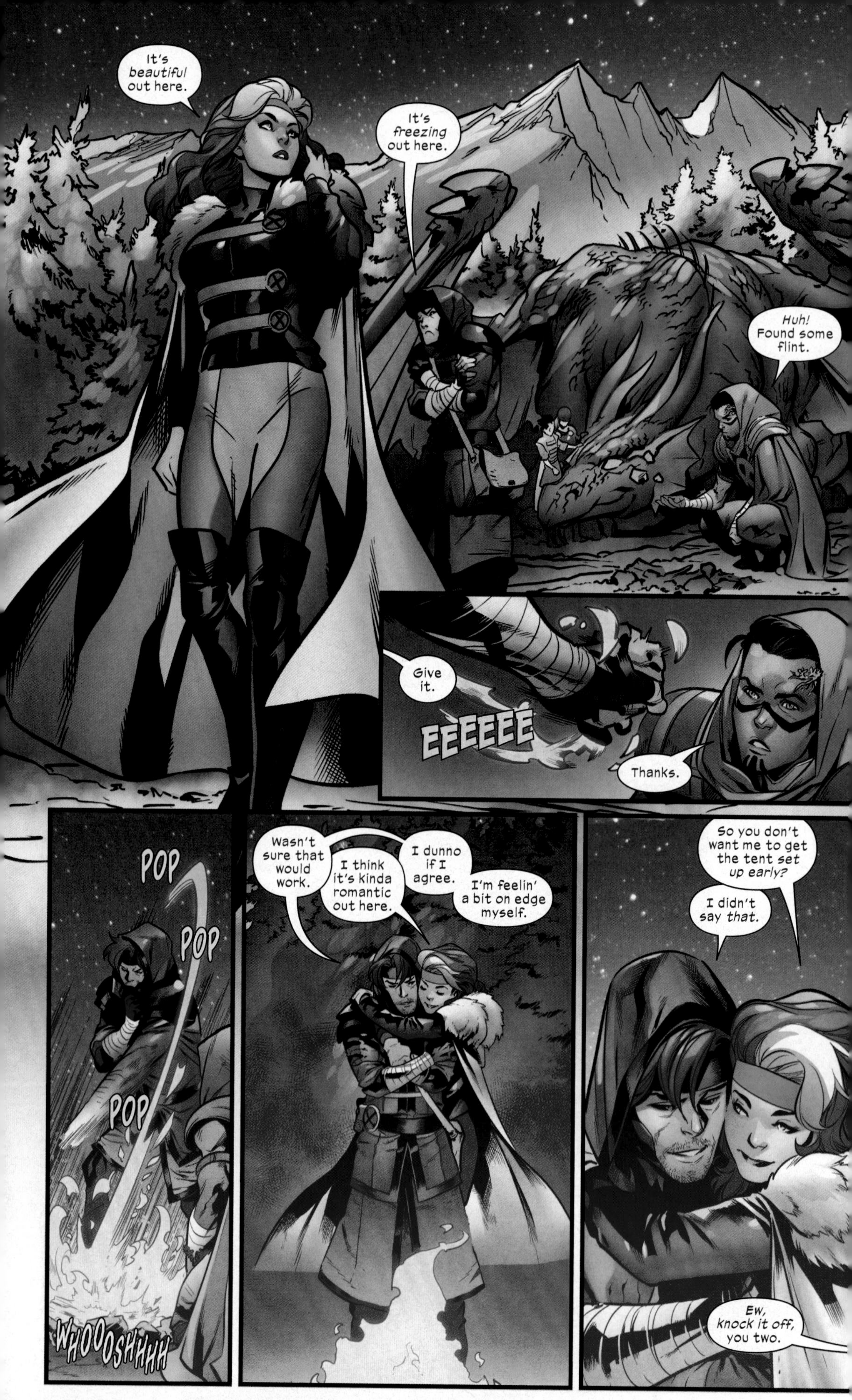

It's *beautiful* out here.
It's *freezing* out here.
Huh! Found some flint.
Give it.
EEEEEE
Thanks.
POP
POP
POP
WHOOOSHHHH
Wasn't sure that would work.
I think it's kinda romantic out here.
I dunno if I agree.
I'm feelin' a bit on edge myself.
So you don't want me to get the tent set *up early?*
I didn't say *that.*
Ew, knock it off, you two.

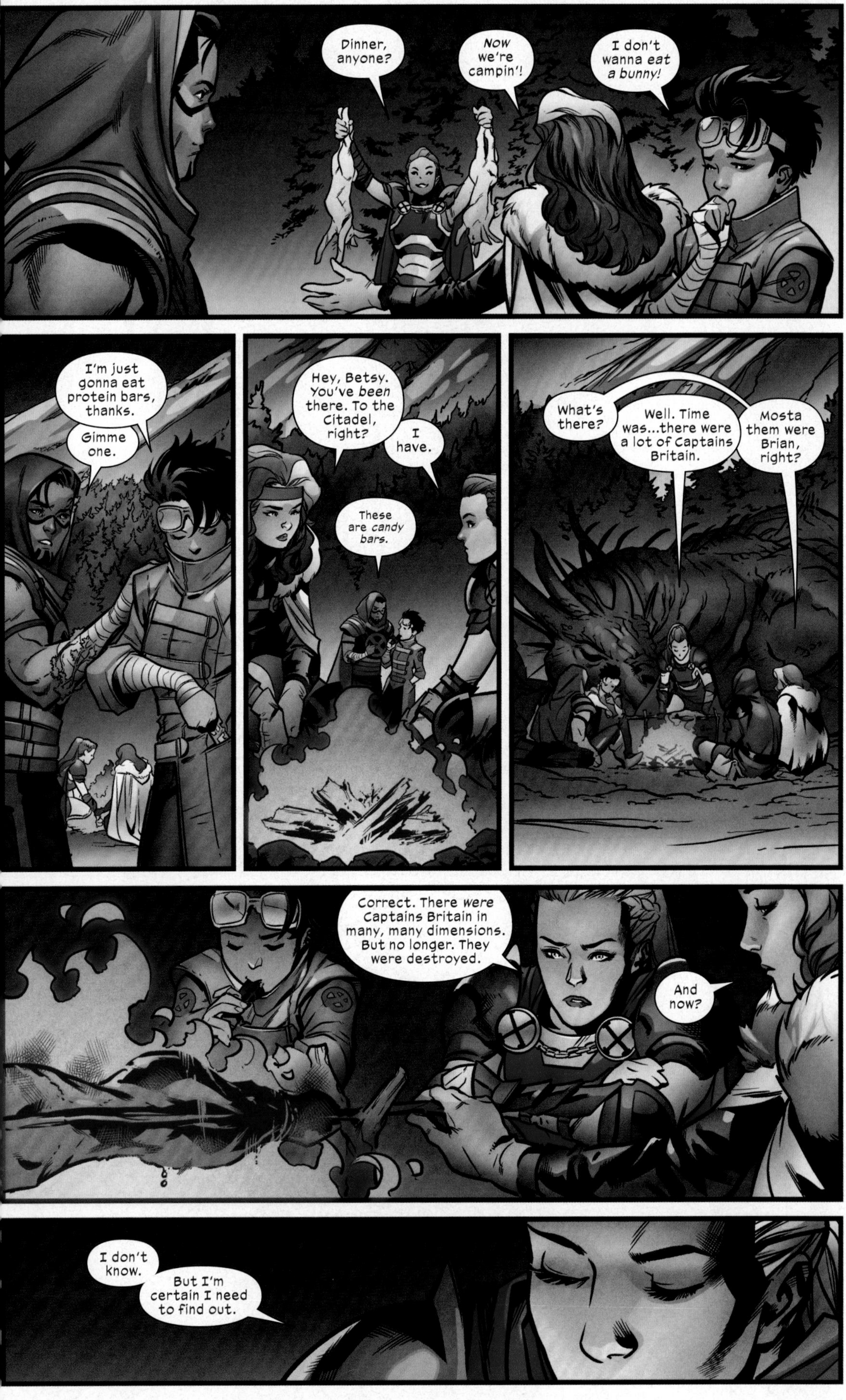

Dinner, anyone?
Now we're campin'!
I don't wanna eat a bunny!
I'm just gonna eat protein bars, thanks.
Gimme one.
Hey, Betsy. You've been there. To the Citadel, right?
I have.
These are candy bars.
What's there?
Well. Time was...there were a lot of Captains Britain.
Mosta them were Brian, right?
Correct. There were Captains Britain in many, many dimensions. But no longer. They were destroyed.
And now?
I don't know.
But I'm certain I need to find out.

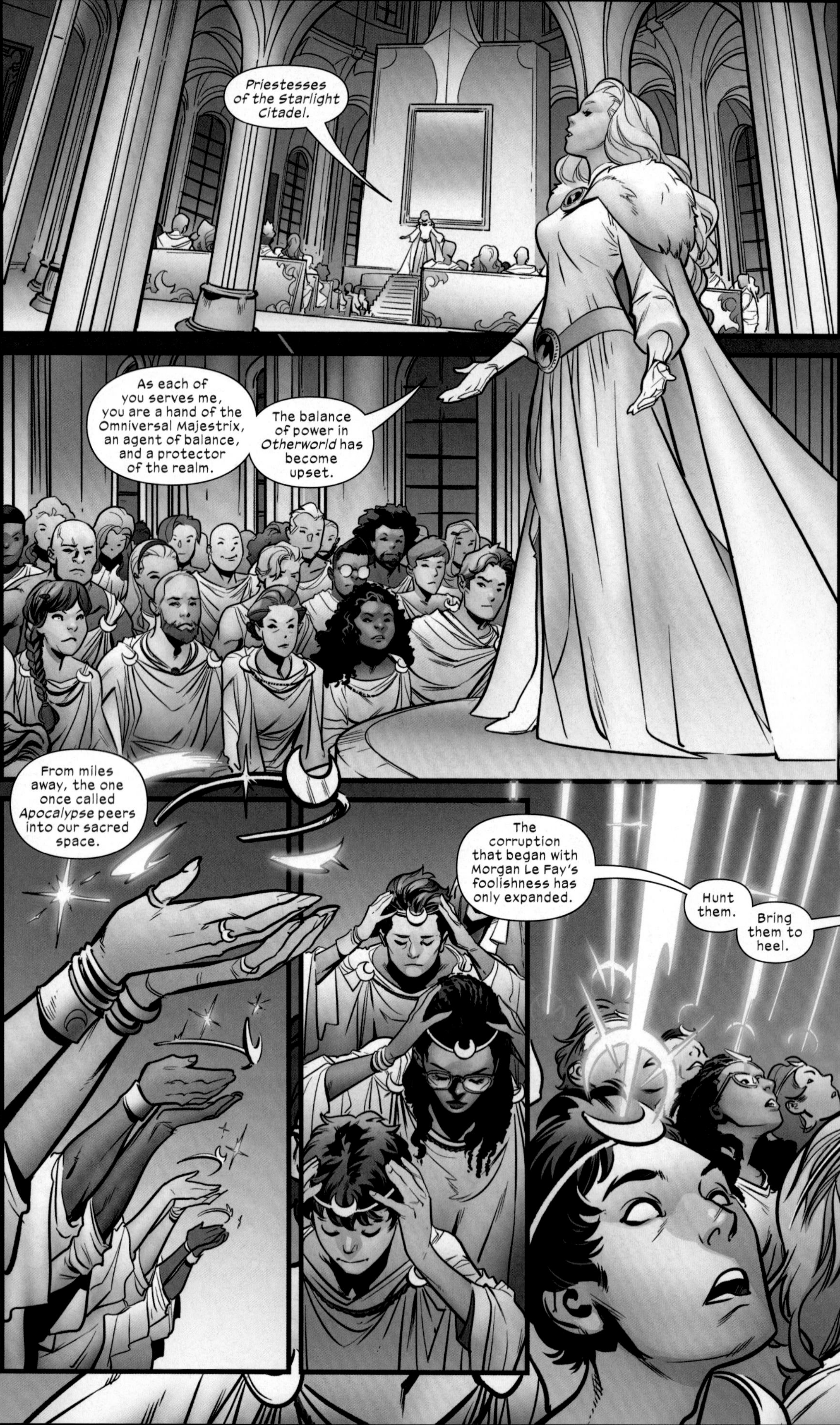

Priestesses of the Starlight Citadel.
As each of you serves me, you are a hand of the Omniversal Majestrix, an agent of balance, and a protector of the realm.
The balance of power in *Otherworld* has become upset.
From miles away, the one once called *Apocalypse* peers into our sacred space.
The corruption that began with Morgan Le Fay's foolishness has only expanded.
Hunt them.
Bring them to heel.

RITE OF INITIATION OF THE WHITE PRIESTESSES: THE MOONLIT DIADEM

[Following the reading of the **SATURNYNIAN MYSTERIES,** the following call-and-response segment of the ritual is to take place during the **RELEASE OF THE 28TH VEIL.**]

SATURNYNE:
See before you the implements of your duty.

Crown thyself in the Moonlight Diadem. See how it transforms you - veiling you in white light so that you may shine into dark places. Anywhere the light can go, you too can appear.

> **PRIESTESSES (all):** *If We Can Be Like the Light.*

SATURNYNE:
Next, your Crescent Bow. Merely reach to the bright sky above and draw down the moon into your hand, pull its light with a slow coaxing - never force - and raise it high. It will shoot far.

Lastly, your ammunition. Your arrows are pulled from the stars' own light and are as innumerable and far-reaching as the stars themselves. They will strike true.

Those who you fight will be limited by the bonds of reality. These chains dissolve in the moon's white light.

The gulf between who you were before and who you are now has never been wider.

Who do you see in the looking glass?

> **PRIESTESSES (all):** *One Who Wants for the Self-Reality.*

SATURNYNE:
Remove the final veil and look once more.

Who do you see in the Looking Glass?

> **PRIESTESSES (all):** *One Who Gives for the All-Reality.*

SATURYNE:
When I call, don your diadem and defend.

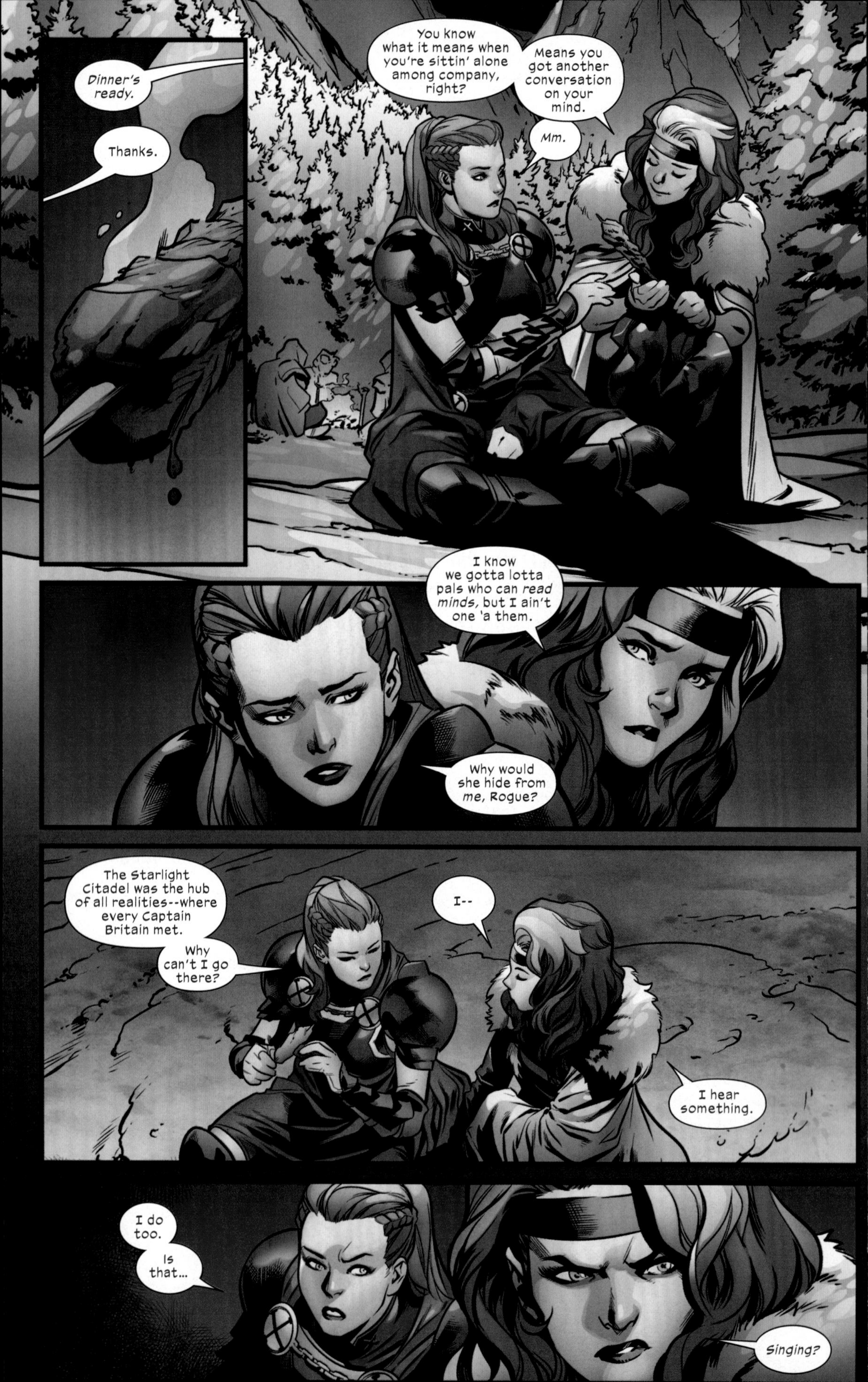
Dinner's ready.
Thanks.
You know what it means when you're sittin' alone among company, right?
Means you got another conversation on your mind.
Mm.
I know we gotta lotta pals who can *read minds*, but I ain't one 'a them.
Why would she hide from *me*, Rogue?
The Starlight Citadel was the hub of all realities--where every Captain Britain met.
Why can't I go there?
I--
I hear something.
I do too.
Is that...
Singing?

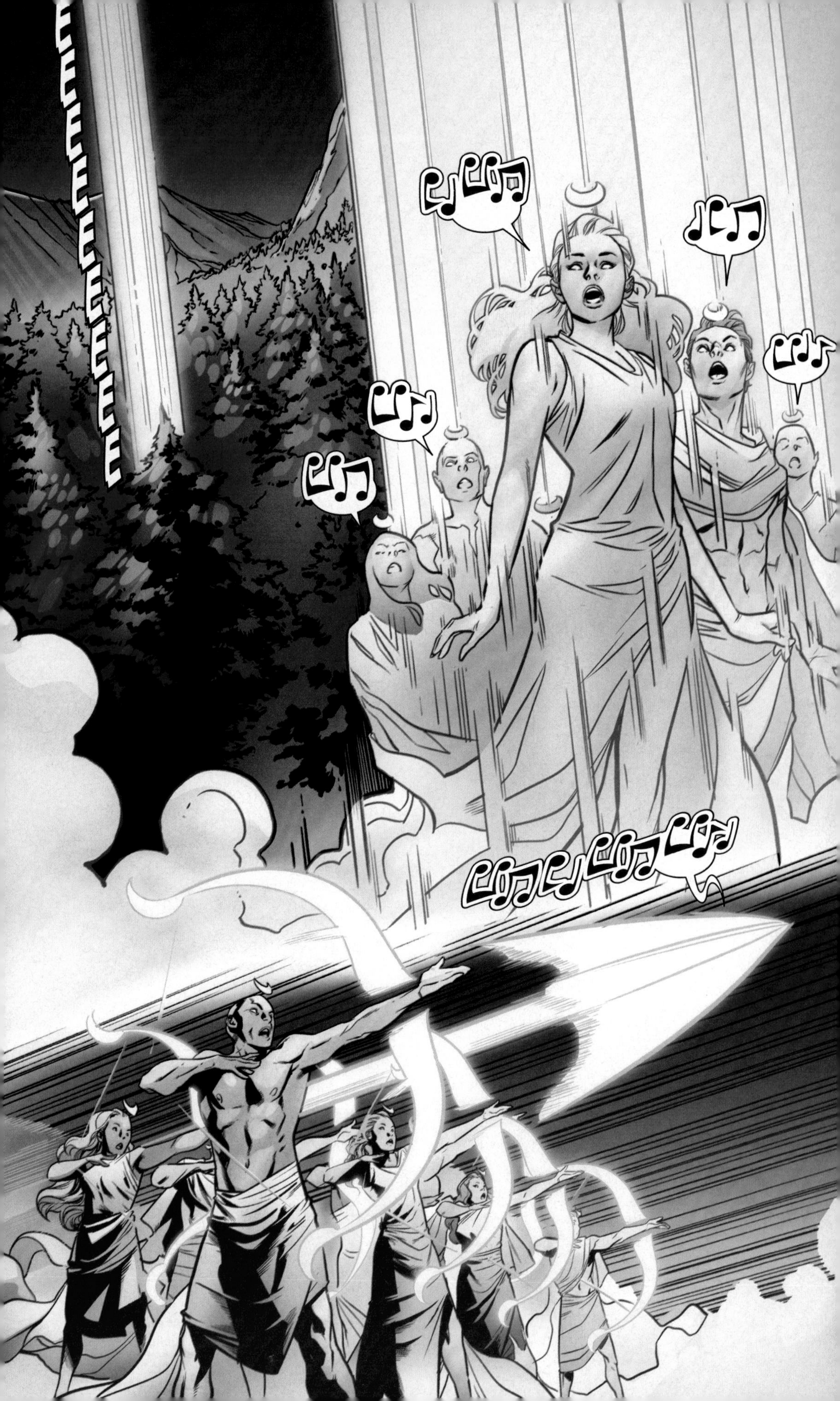

EEEEEEEEEEEEE

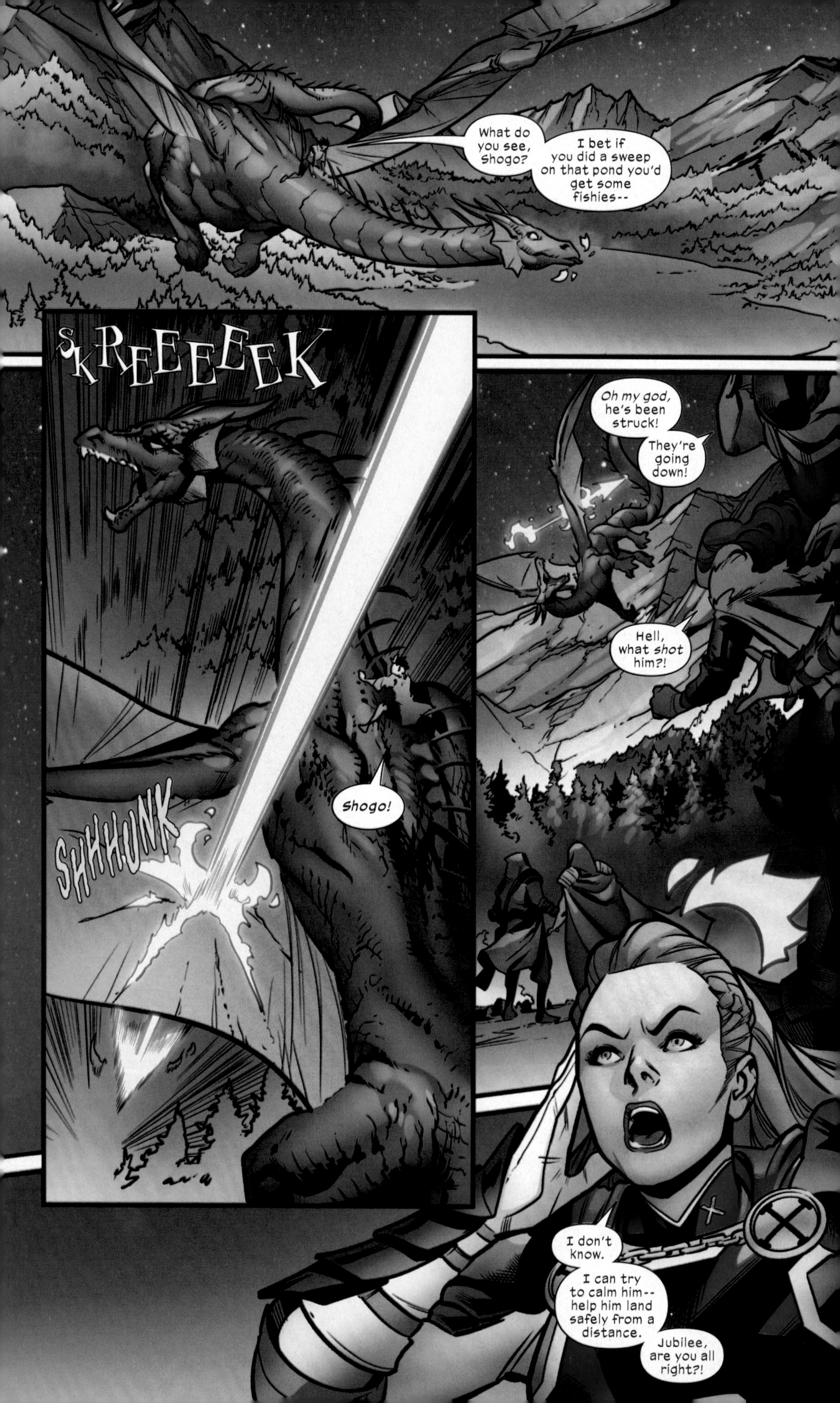
What do you see, Shogo?
I bet if you did a sweep on that pond you'd get some fishies--
SKREEEEEK
Shogo!
SHHHUNK
Oh my god, he's been struck!
They're going down!
Hell, what shot him?!
I don't know.
I can try to calm him-- help him land safely from a distance.
Jubilee, are you all right?!

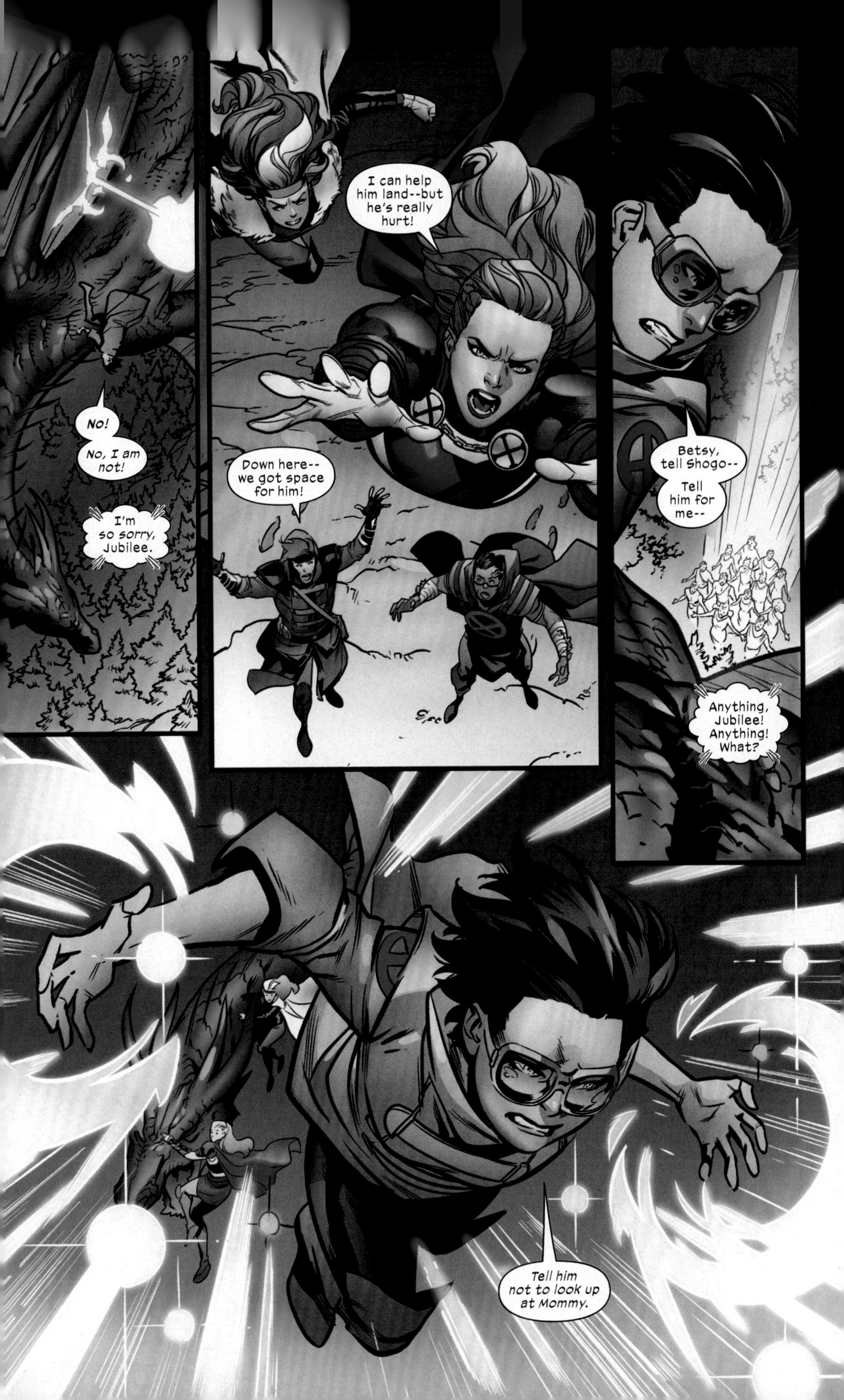
No!
No, I am not!
I'm so sorry, Jubilee.
I can help him land--but he's really hurt!
Down here--we got space for him!
Betsy, tell Shogo--
Tell him for me--
Anything, Jubilee! Anything! What?
Tell him not to look up at Mommy.

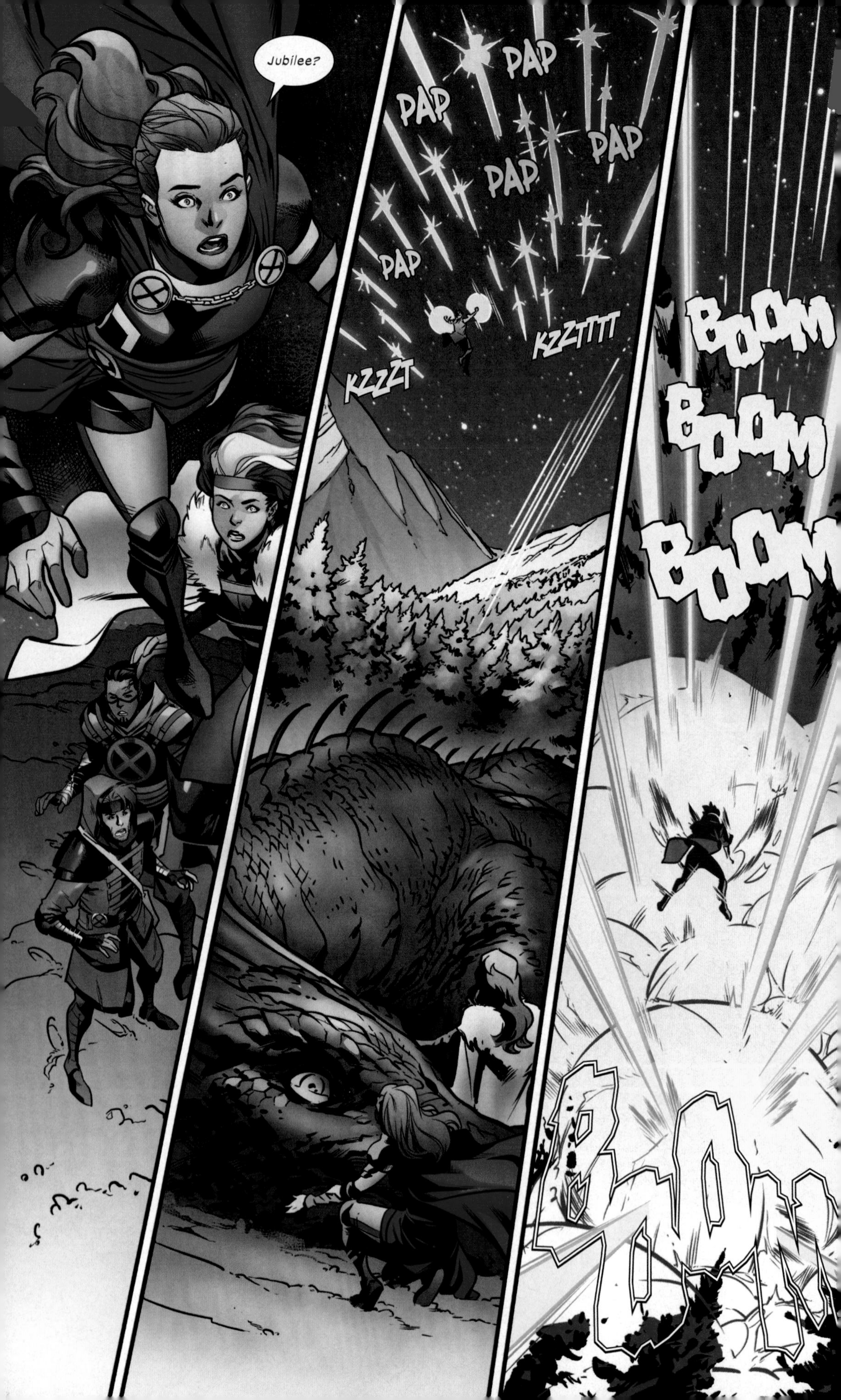
Jubilee?
PAP
PAP
PAP
PAP
PAP
KZZZT
KZZTTTT
BOOM
BOOM
BOOM
BOOM

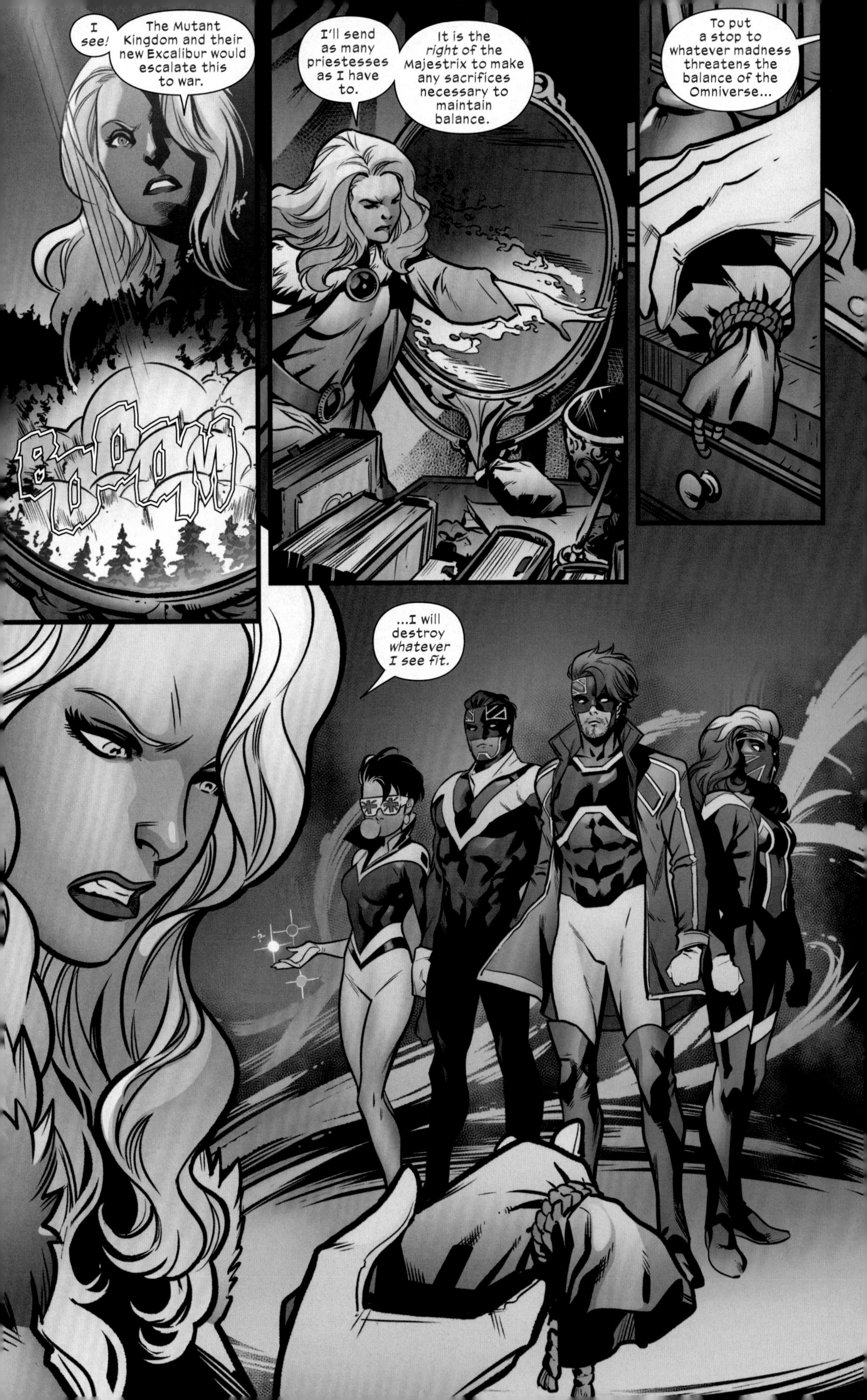

I see!
The Mutant Kingdom and their new Excalibur would escalate this to war.
BOOM
I'll send as many priestesses as I have to.
It is the right of the Majestrix to make any sacrifices necessary to maintain balance.
To put a stop to whatever madness threatens the balance of the Omniverse...
...I will destroy whatever I see fit.

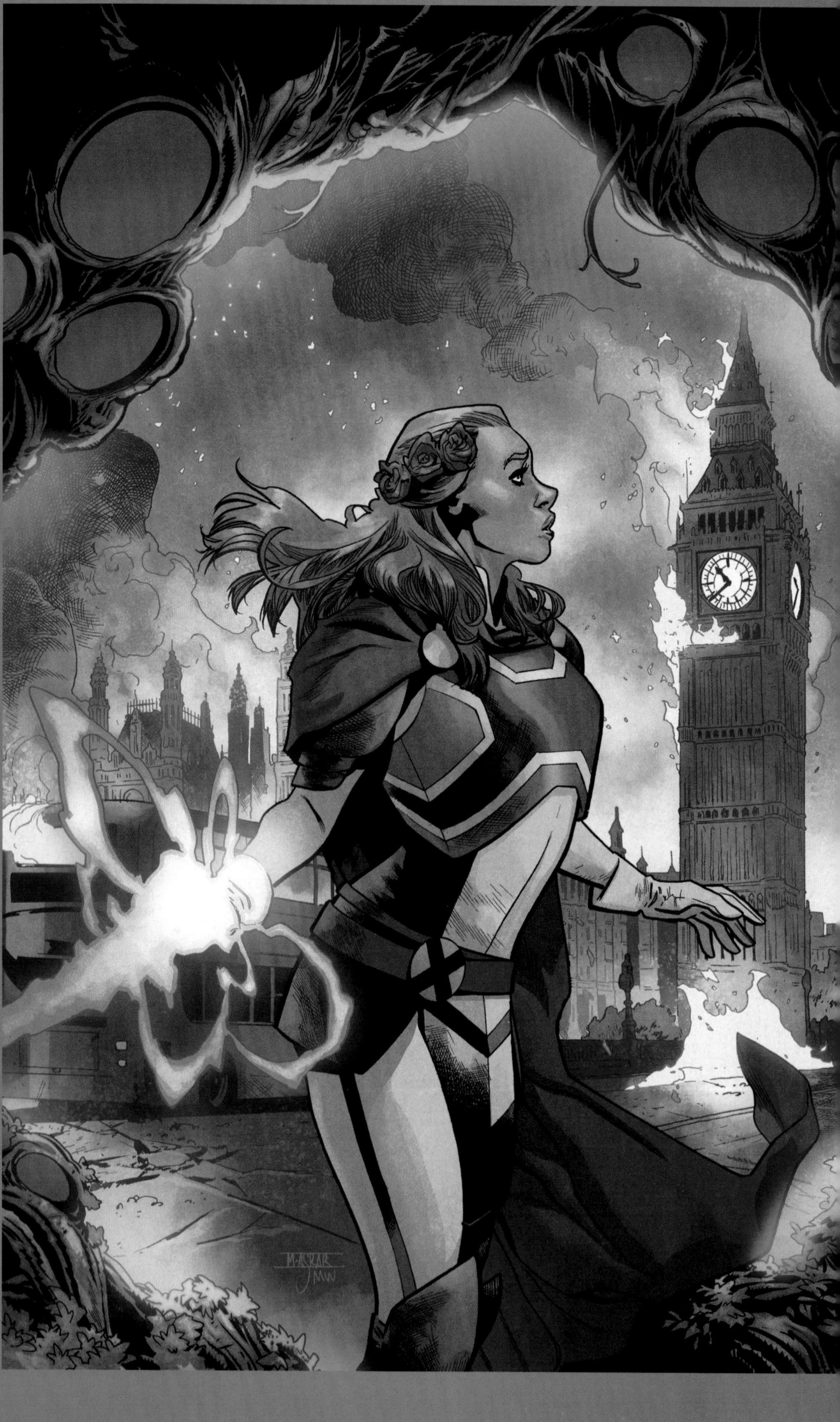

A Crooked World

LONDON: PREPARE FOR WAR

RECENT INTELLIGENCE SUGGESTS THE ISLAND-NATION OF KRAKOA MOVES TOWARD AGGRESSIVE ACTION. REPORTS SUGGEST RECENT ATTACKS CAN BE SOURCED TO MUTANT-SPECIFIC VEGETATION.

Intelligence suggests burning of mutant vegetation until authorities can be present.

Protect and survive!

SEE A MUTANT?
TELL A HUMAN

FOR QUEEN AND COUNTRY

THE HUMAN RACE IS IN PERIL

DEFEND IT WITH ALL YOUR MIGHT

-- *Minister of Information, Reuben Brousseau*

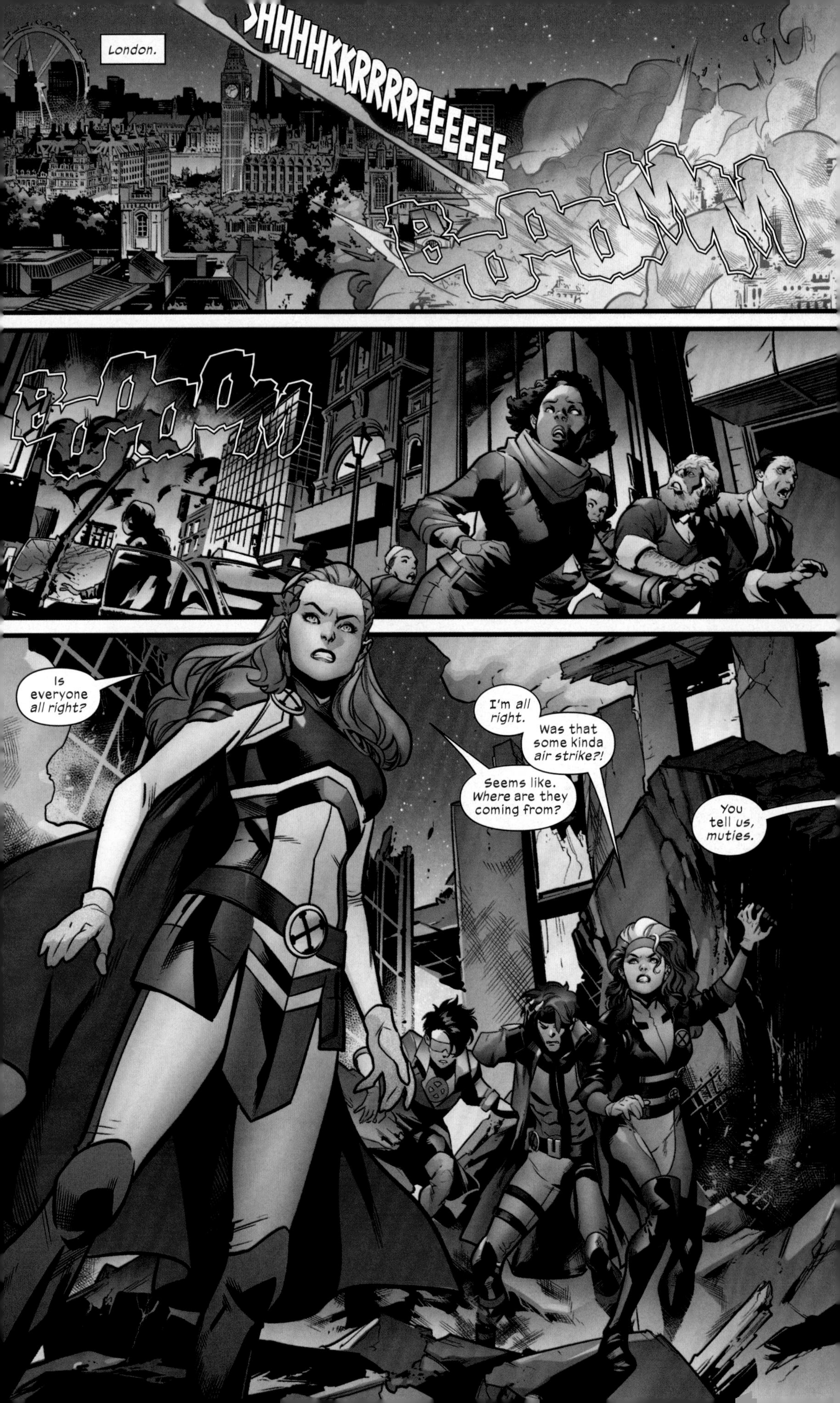
London.
SHHHHKKRRRRREEEEEE
BOOOMM
BOOOM
Is everyone all right?
I'm all right.
Was that some kinda air strike?!
Seems like. Where are they coming from?
You tell us, muties.

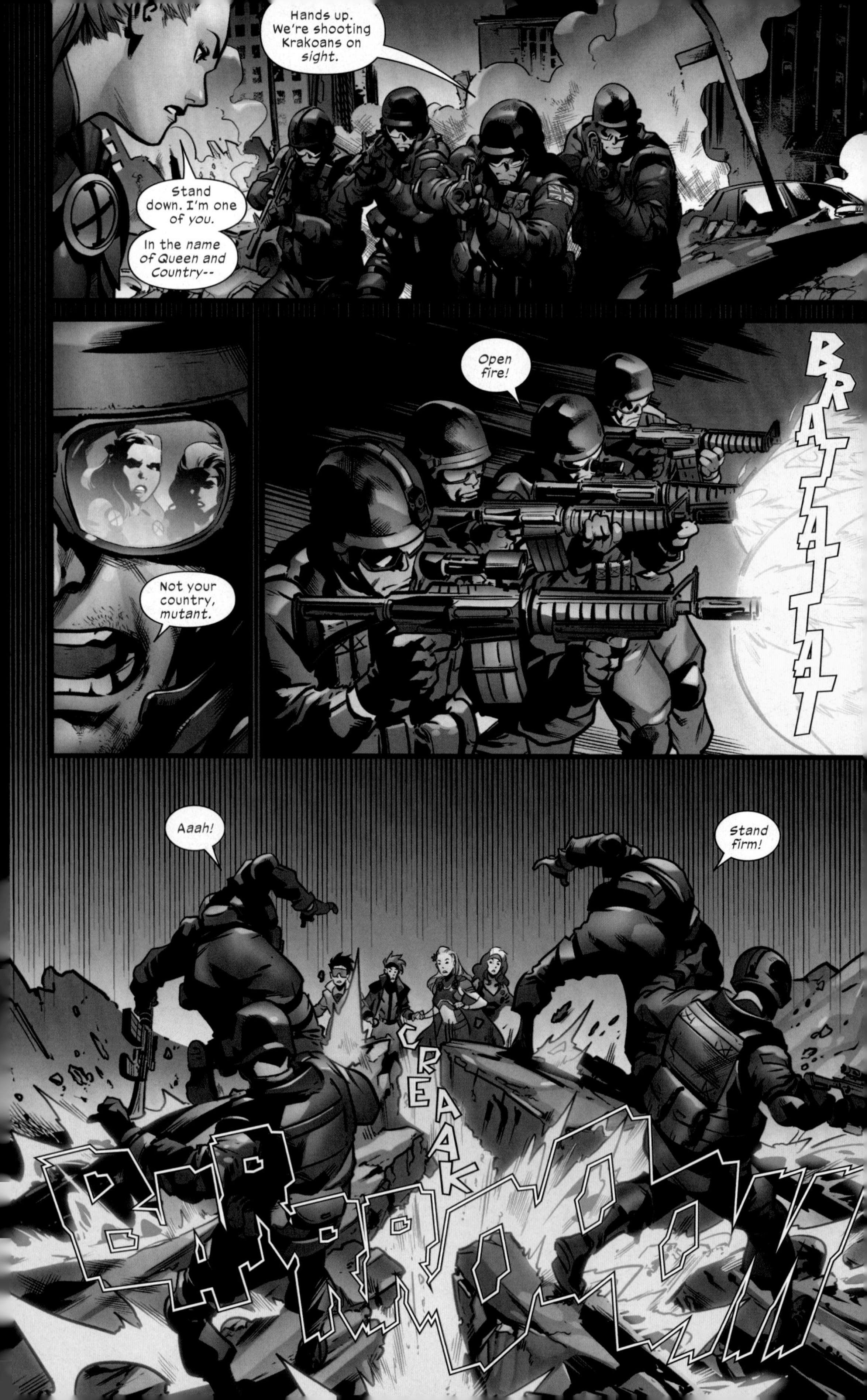
Hands up. We're shooting Krakoans on sight.
Stand down. I'm one of you.
In the name of Queen and Country--
Not your country, mutant.
Open fire!
BRATATATAT
Aaah!
Stand firm!
CREAAK
BRRROOOOM!

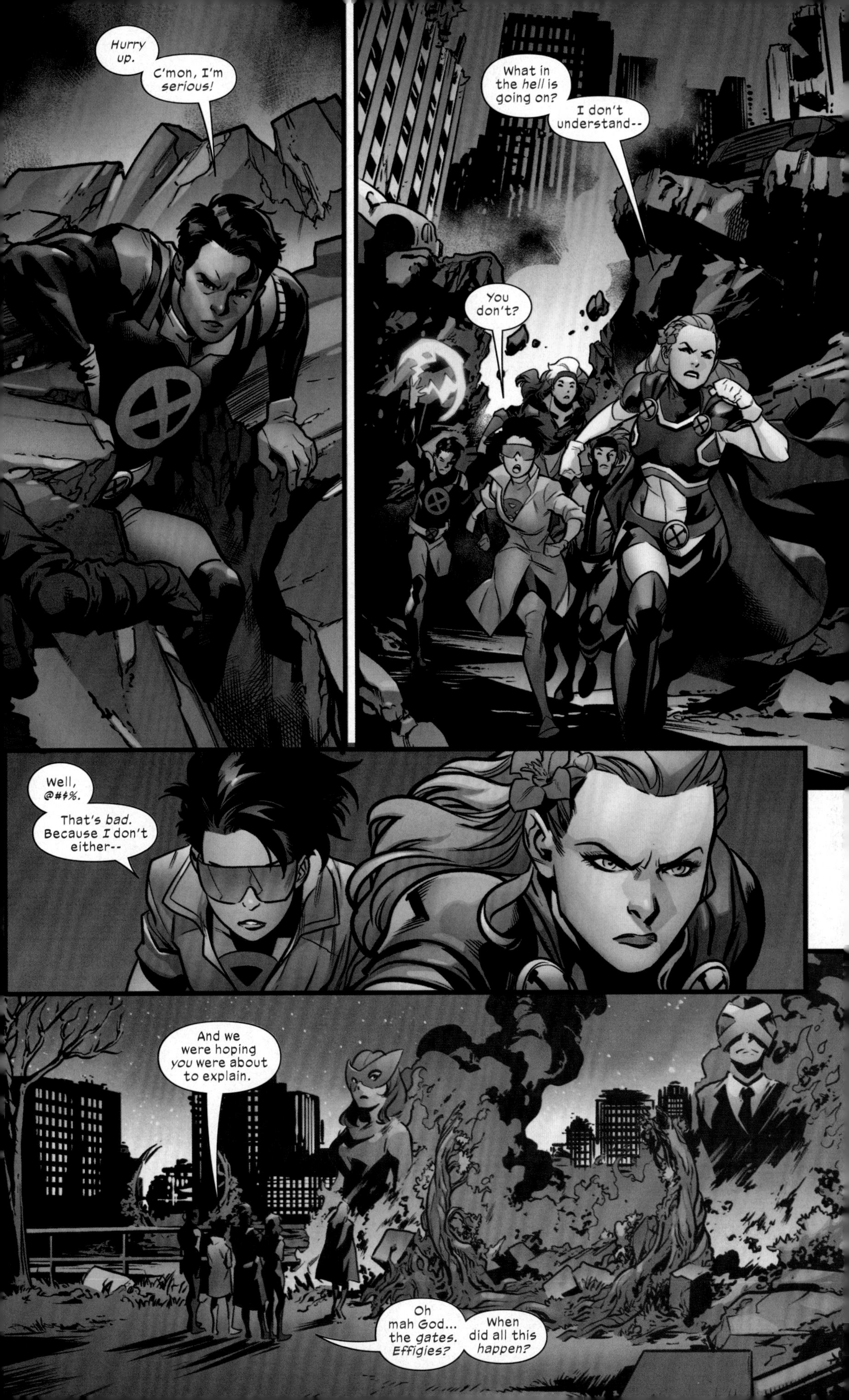
Hurry up.
C'mon, I'm serious!
What in the hell is going on?
I don't understand--
You don't?
Well, @#$%.
That's bad. Because I don't either--
And we were hoping you were about to explain.
Oh mah God... the gates. Effigies?
When did all this happen?

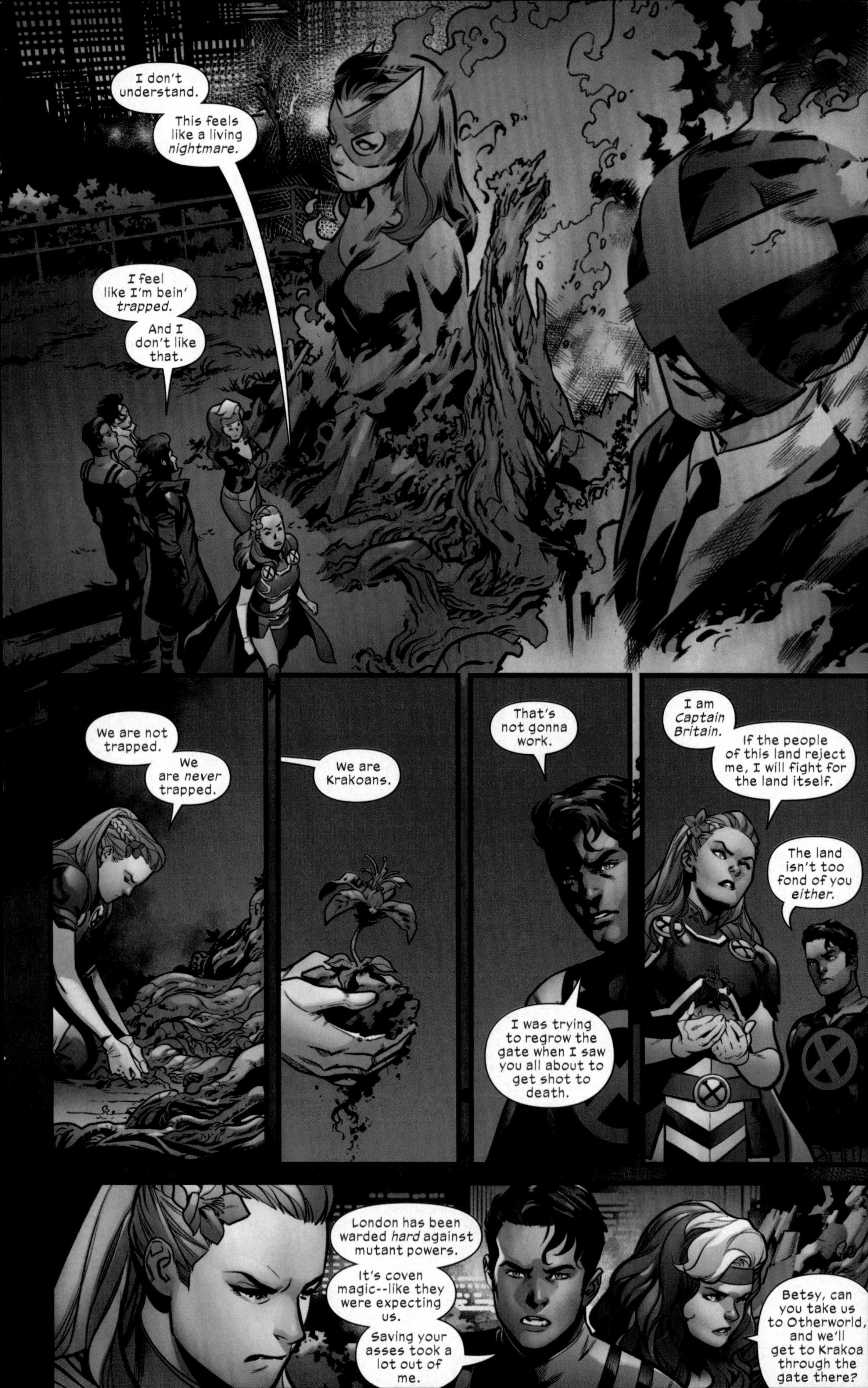
I don't understand.
This feels like a living nightmare.
I feel like I'm bein' trapped.
And I don't like that.
We are not trapped.
We are never trapped.
We are Krakoans.
That's not gonna work.
I was trying to regrow the gate when I saw you all about to get shot to death.
I am Captain Britain.
If the people of this land reject me, I will fight for the land itself.
The land isn't too fond of you either.
London has been warded hard against mutant powers.
It's coven magic--like they were expecting us.
Saving your asses took a lot out of me.
Betsy, can you take us to Otherworld, and we'll get to Krakoa through the gate there?

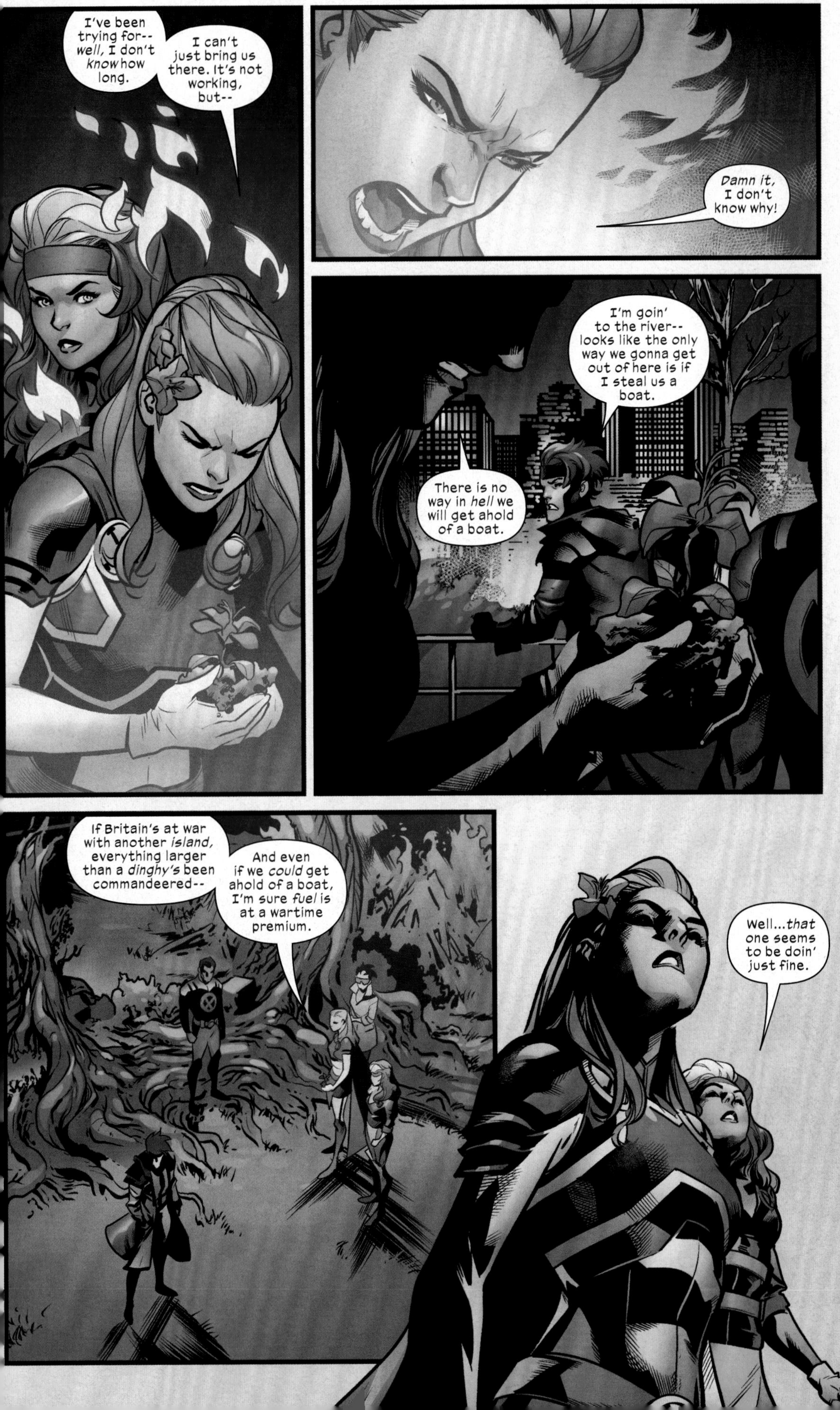
I've been trying for-- well, I don't know how long.
I can't just bring us there. It's not working, but--
Damn it, I don't know why!
I'm goin' to the river-- looks like the only way we gonna get out of here is if I steal us a boat.
There is no way in hell we will get ahold of a boat.
If Britain's at war with another island, everything larger than a dinghy's been commandeered--
And even if we could get ahold of a boat, I'm sure fuel is at a wartime premium.
Well...that one seems to be doin' just fine.

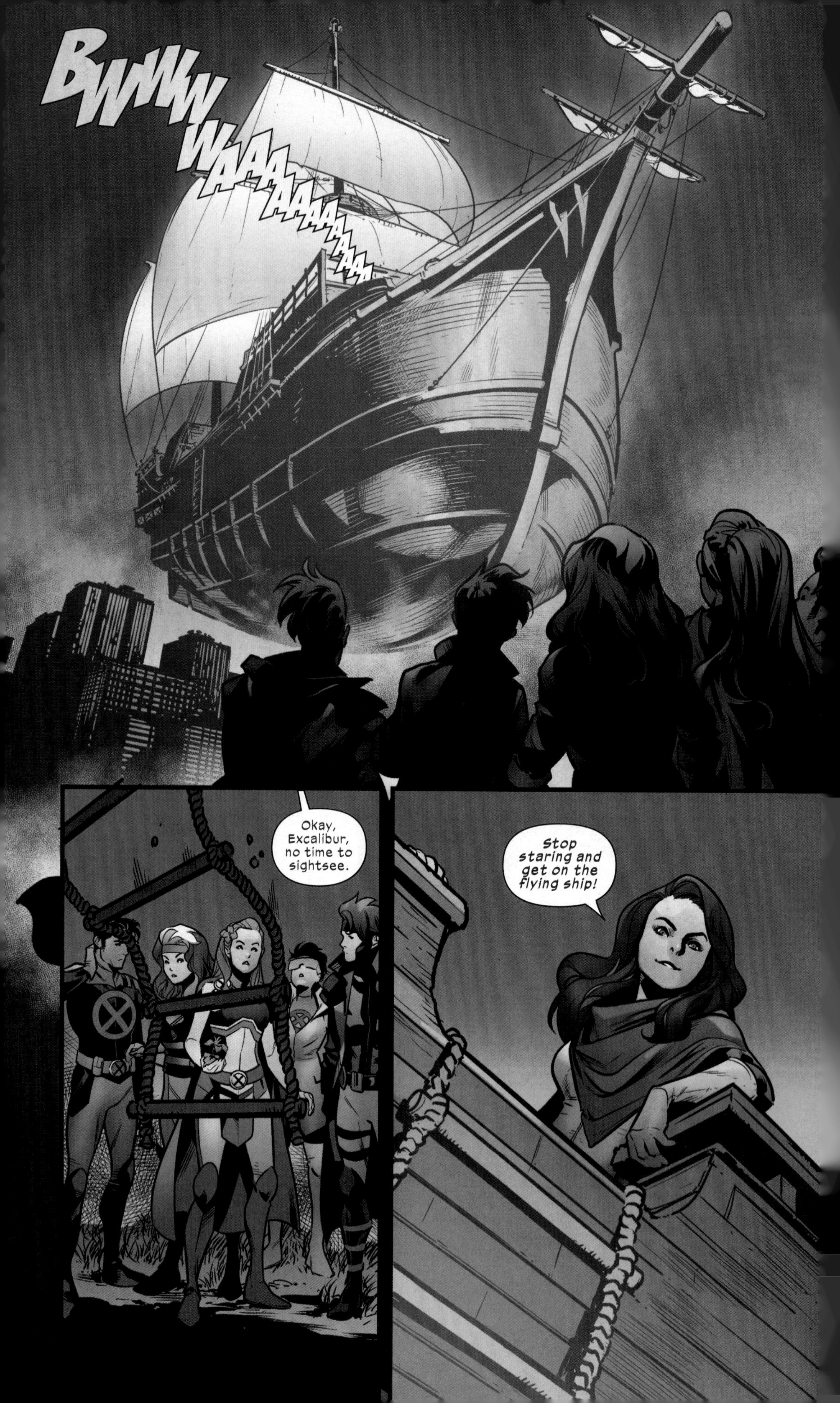
BWWWWAAAAAAAAAAAM
Okay, Excalibur, no time to sightsee.
Stop staring and get on the flying ship!

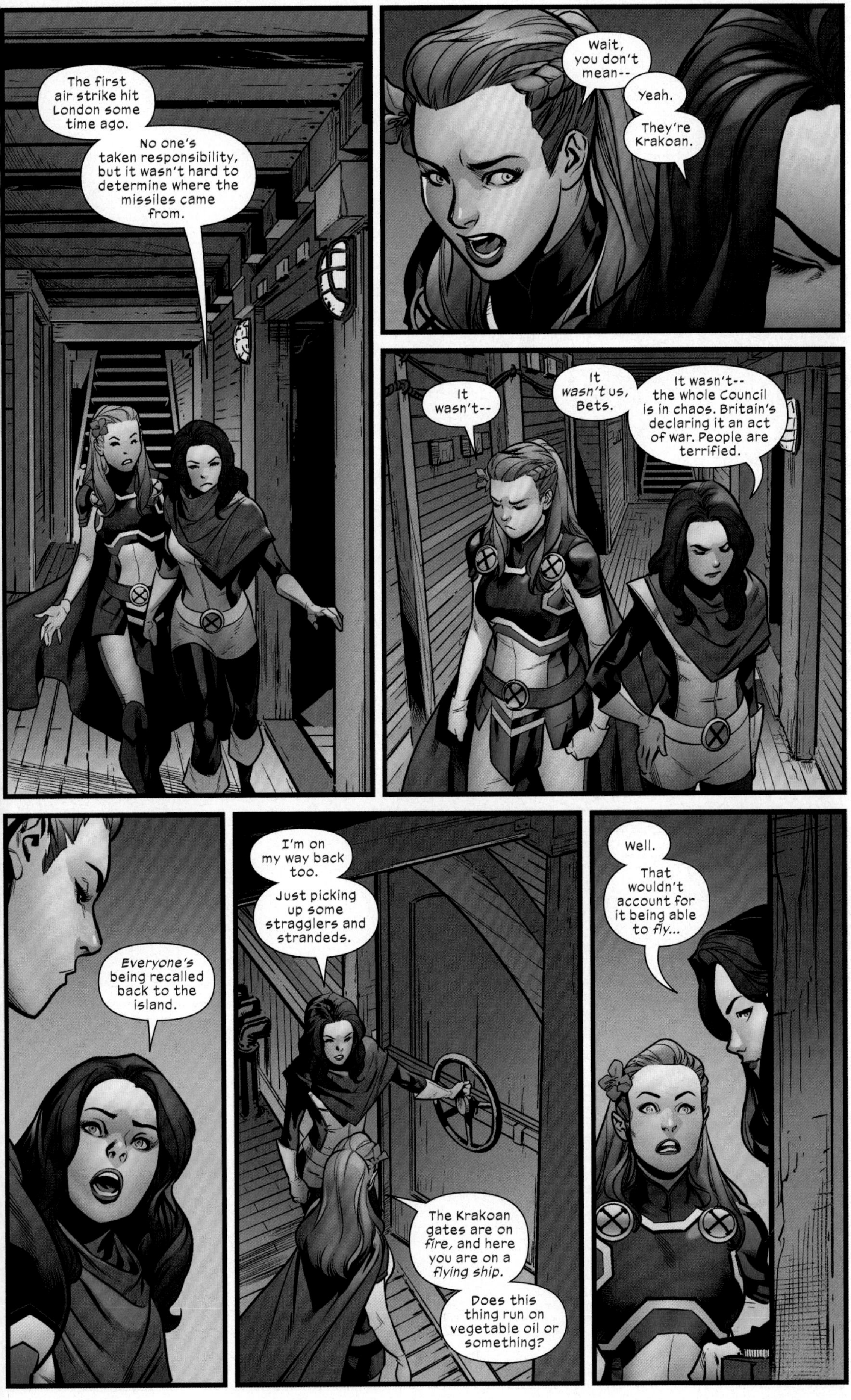

The first air strike hit London some time ago.
No one's taken responsibility, but it wasn't hard to determine where the missiles came from.
Wait, you don't mean--
Yeah.
They're Krakoan.
It wasn't--
It *wasn't* us, Bets.
It wasn't-- the whole Council is in chaos. Britain's declaring it an act of war. People are terrified.
Everyone's being recalled back to the island.
I'm on my way back too.
Just picking up some stragglers and strandeds.
The Krakoan gates are on *fire,* and here you are on a *flying ship.*
Does this thing run on vegetable oil or something?
Well.
That wouldn't account for it being able to *fly...*

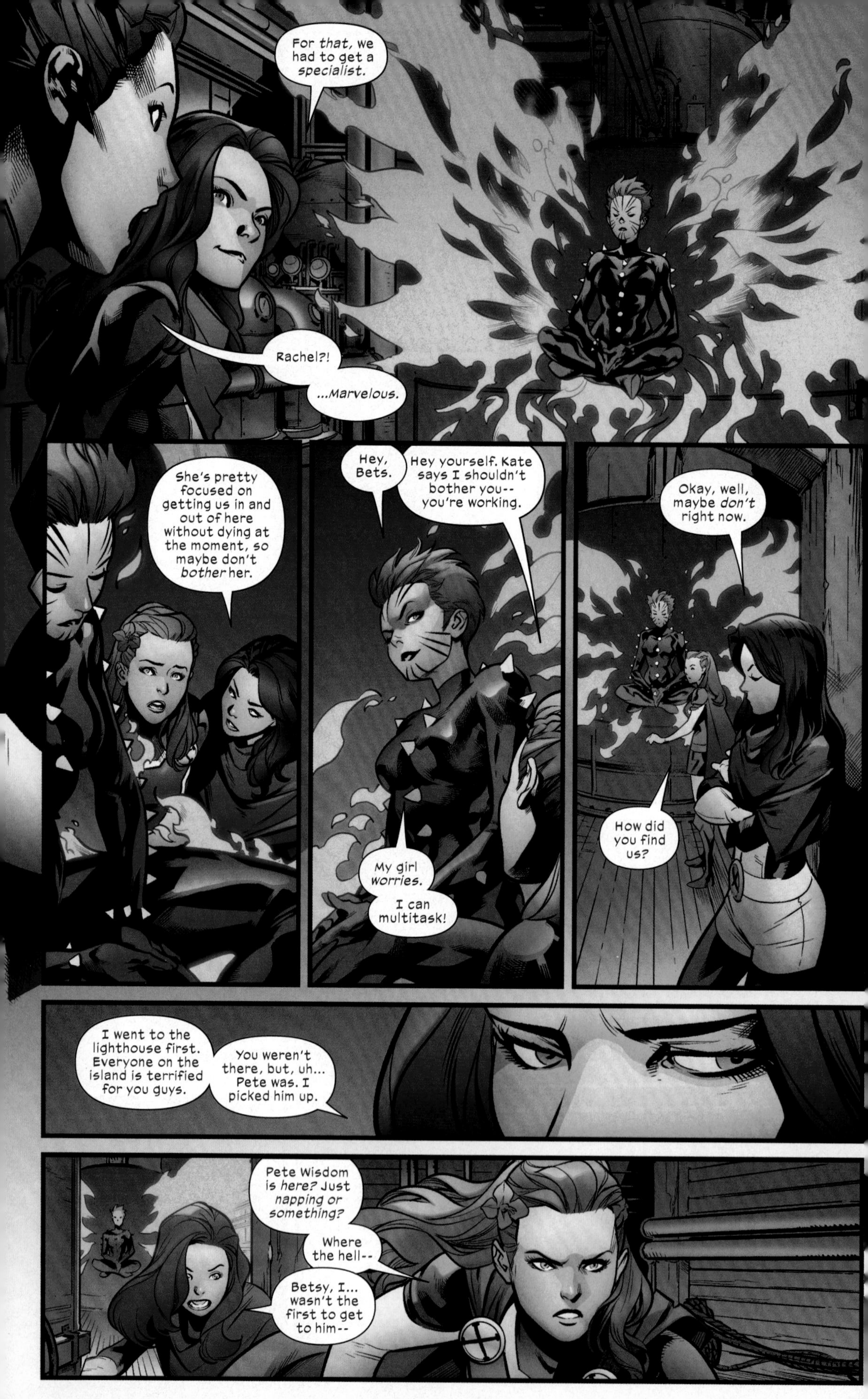
For *that*, we had to get a *specialist*.
Rachel?!
...*Marvelous.*
She's pretty focused on getting us in and out of here without dying at the moment, so maybe don't *bother* her.
Hey, Bets.
Hey yourself. Kate says I shouldn't bother you-- you're working.
My girl *worries*.
I can multitask!
Okay, well, maybe *don't* right now.
How did you find us?
I went to the lighthouse first. Everyone on the island is terrified for you guys.
You weren't there, but, uh... Pete was. I picked him up.
Pete Wisdom is *here?* Just *napping or something?*
Where the hell--
Betsy, I... wasn't the first to get to him--

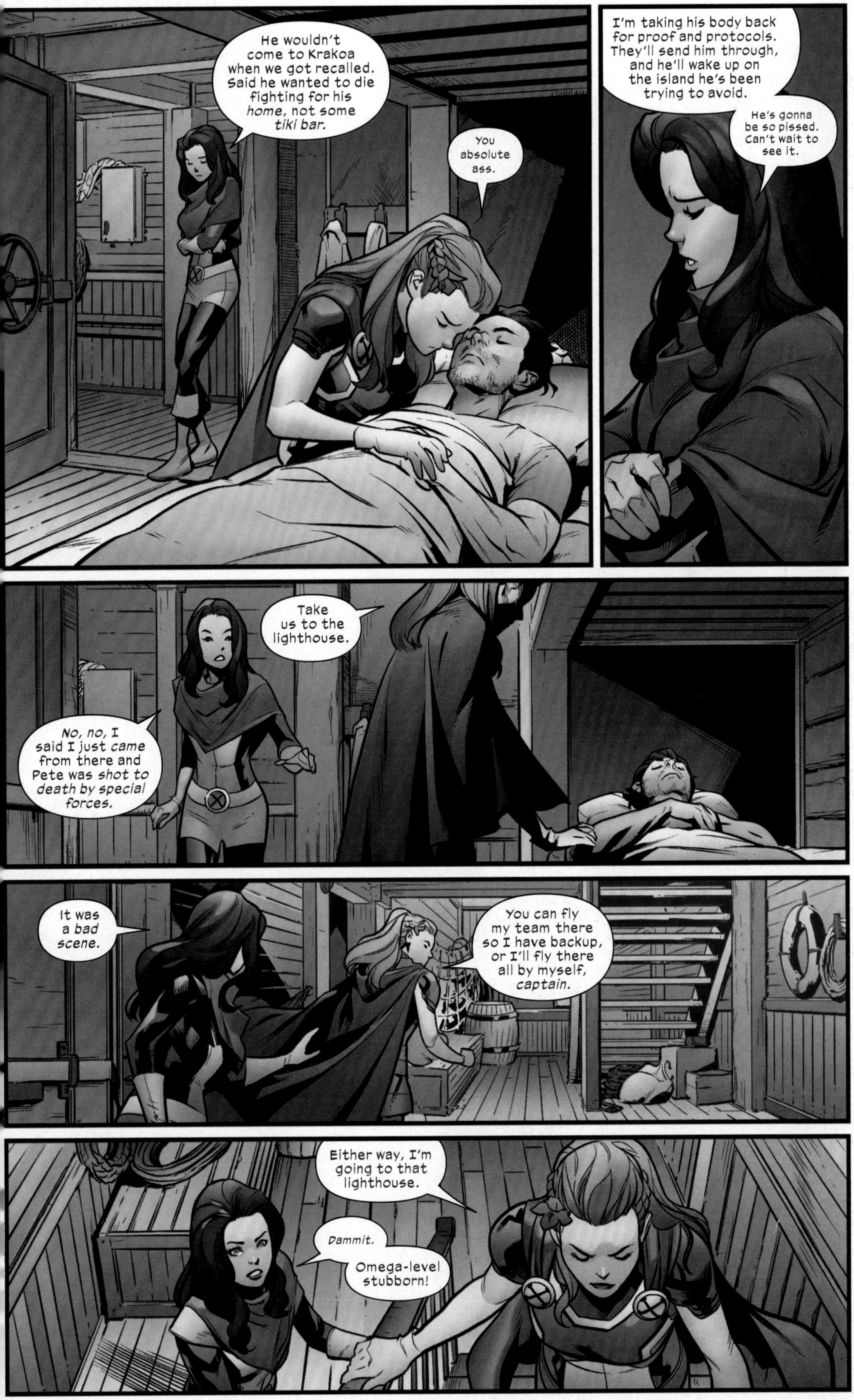
He wouldn't come to Krakoa when we got recalled. Said he wanted to die fighting for his *home*, not some *tiki bar*.
You absolute ass.
I'm taking his body back for proof and protocols. They'll send him through, and he'll wake up on the island he's been trying to avoid.
He's gonna be so pissed. Can't wait to see it.
Take us to the lighthouse.
No, no, I said I just *came* from there and Pete was *shot to death by special forces.*
It was a *bad* scene.
You can fly my team there so I have backup, or I'll fly there all by myself, *captain.*
Either way, I'm going to that lighthouse.
Dammit.
Omega-level stubborn!

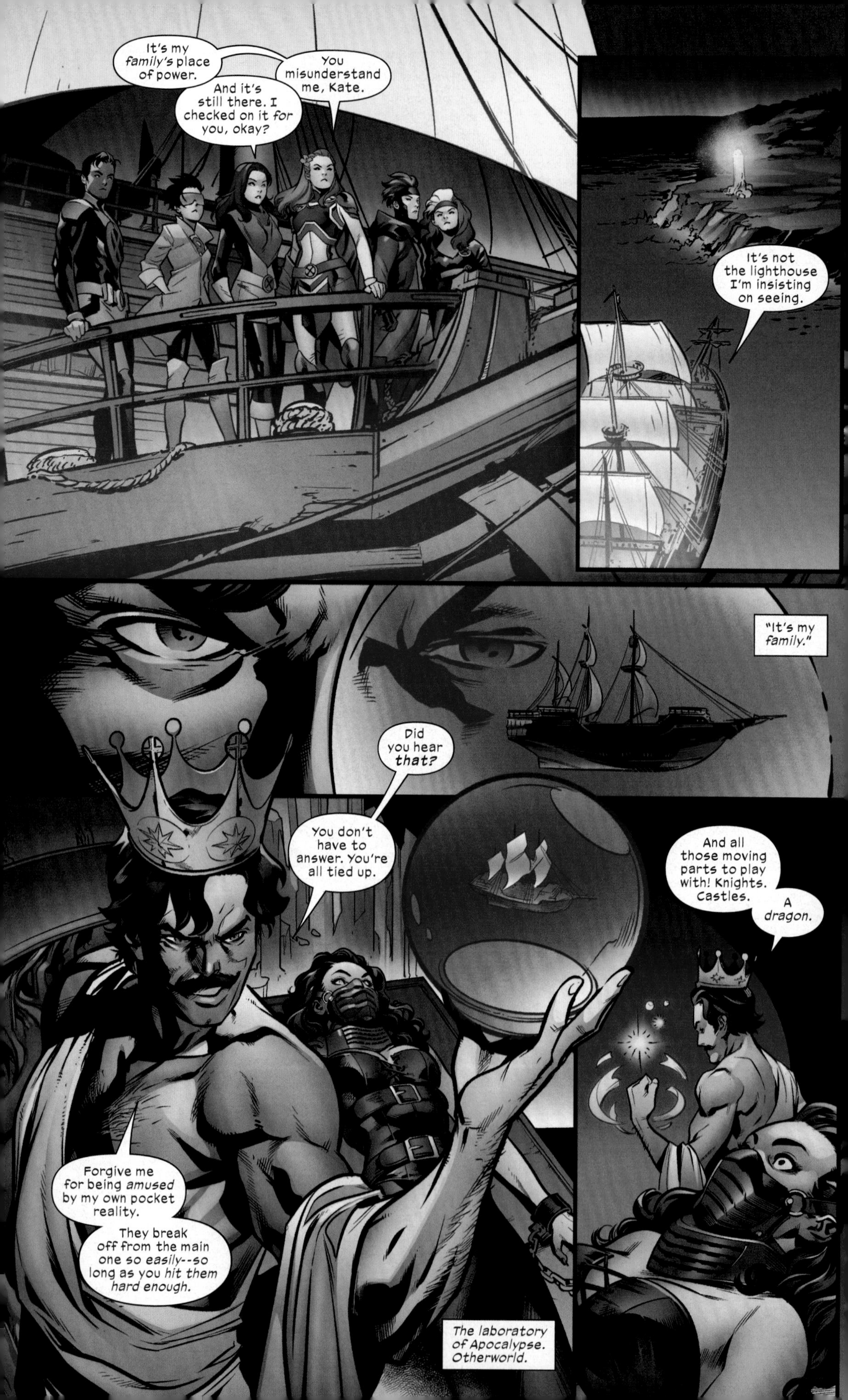
It's my *family's* place of power.
You misunderstand me, Kate.
And it's still there. I checked on it *for* you, okay?
It's not the lighthouse I'm insisting on seeing.
"It's my *family*."
Did you hear *that?*
You don't have to answer. You're all tied up.
Forgive me for being *amused* by my own pocket reality.
They break off from the main one so *easily*--so long as you *hit them hard enough.*
The laboratory of Apocalypse. Otherworld.
And all those moving parts to play with! Knights. Castles.
A *dragon.*

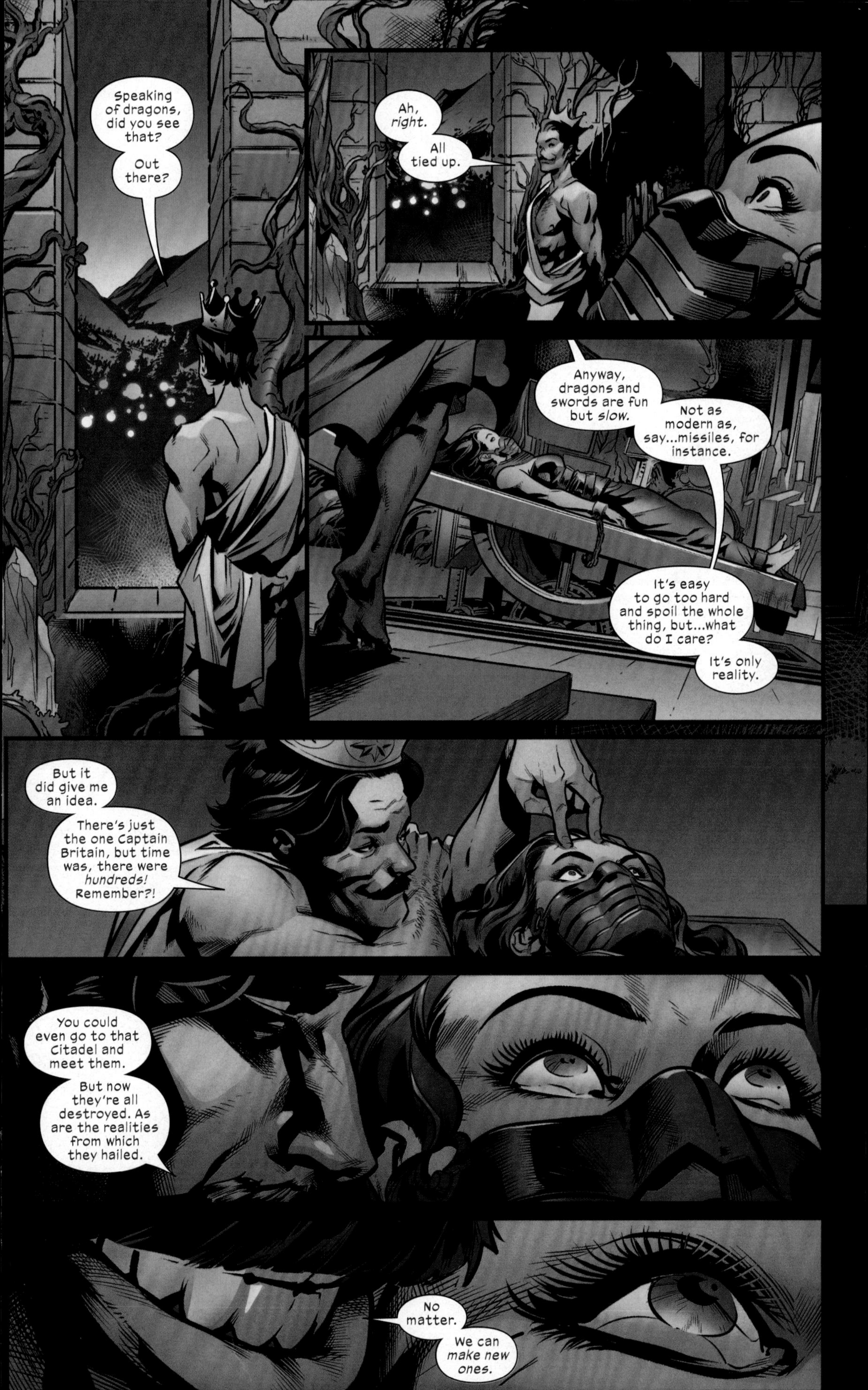
Speaking of dragons, did you see that?
Out there?
Ah, *right*.
All tied up.
Anyway, dragons and swords are fun but *slow*.
Not as modern as, say...missiles, for instance.
It's easy to go too hard and spoil the whole thing, but...what do I care?
It's only reality.
But it did give me an idea.
There's just the one Captain Britain, but time was, there were *hundreds!* Remember?!
You could even go to that Citadel and meet them.
But now they're all destroyed. As are the realities from which they hailed.
No matter.
We can *make new ones*.

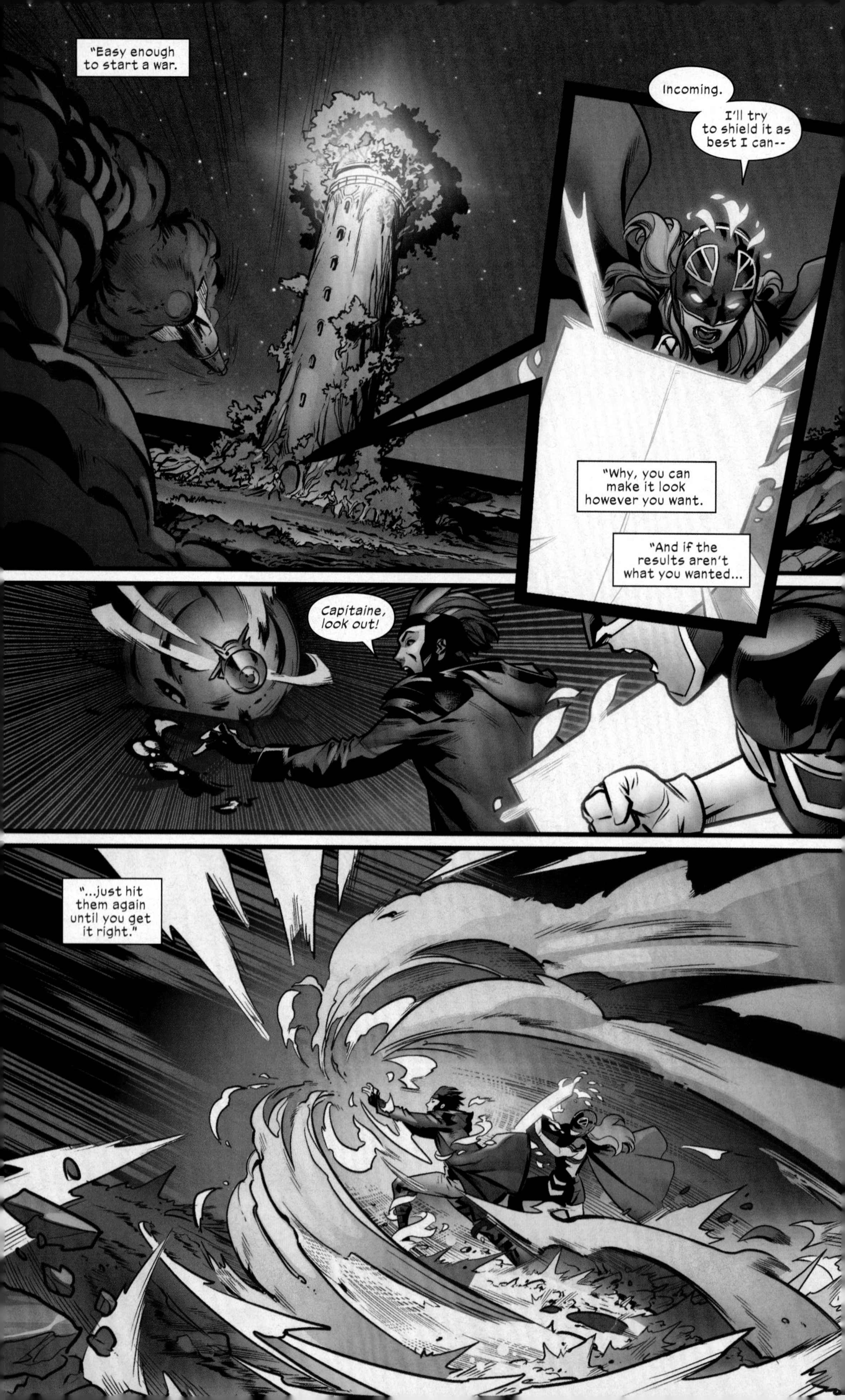
"Easy enough to start a war.
Incoming.
I'll try to shield it as best I can--
"Why, you can make it look however you want.
"And if the results aren't what you wanted...
Capitaine, look out!
"...just hit them again until you get it right."

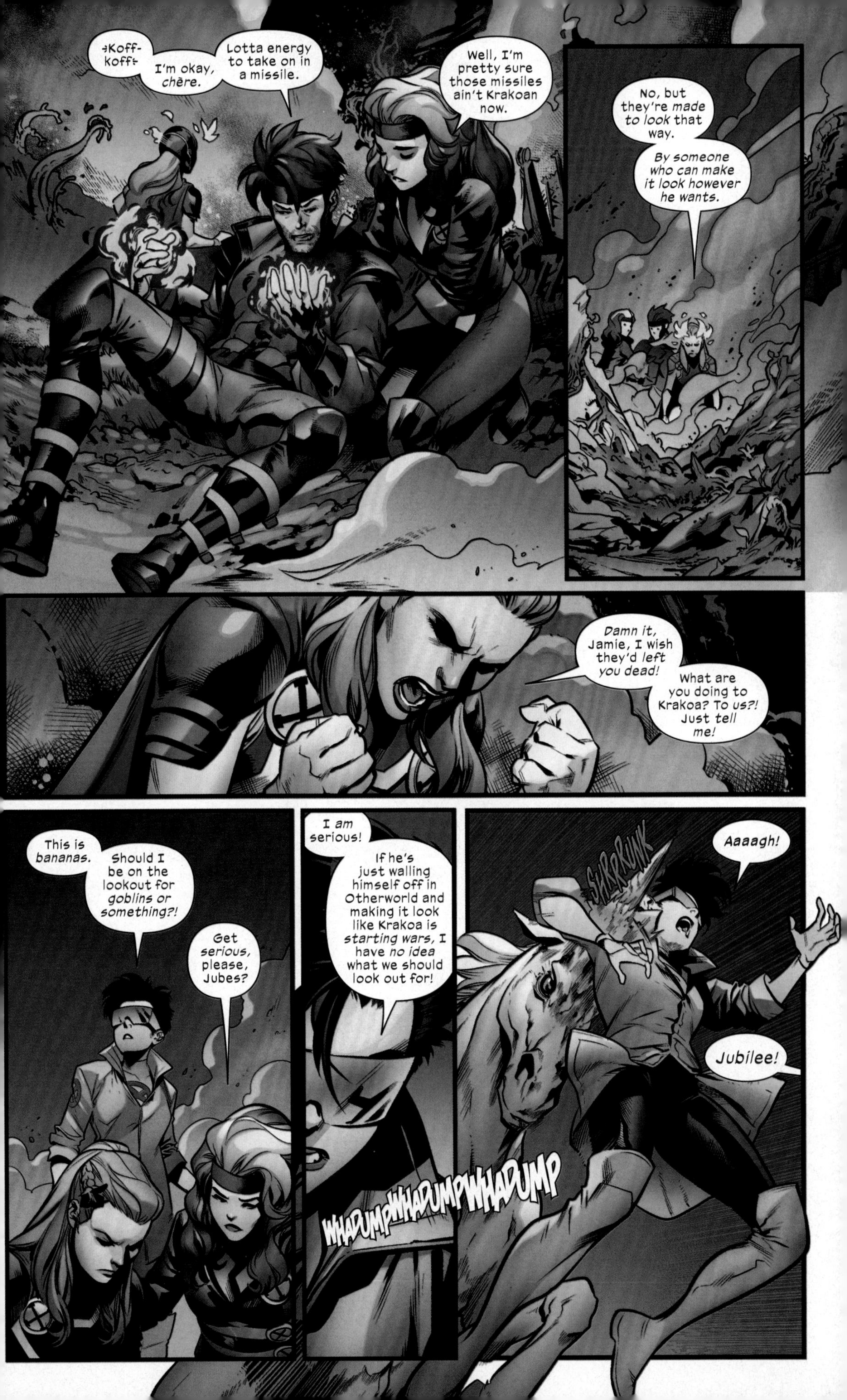

-Koff-koff-
I'm okay, *chère*.
Lotta energy to take on in a missile.
Well, I'm pretty sure those missiles ain't Krakoan now.
No, but they're *made to look* that way.
By someone who can make it look however he wants.
Damn it, Jamie, I wish they'd left you dead!
What are you doing to Krakoa? To us?! Just tell me!
This is *bananas*.
Should I be on the lookout for *goblins or something?!*
Get *serious*, please, Jubes?
I *am* serious!
If he's just walling himself off in Otherworld and making it look like Krakoa is *starting wars*, I have *no idea* what we should look out for!
WHADUMPWHADUMPWHADUMP
SPARRUNK
Aaaagh!
Jubilee!

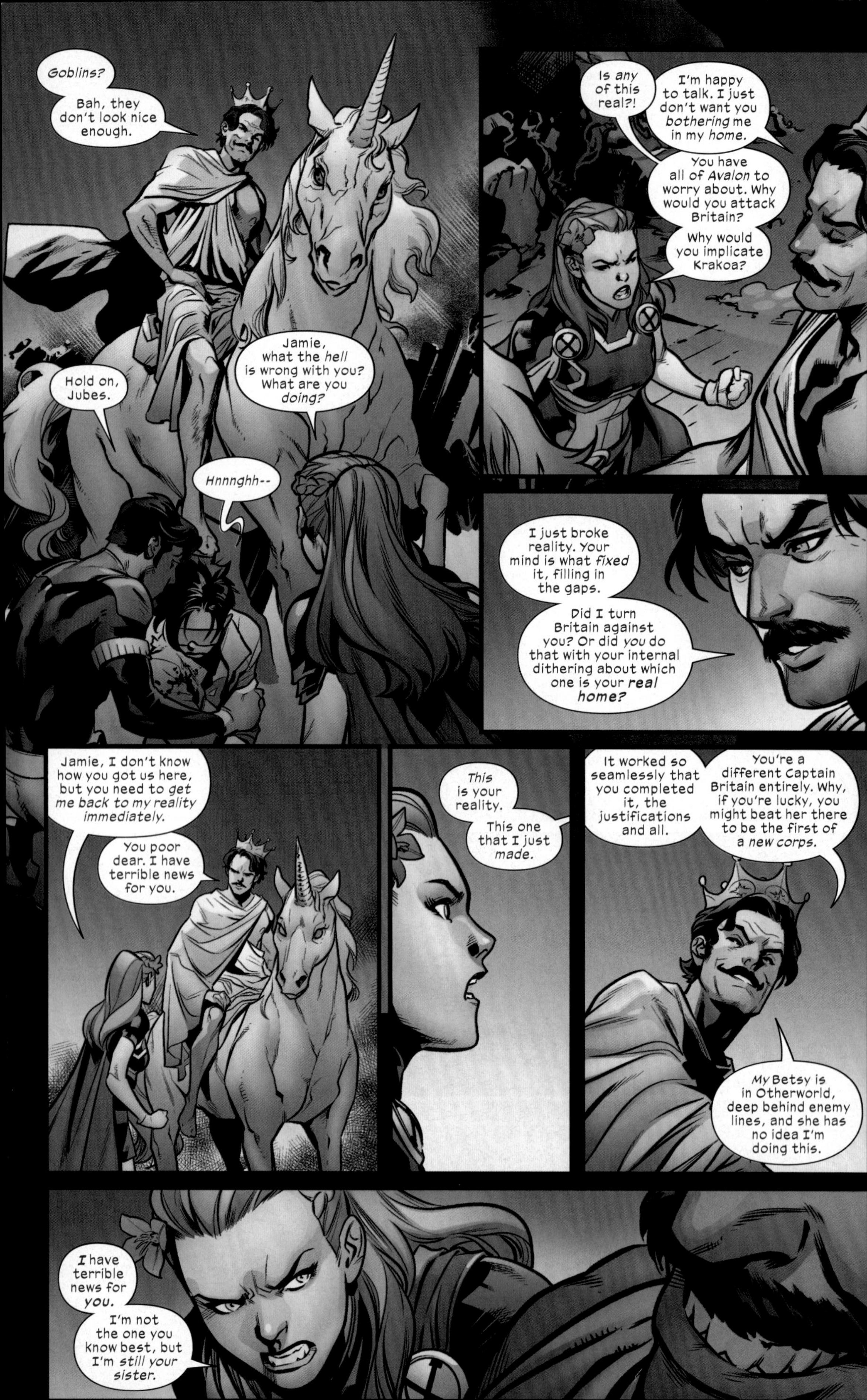
Goblins?
Bah, they don't look nice enough.
Hold on, Jubes.
Jamie, what the hell is wrong with you? What are you doing?
Hnnnghh--
Is any of this real?!
I'm happy to talk. I just don't want you bothering me in my home.
You have all of Avalon to worry about. Why would you attack Britain?
Why would you implicate Krakoa?
I just broke reality. Your mind is what fixed it, filling in the gaps.
Did I turn Britain against you? Or did you do that with your internal dithering about which one is your real home?
Jamie, I don't know how you got us here, but you need to get me back to my reality immediately.
You poor dear. I have terrible news for you.
This is your reality.
This one that I just made.
It worked so seamlessly that you completed it, the justifications and all.
You're a different Captain Britain entirely. Why, if you're lucky, you might beat her there to be the first of a new corps.
My Betsy is in Otherworld, deep behind enemy lines, and she has no idea I'm doing this.
I have terrible news for you.
I'm not the one you know best, but I'm still your sister.

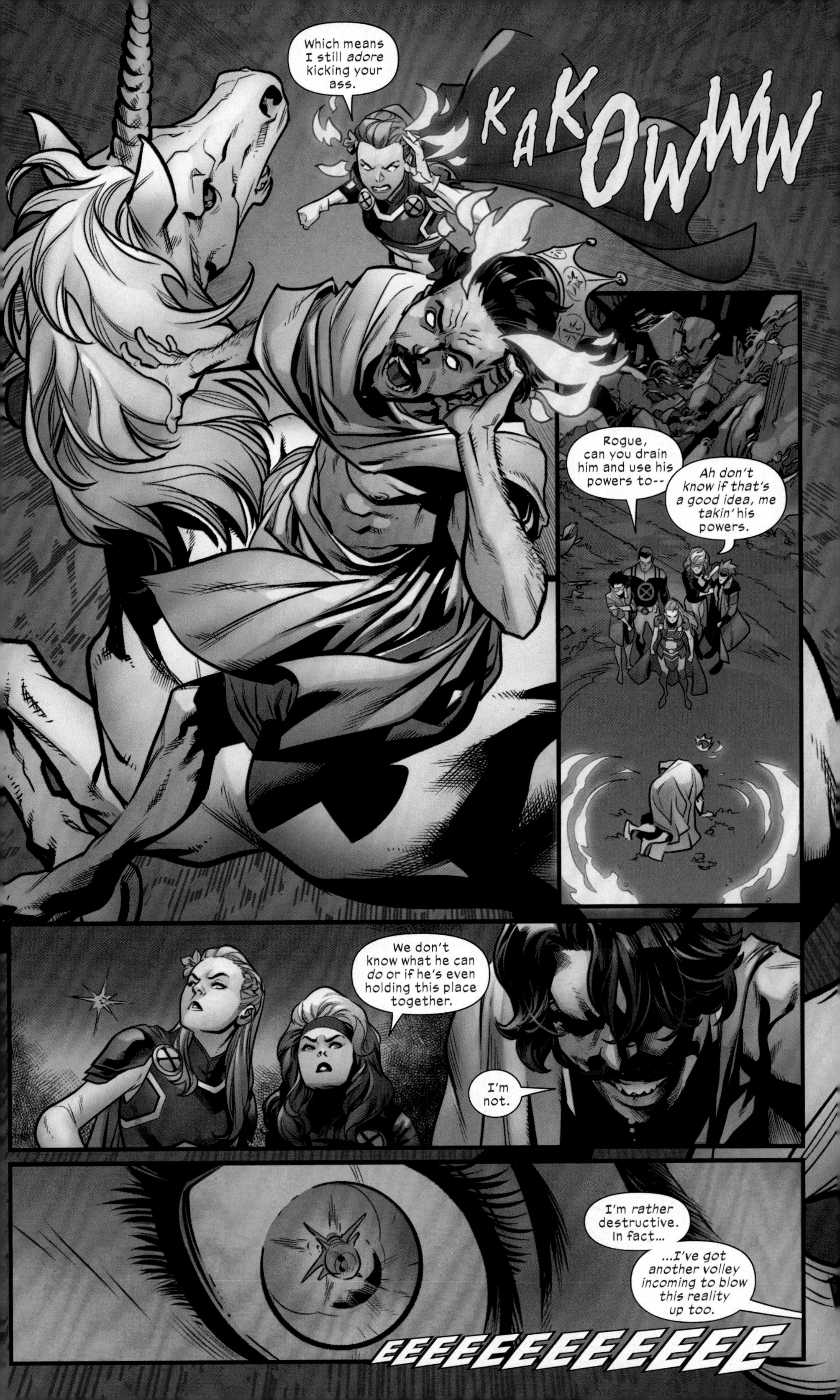

Which means I still *adore* kicking your ass.
KAKOWMW
Rogue, can you drain him and use his powers to--
Ah don't know if that's a good idea, me takin' his powers.
We don't know what he can *do* or if he's even holding this place together.
I'm not.
I'm *rather* destructive. In fact...
...I've got another volley incoming to blow this reality up too.
EEEEEEEEEEEEEE

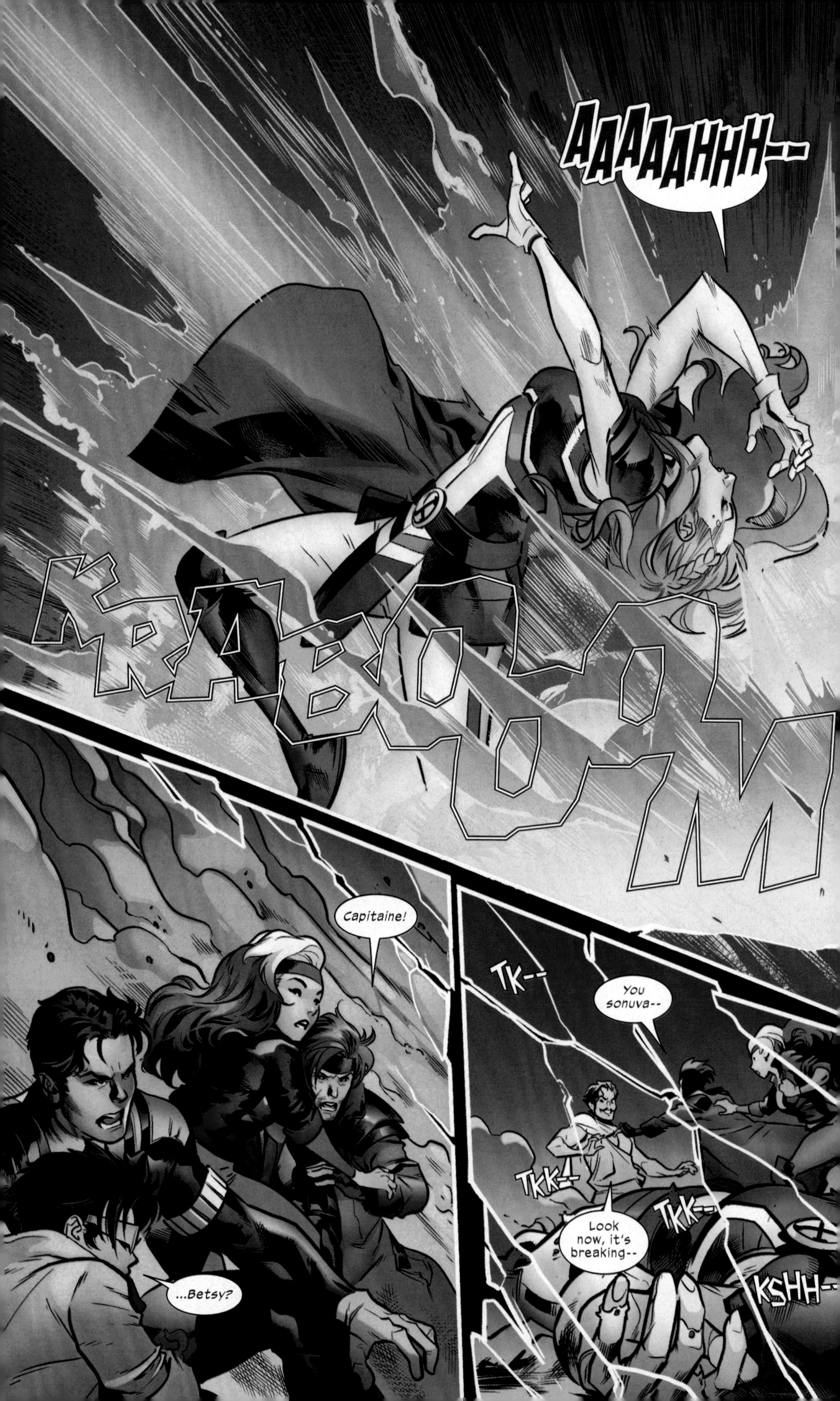
AAAAAHHH--
KRABOOOOOM
Capitaine!
...Betsy?
TK--
You sonuva--
TKK--
Look now, it's breaking--
TKK--
KSHH--

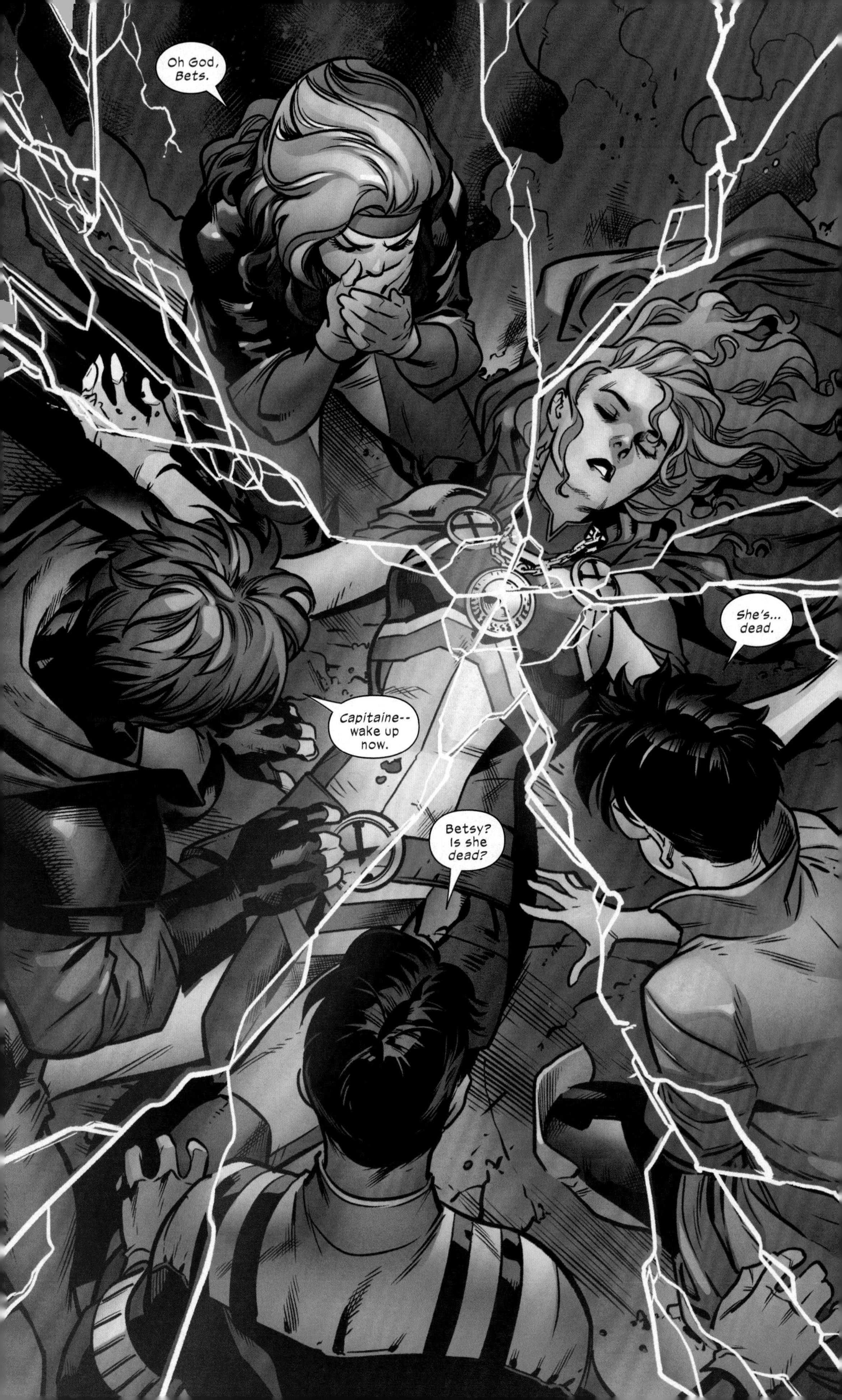
Oh God, Bets.
She's... dead.
Capitaine-- wake up now.
Betsy? Is she dead?

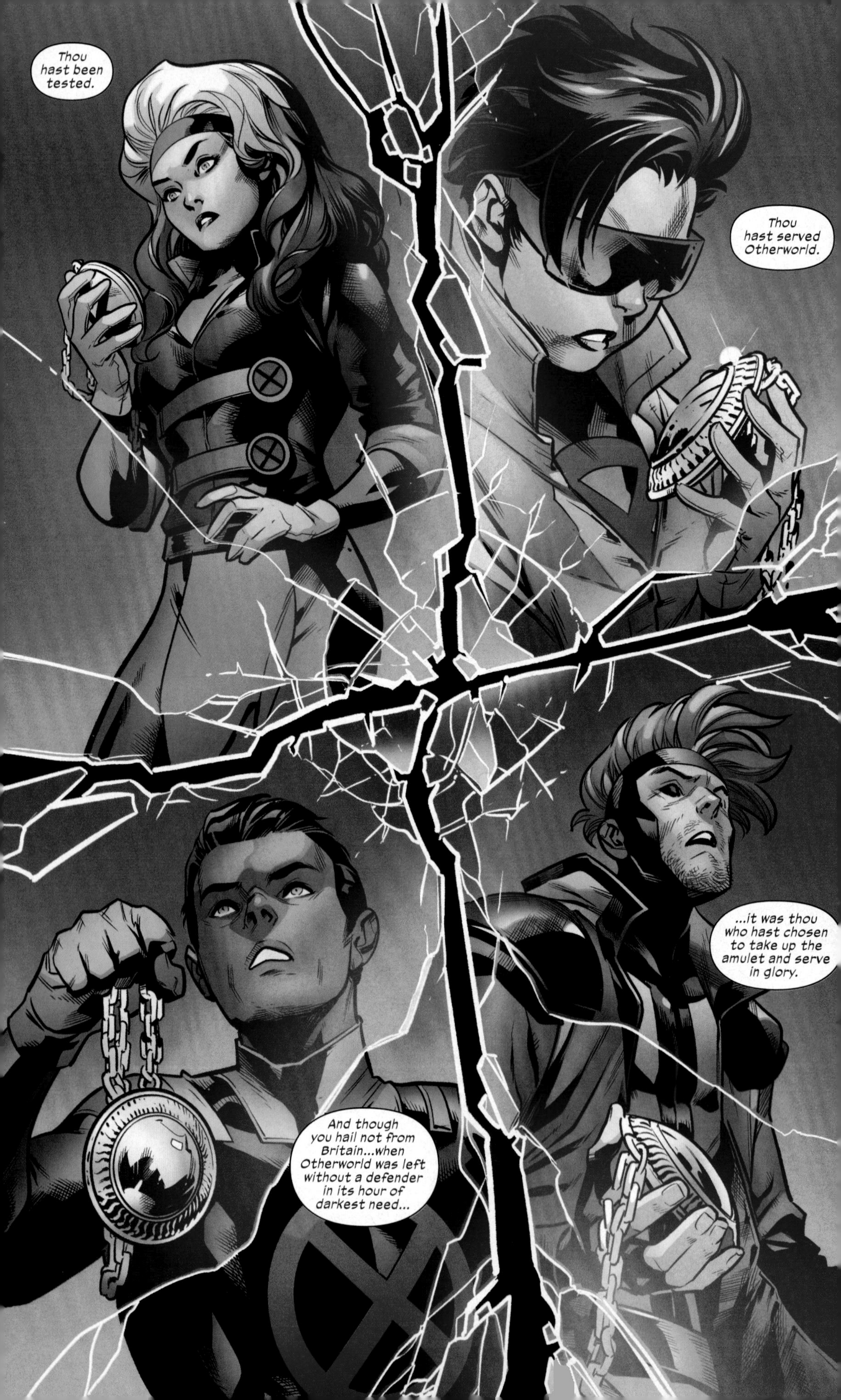
Thou hast been tested.
Thou hast served Otherworld.
And though you hail not from Britain...when Otherworld was left without a defender in its hour of darkest need...
...it was thou who hast chosen to take up the amulet and serve in glory.

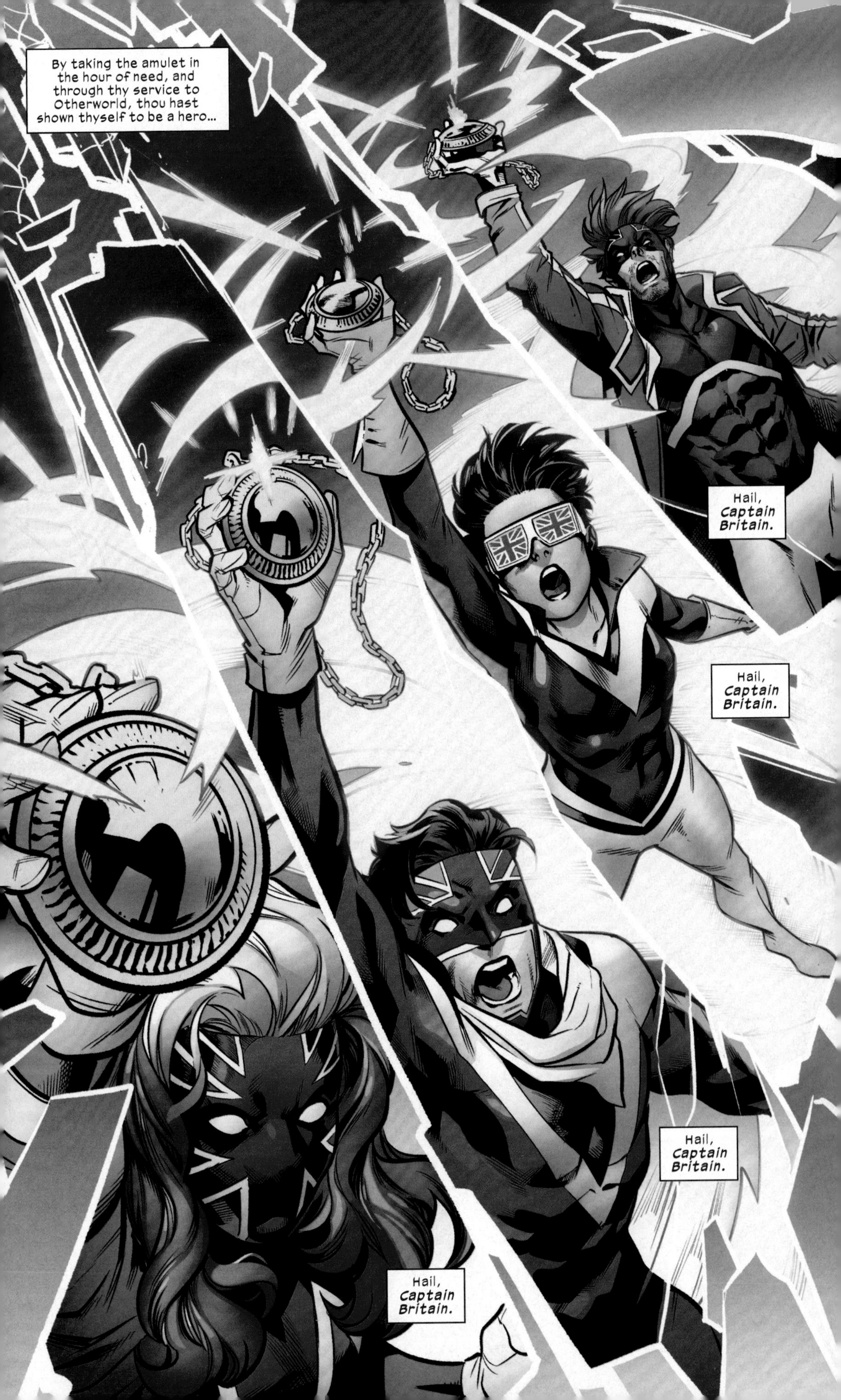
By taking the amulet in the hour of need, and through thy service to Otherworld, thou hast shown thyself to be a hero...
Hail, Captain Britain.
Hail, Captain Britain.
Hail, Captain Britain.
Hail, Captain Britain.

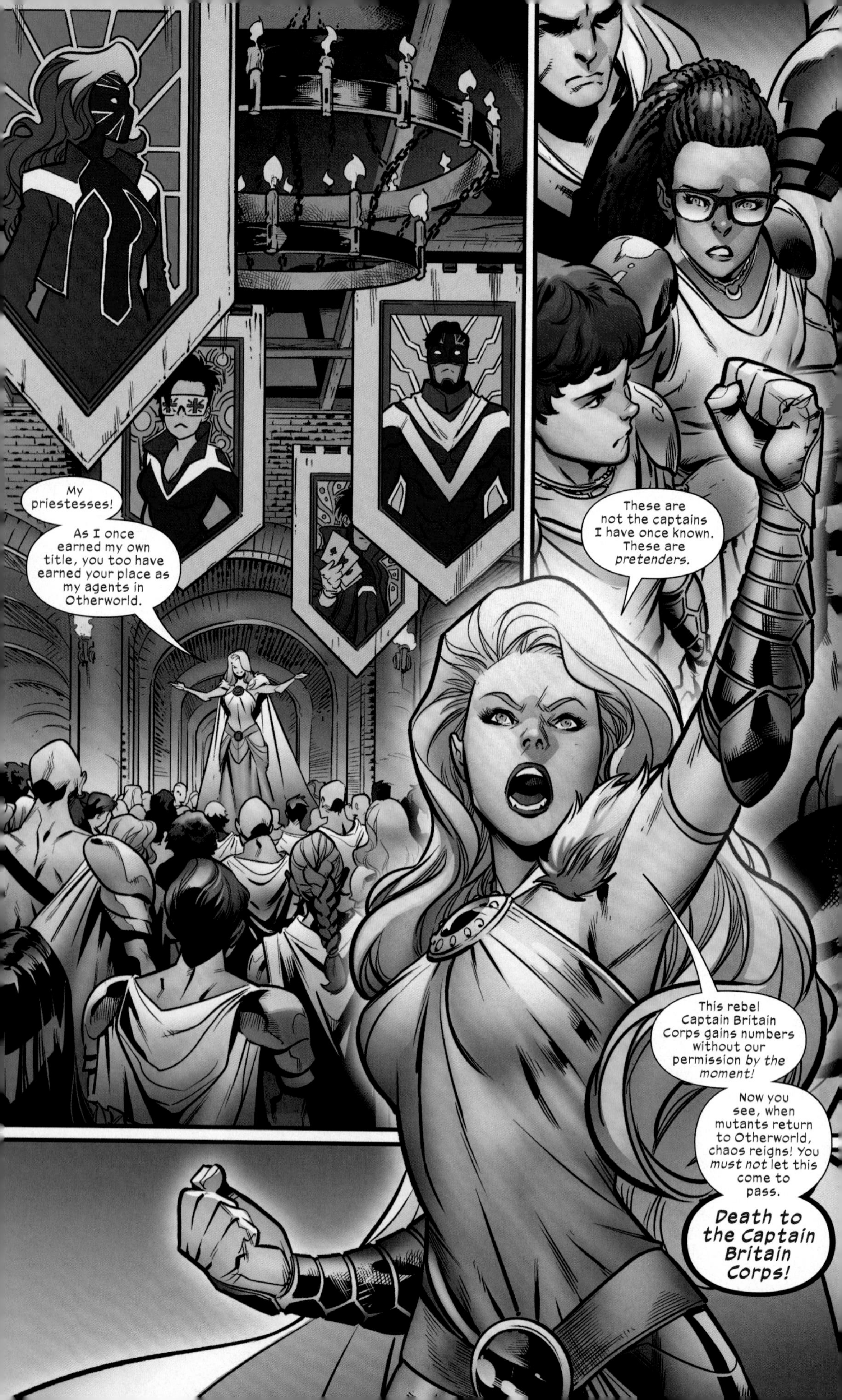
My priestesses!
As I once earned my own title, you too have earned your place as my agents in Otherworld.
These are not the captains I have once known. These are *pretenders.*
This rebel Captain Britain Corps gains numbers without our permission *by the moment!*
Now you see, when mutants return to Otherworld, chaos reigns! You *must not* let this come to pass.
Death to the Captain Britain Corps!

INCURSION

Omega-level reality-warping mutant King Jamie Braddock of Avalon commits a series of attacks on the very fabric of reality. Each one causes a fracture, including a ripple effect that causes reality to 'backfill' with memories and justifications of its own existence. The incursion goes largely unnoticed by the denizens of the home reality.

Traditionally, the accolade of Captain Britain has been chosen by a direct offer from Otherworld leadership to a member of the Braddock family or, rarely, another who would take their place.

King Jamie's method is quite unprecedented.

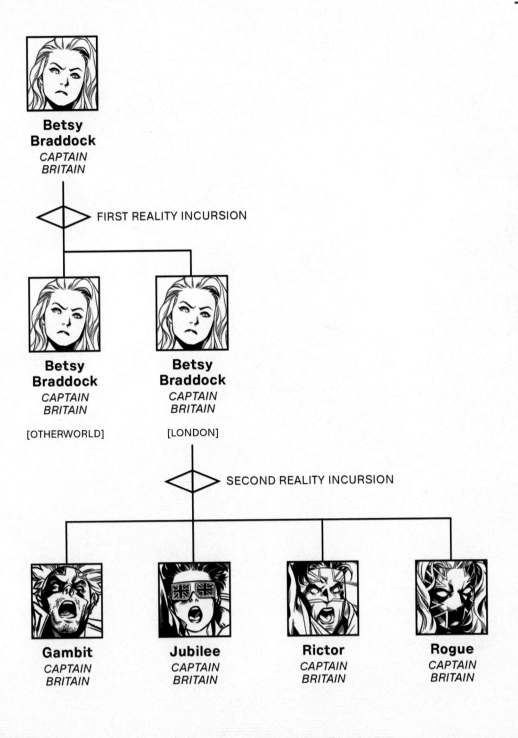

Betsy Braddock
CAPTAIN BRITAIN

FIRST REALITY INCURSION

Betsy Braddock
CAPTAIN BRITAIN

[OTHERWORLD]

Betsy Braddock
CAPTAIN BRITAIN

[LONDON]

SECOND REALITY INCURSION

Gambit
CAPTAIN BRITAIN

Jubilee
CAPTAIN BRITAIN

Rictor
CAPTAIN BRITAIN

Rogue
CAPTAIN BRITAIN

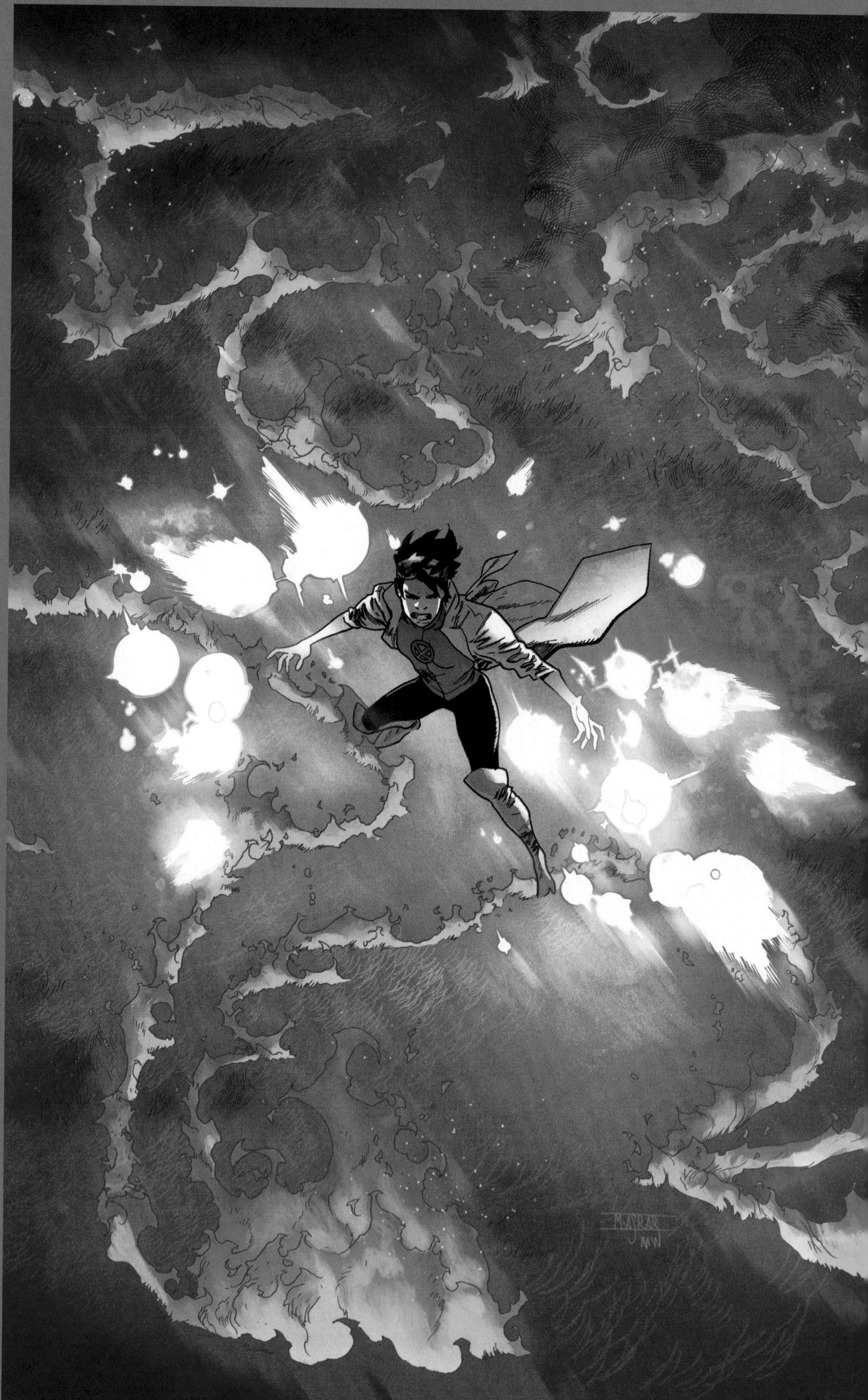

Blood of the Changeling

11

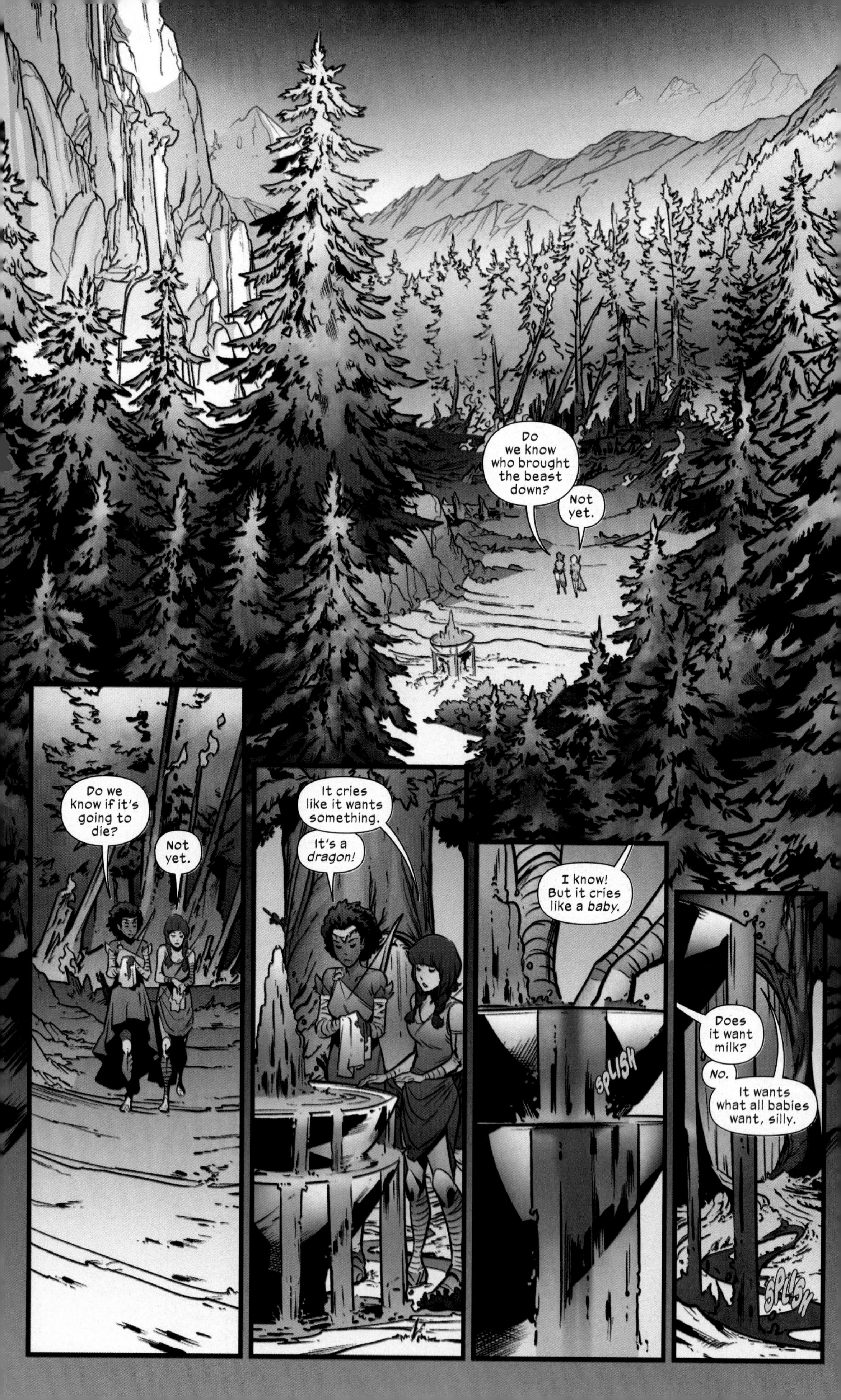
Do we know who brought the beast down?
Not yet.
Do we know if it's going to die?
Not yet.
It cries like it wants something.
It's a *dragon!*
I know! But it cries like a *baby.*
SPLISH
Does it want milk?
No.
It wants what all babies want, silly.
SPLISH

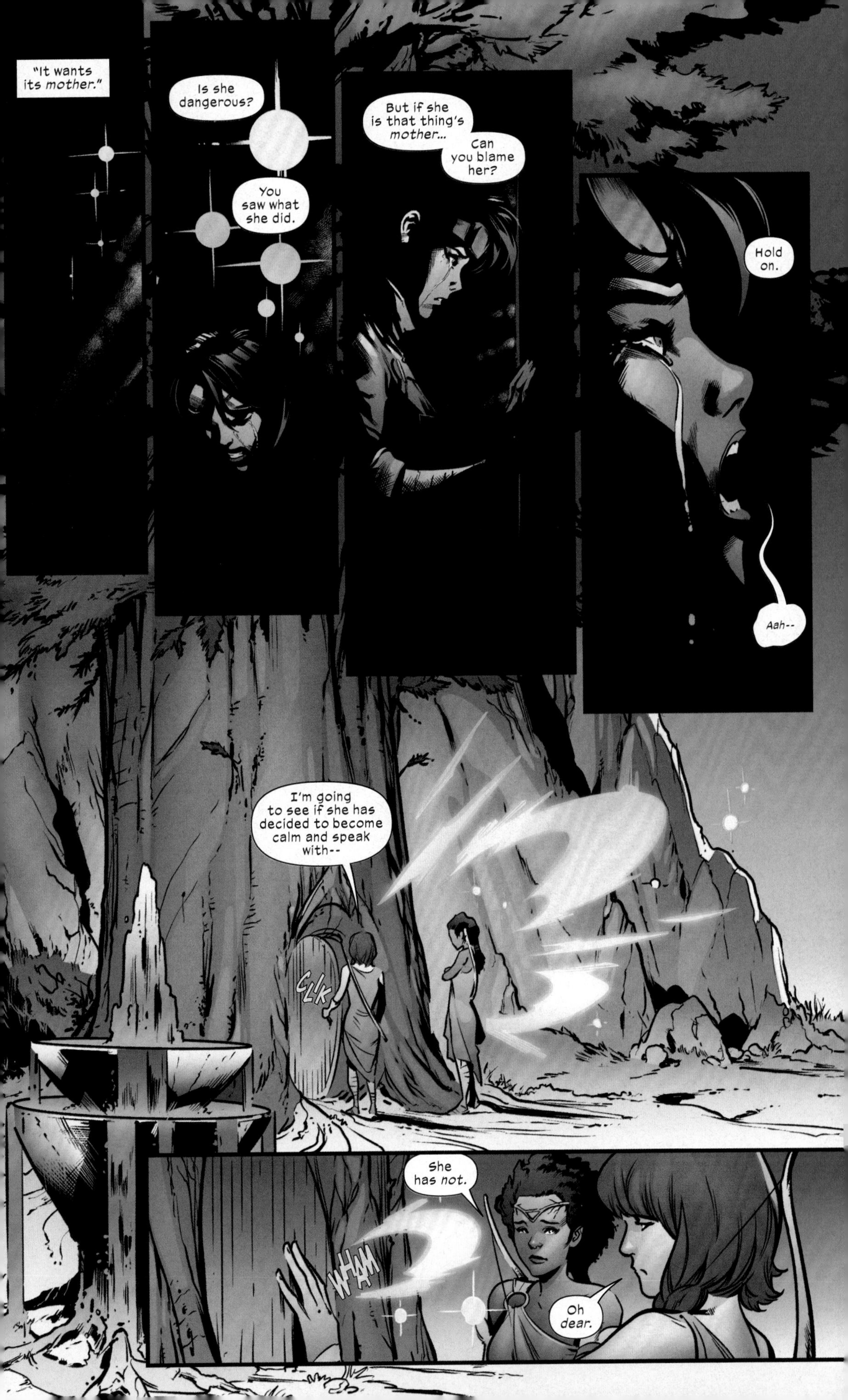
"It wants its *mother*."
Is she dangerous?
You saw what she did.
But if she is that thing's *mother*...
Can you blame her?
Hold on.
Aah--
I'm going to see if she has decided to become calm and speak with--
CLIK
She has *not*.
WHAM
Oh dear.

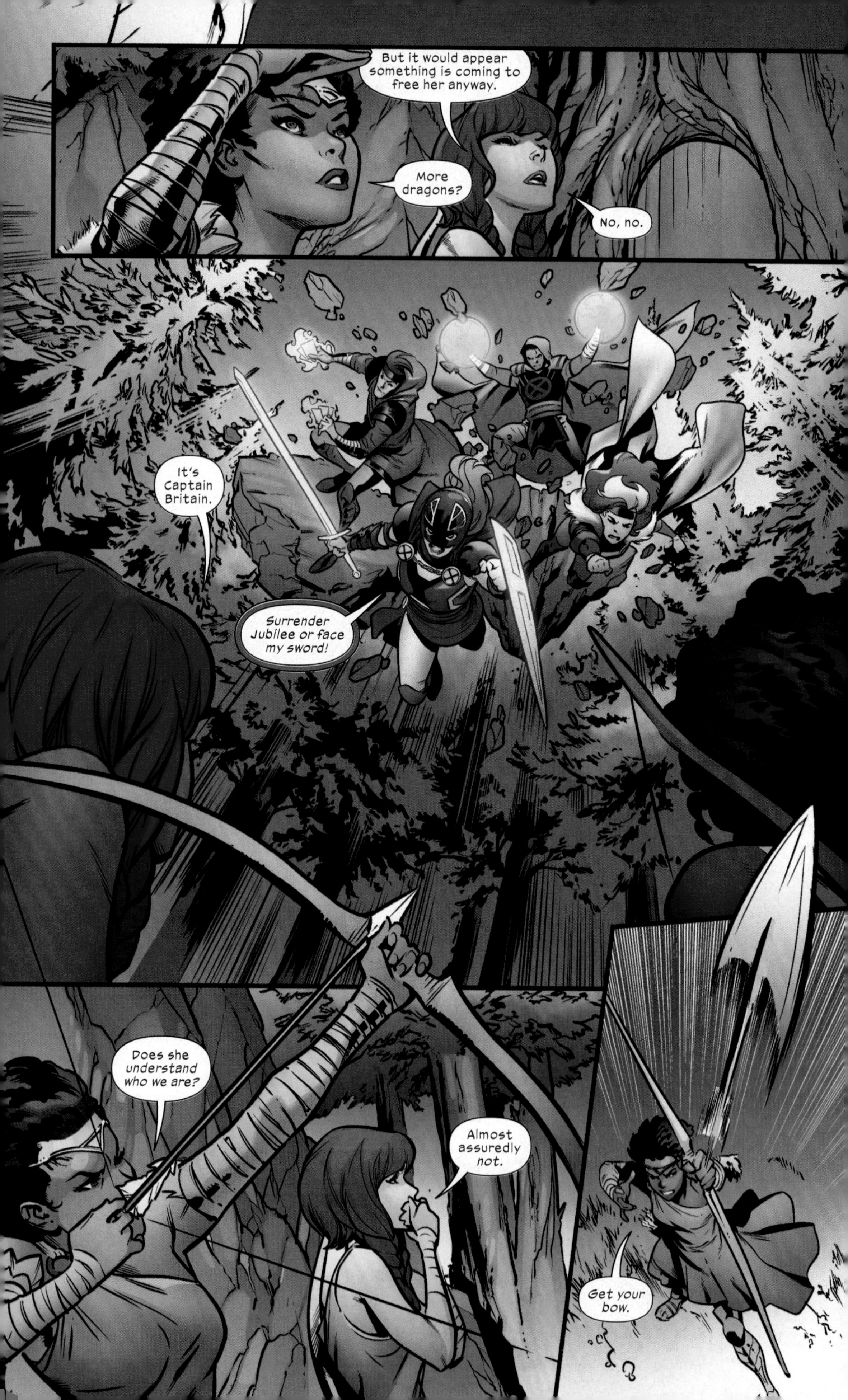
But it would appear something is coming to free her anyway.
More dragons?
No, no.
It's Captain Britain.
Surrender Jubilee or face my sword!
Does she understand who we are?
Almost assuredly not.
Get your bow.

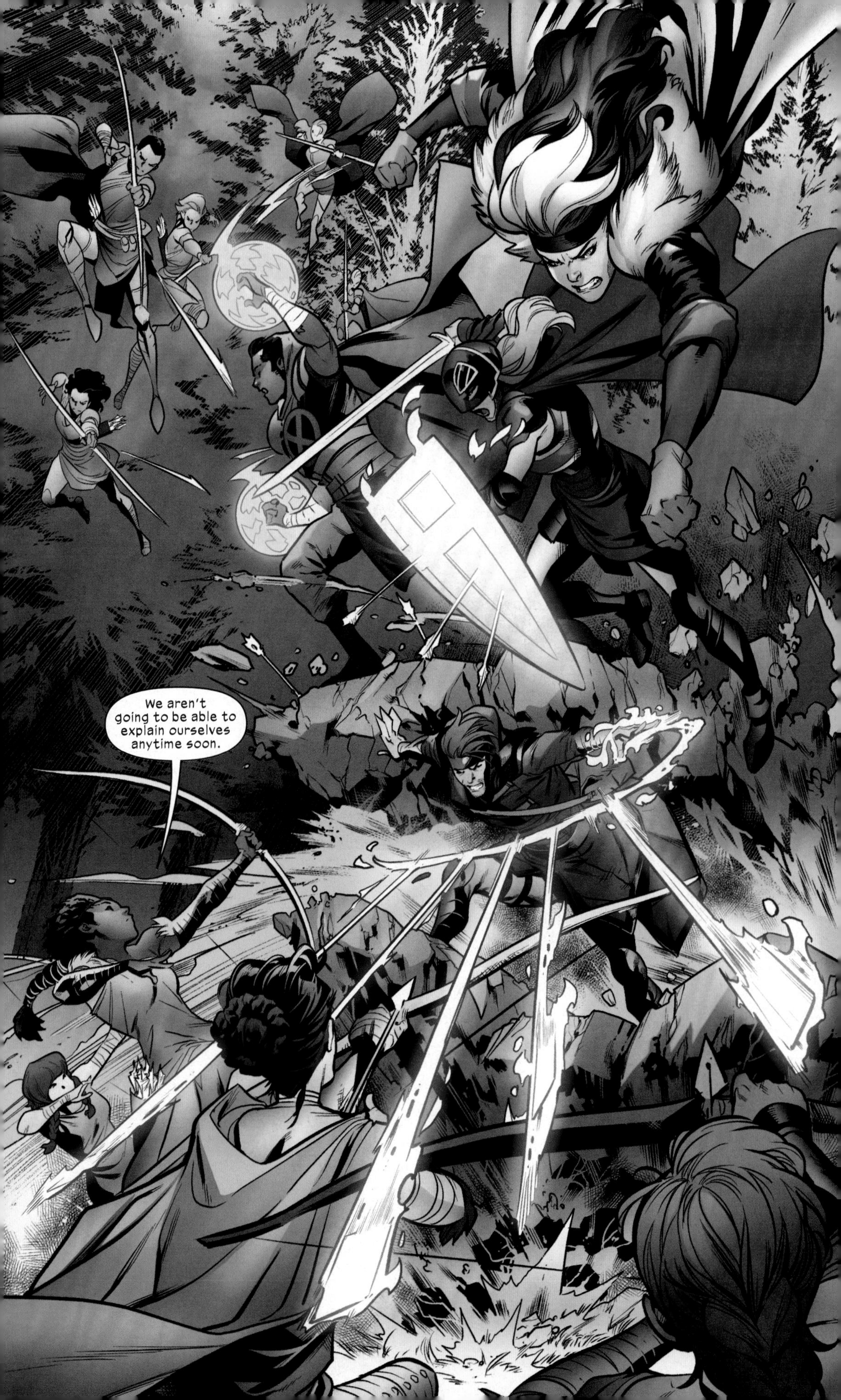
We aren't going to be able to explain ourselves anytime soon.

PRIESTESSES OF OPAL LUNA SATURNYNE

Students and devotees to Saturnyne, the priestesses are organized in two castes -- those of the *White*, who have chosen to live within the walls of the Citadel and the surrounding province, and those of the *Green*, who have taken their training and knowledge to the lands outside of the Citadel and chosen to enact Saturnyne's *intent* rather than her direct *will*. By living alongside the wild thickets that act as buffers between the province of Avalon (or other provinces) and the province of Saturnyne, they are known to act as healers, hunters and keepers of the land.

Priestesses of the White only leave their lady's tower by donning their crescent diadems and taking a nearly faceless form, obscuring their own identity so that they may act in anonymous accordance with Lady Saturnyne's will.

Priestesses of the Green follow Saturnyne's teaching and intent, believing balance to be a nuanced thing that cannot be corrected by distant declaration and requiring attention, action and presence.

Despite their differences, the **Green** are not viewed as heretical; rather, Majestrix allows them, viewing them as a necessary opposition to her own actions, as all things must have opposition.

Occasionally the **White** and the **Green** come into contention when orders given to priestesses for the **White** (ex: "stop Captain Britain and her cohorts," "slay that dragon," etc.) find themselves in conflict with the **Green**'s more *moderate* views, who tend to follow a less draconic code of ethics, such as "if you find a wounded dragon in the woods, nurse it back to health," or "if a woman is causing explosions in the forest, imprison her until she calms down a bit."

Typically the **Green** will fight their enemies, as they say, "only till their sides stitch," meaning until **weariness from battle calms the temper and brings about necessary parlay.**

—

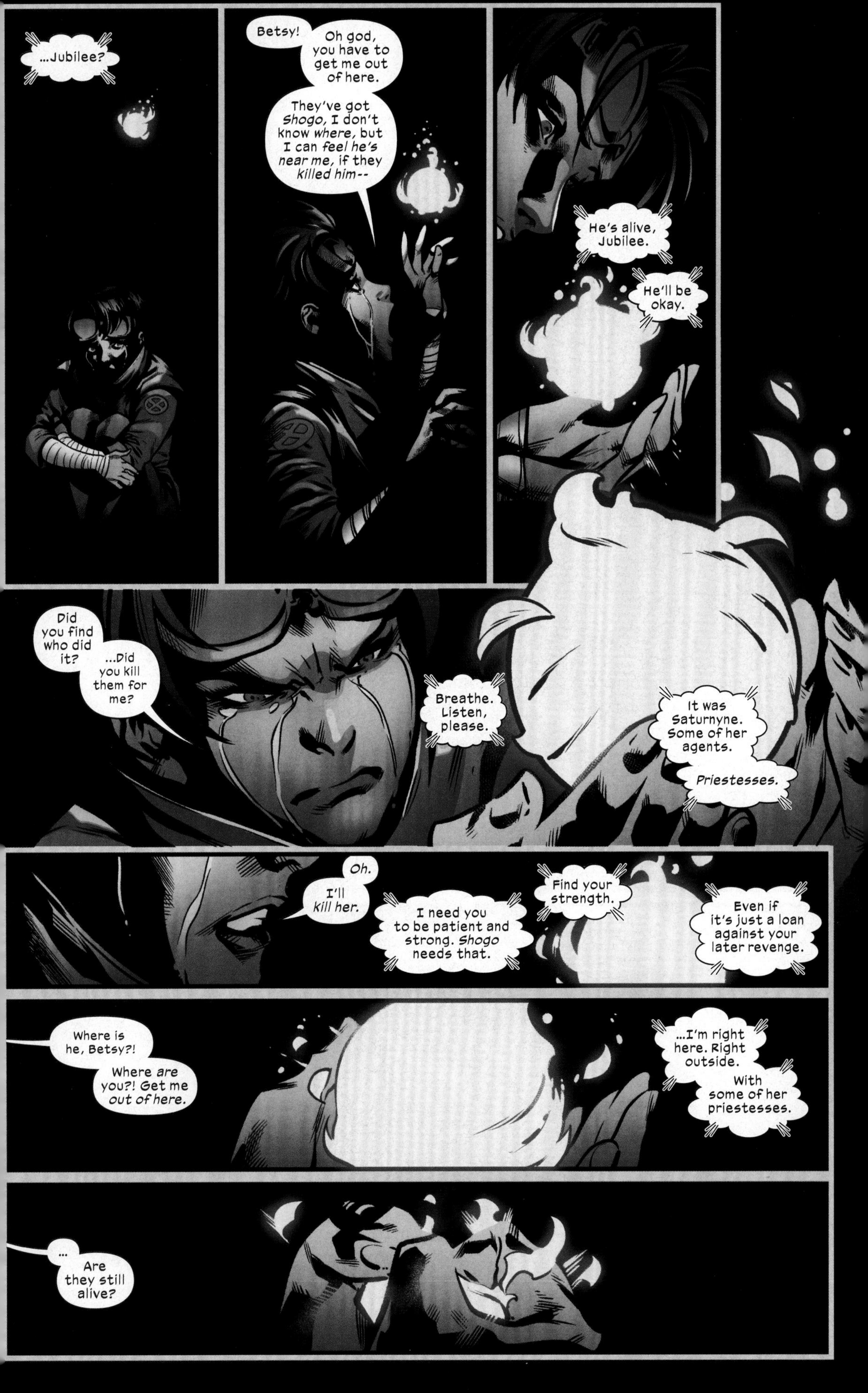
...Jubilee?
Betsy!
Oh god, you have to get me out of here.
They've got *Shogo*, I don't know *where*, but I can *feel he's near me*, if they *killed him*--
He's alive, Jubilee.
He'll be okay.
Did you find who did it?
...Did you kill them for me?
Breathe. Listen, please.
It was Saturnyne. Some of her agents.
Priestesses.
Oh.
I'll *kill her.*
I need you to be patient and strong. *Shogo* needs that.
Find your strength.
Even if it's just a loan against your later revenge.
Where is he, Betsy?!
Where *are* you?! Get me *out of here.*
...I'm right here. Right outside.
With some of her priestesses.
...
Are they still alive?

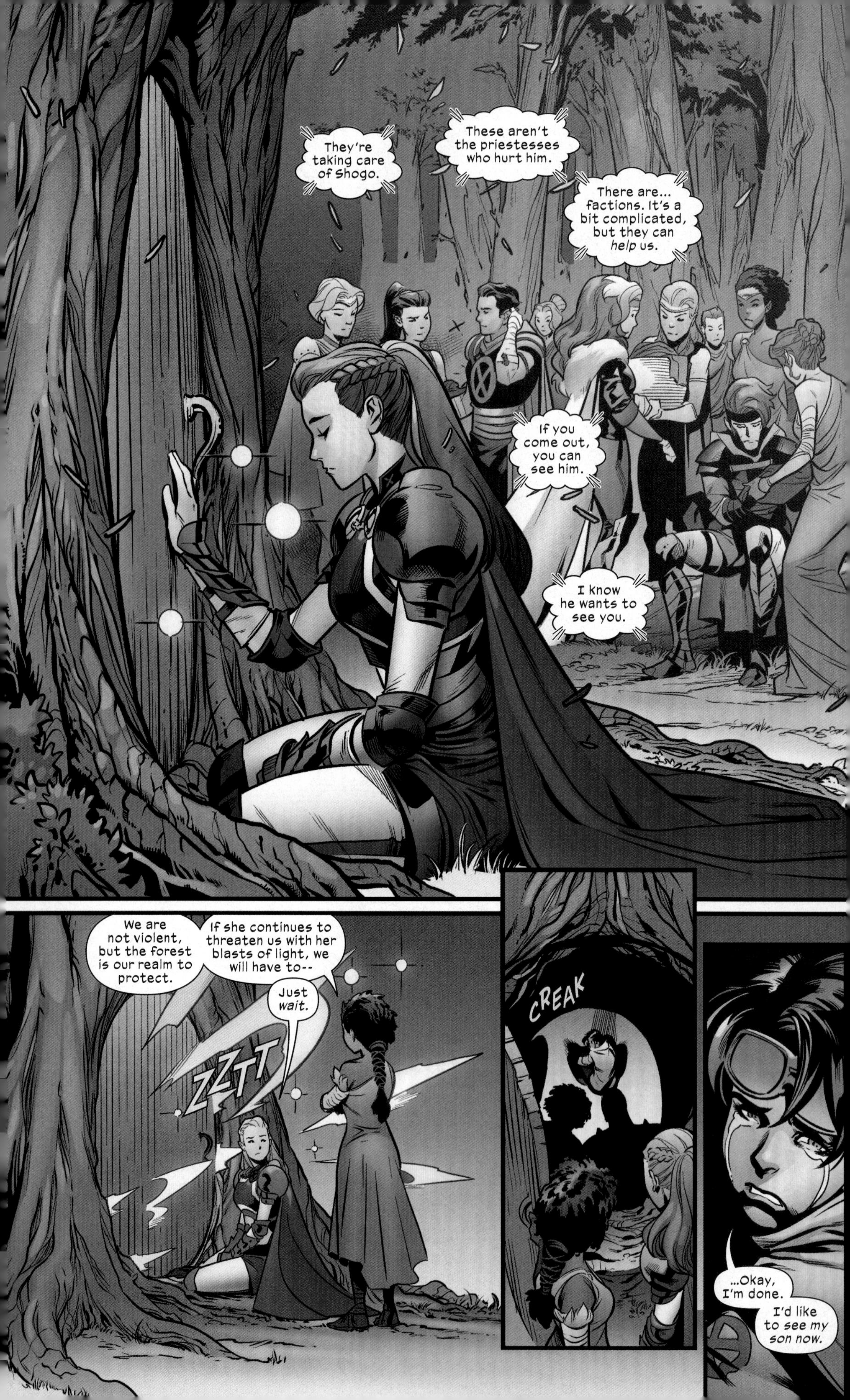
They're taking care of Shogo.
These aren't the priestesses who hurt him.
There are... factions. It's a bit complicated, but they can *help* us.
If you come out, you can see him.
I know he wants to see you.
We are not violent, but the forest is our realm to protect.
If she continues to threaten us with her blasts of light, we will have to--
Just *wait.*
ZZTT
CREAK
...Okay, I'm done.
I'd like to see my son now.

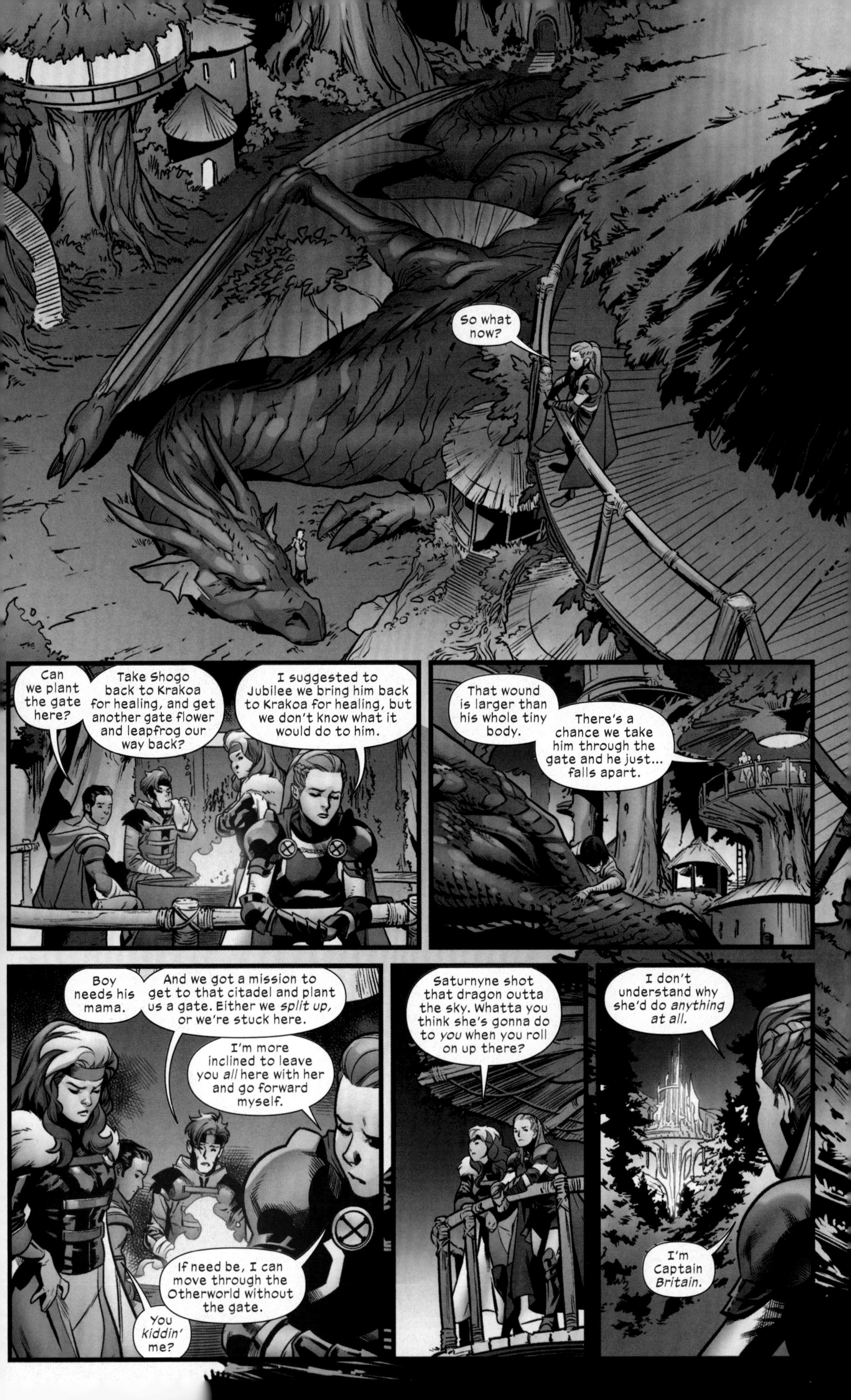
So what now?
Can we plant the gate here?
Take Shogo back to Krakoa for healing, and get another gate flower and leapfrog our way back?
I suggested to Jubilee we bring him back to Krakoa for healing, but we don't know what it would do to him.
That wound is larger than his whole tiny body.
There's a chance we take him through the gate and he just... falls apart.
Boy needs his mama.
And we got a mission to get to that citadel and plant us a gate. Either we *split up,* or we're stuck here.
I'm more inclined to leave you *all* here with her and go forward myself.
If need be, I can move through the Otherworld without the gate.
You *kiddin'* me?
Saturnyne shot that dragon outta the sky. Whatta you think she's gonna do to *you* when you roll on up there?
I don't understand why she'd do *anything at all.*
I'm Captain *Britain.*

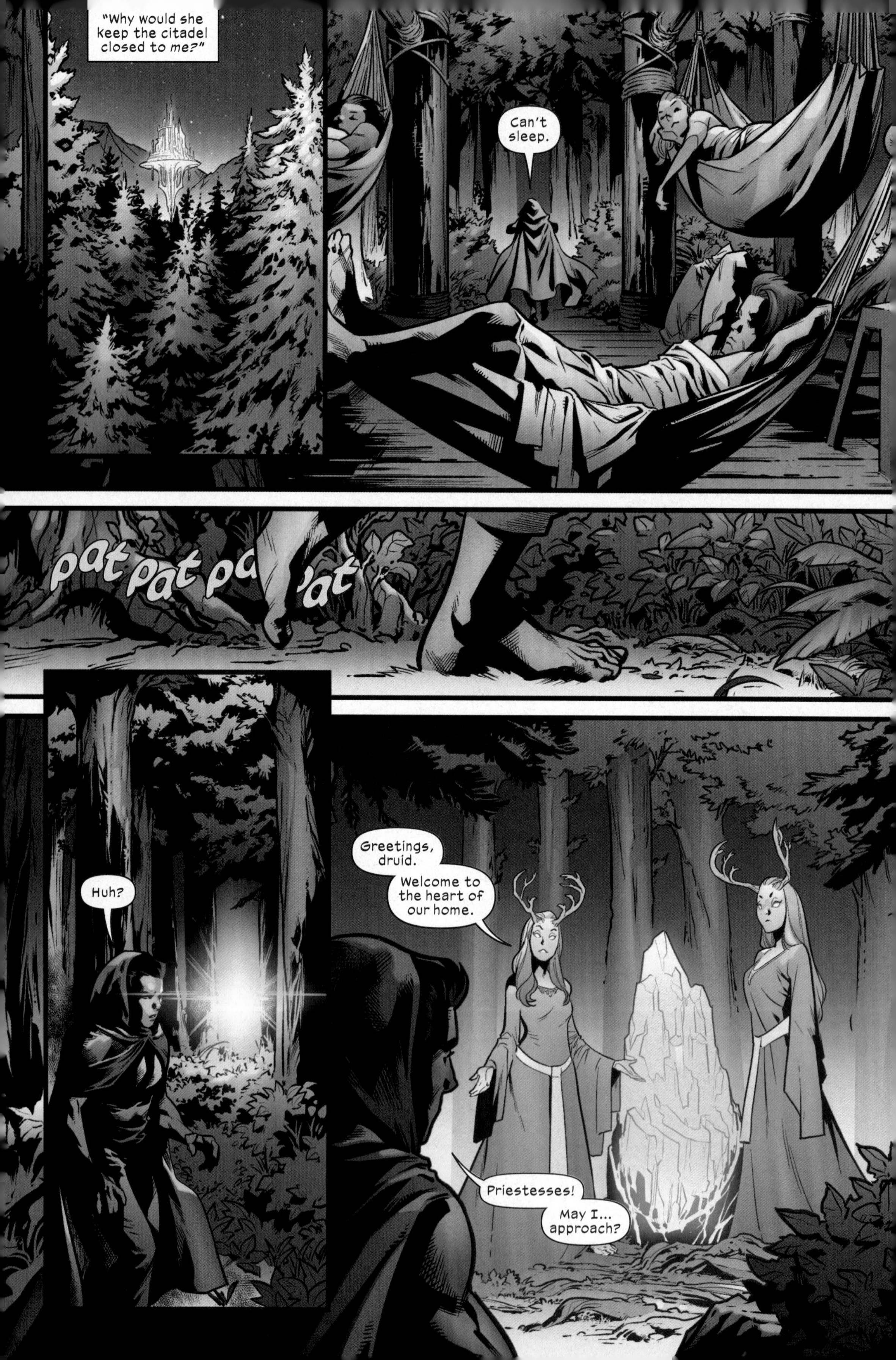
"Why would she keep the citadel closed to *me?*"
Can't sleep.
pat pat pa pat
Huh?
Greetings, druid.
Welcome to the heart of our home.
Priestesses!
May I... approach?

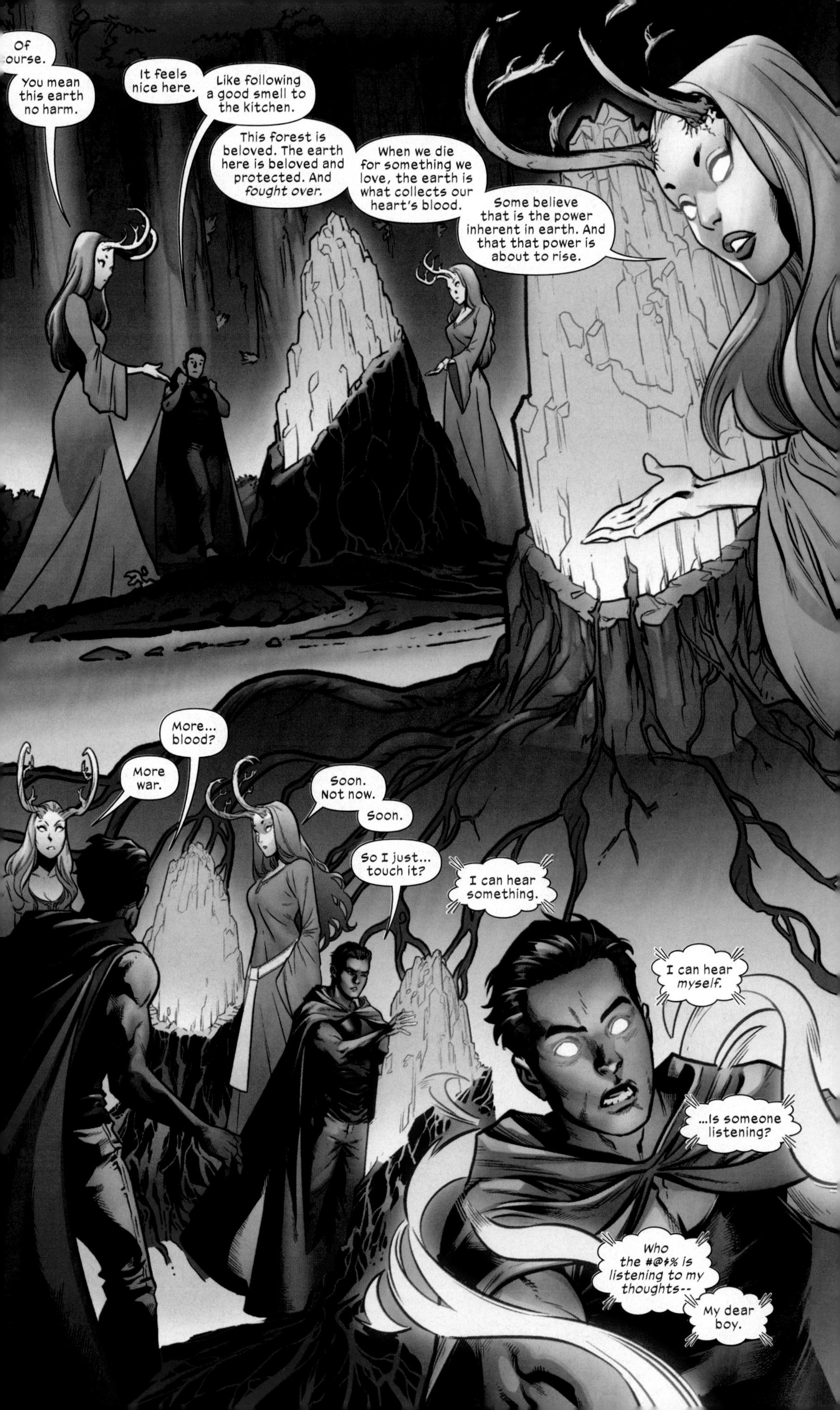

Of course.
You mean this earth no harm.
It feels nice here.
Like following a good smell to the kitchen.
This forest is beloved. The earth here is beloved and protected. And *fought over.*
When we die for something we love, the earth is what collects our heart's blood.
Some believe that is the power inherent in earth. And that that power is about to rise.
More... blood?
More war.
Soon. Not now.
Soon.
So I just... touch it?
I can hear something.
I can hear *myself.*
...Is someone listening?
Who the #@$% is listening to my thoughts--
My dear boy.

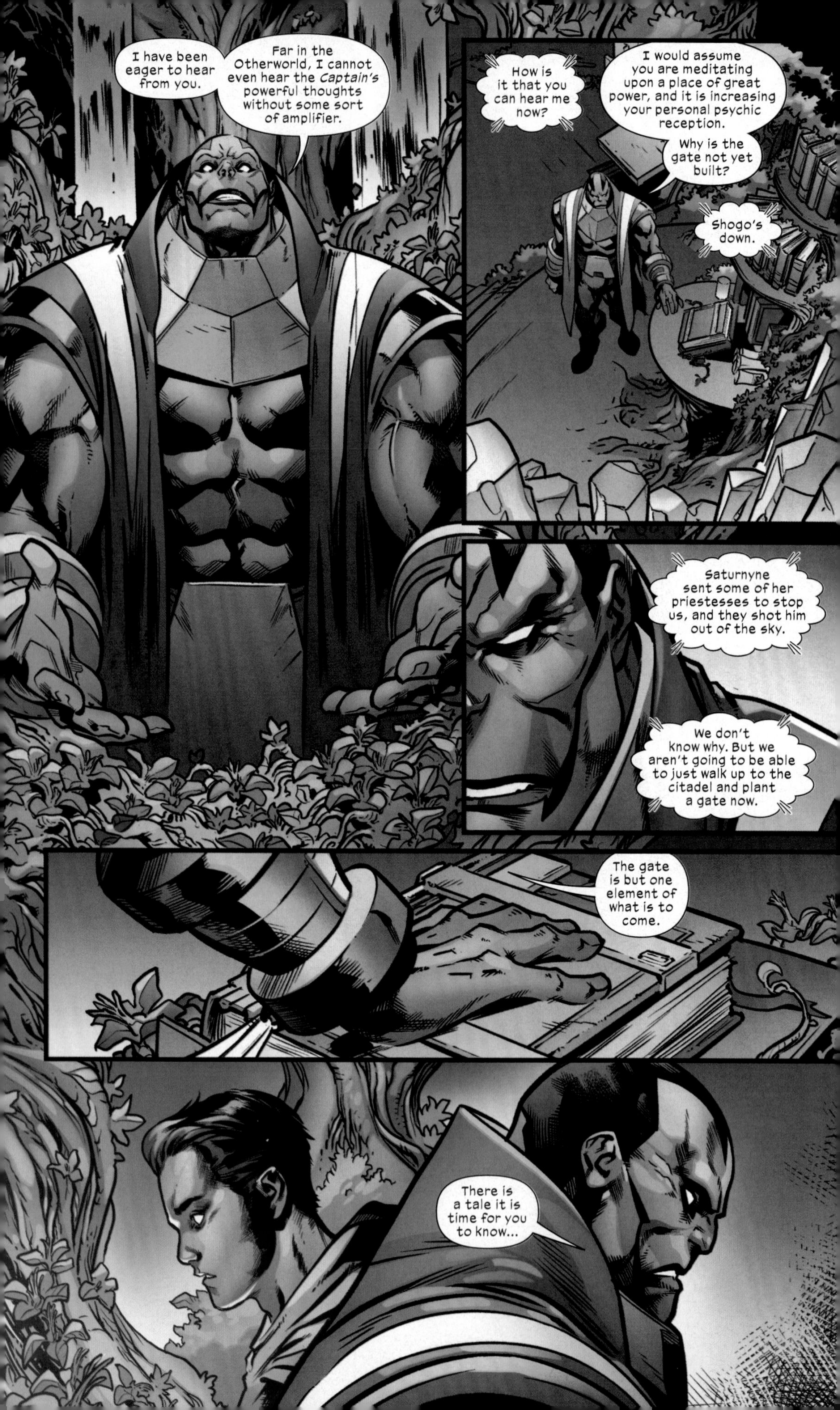

I have been eager to hear from you.
Far in the Otherworld, I cannot even hear the *Captain's* powerful thoughts without some sort of amplifier.
How is it that you can hear me now?
I would assume you are meditating upon a place of great power, and it is increasing your personal psychic reception.
Why is the gate not yet built?
Shogo's down.
Saturnyne sent some of her priestesses to stop us, and they shot him out of the sky.
We don't know why. But we aren't going to be able to just walk up to the citadel and plant a gate now.
The gate is but one element of what is to come.
There is a tale it is time for you to know...

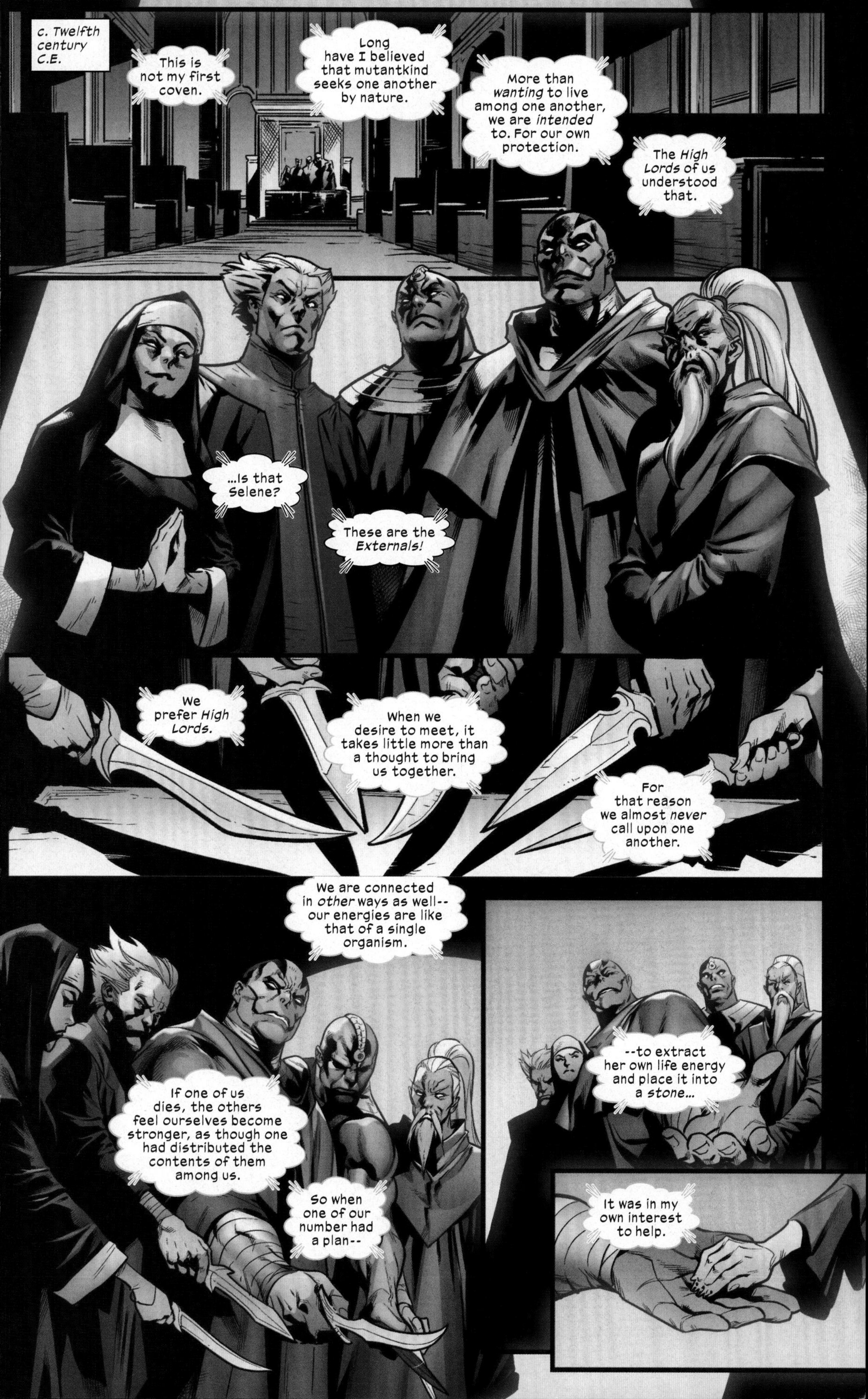
c. Twelfth century C.E.
This is not my first coven.
Long have I believed that mutantkind seeks one another by nature.
More than *wanting* to live among one another, we are *intended* to. For our own protection.
The *High Lords* of us understood that.
...Is that Selene?
These are the *Externals!*
We prefer *High Lords.*
When we desire to meet, it takes little more than a thought to bring us together.
For that reason we almost *never* call upon one another.
We are connected in *other* ways as well--our energies are like that of a single organism.
If one of us dies, the others feel ourselves become stronger, as though one had distributed the contents of them among us.
So when one of our number had a plan--
--to extract her own life energy and place it into a *stone*...
It was in my own interest to help.

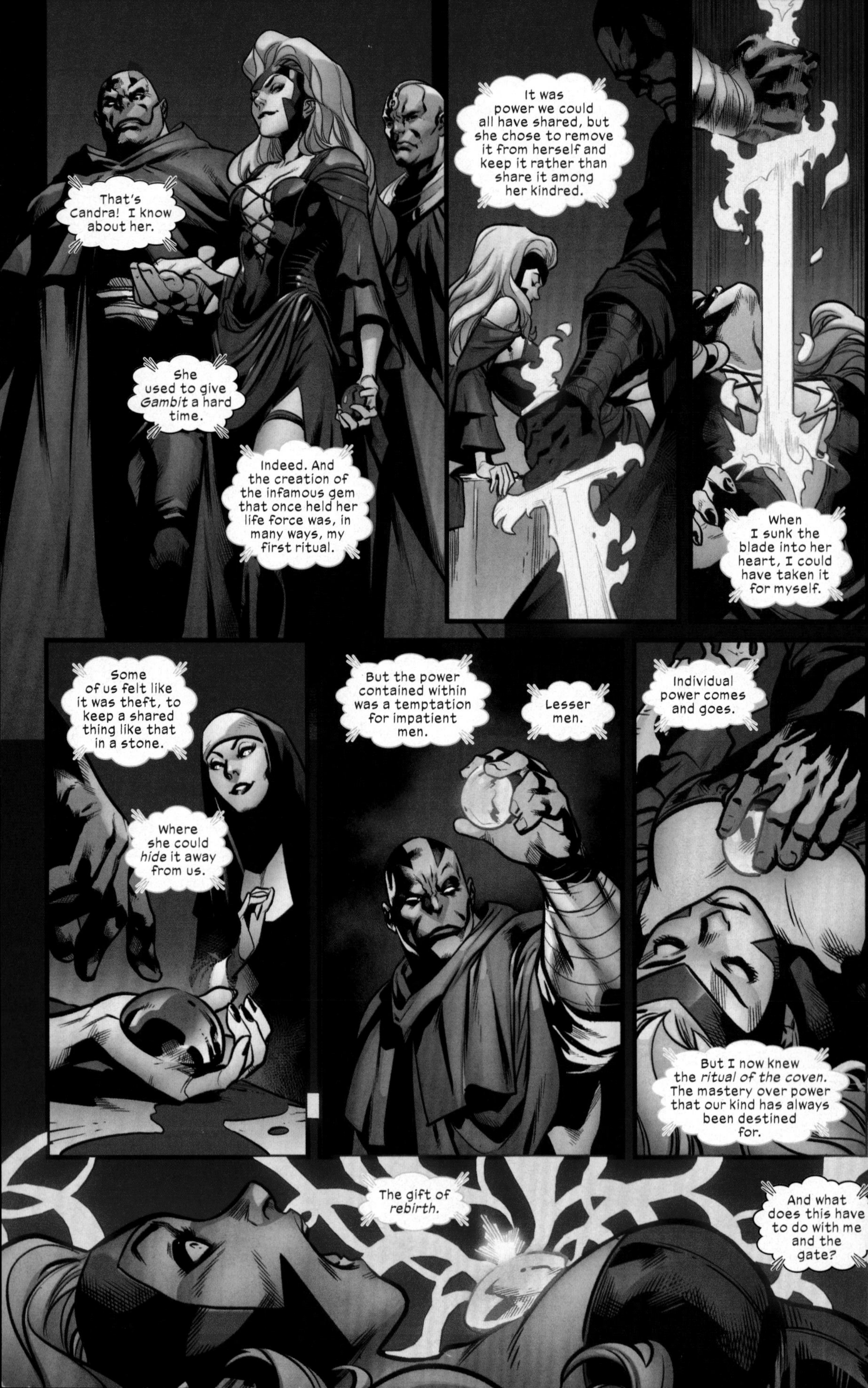
That's Candra! I know about her.
She used to give *Gambit* a hard time.
Indeed. And the creation of the infamous gem that once held her life force was, in many ways, my *first ritual.*
It was power we could all have shared, but she chose to remove it from herself and keep it rather than share it among her kindred.
When I sunk the blade into her heart, I could have taken it for myself.
Some of us felt like it was theft, to keep a shared thing like that in a stone.
Where she could *hide* it away from us.
But the power contained within was a temptation for impatient men.
Lesser men.
Individual power comes and goes.
But I now knew the *ritual of the coven.* The mastery over power that our kind has always been destined for.
The gift of *rebirth.*
And what does this have to do with me and the gate?

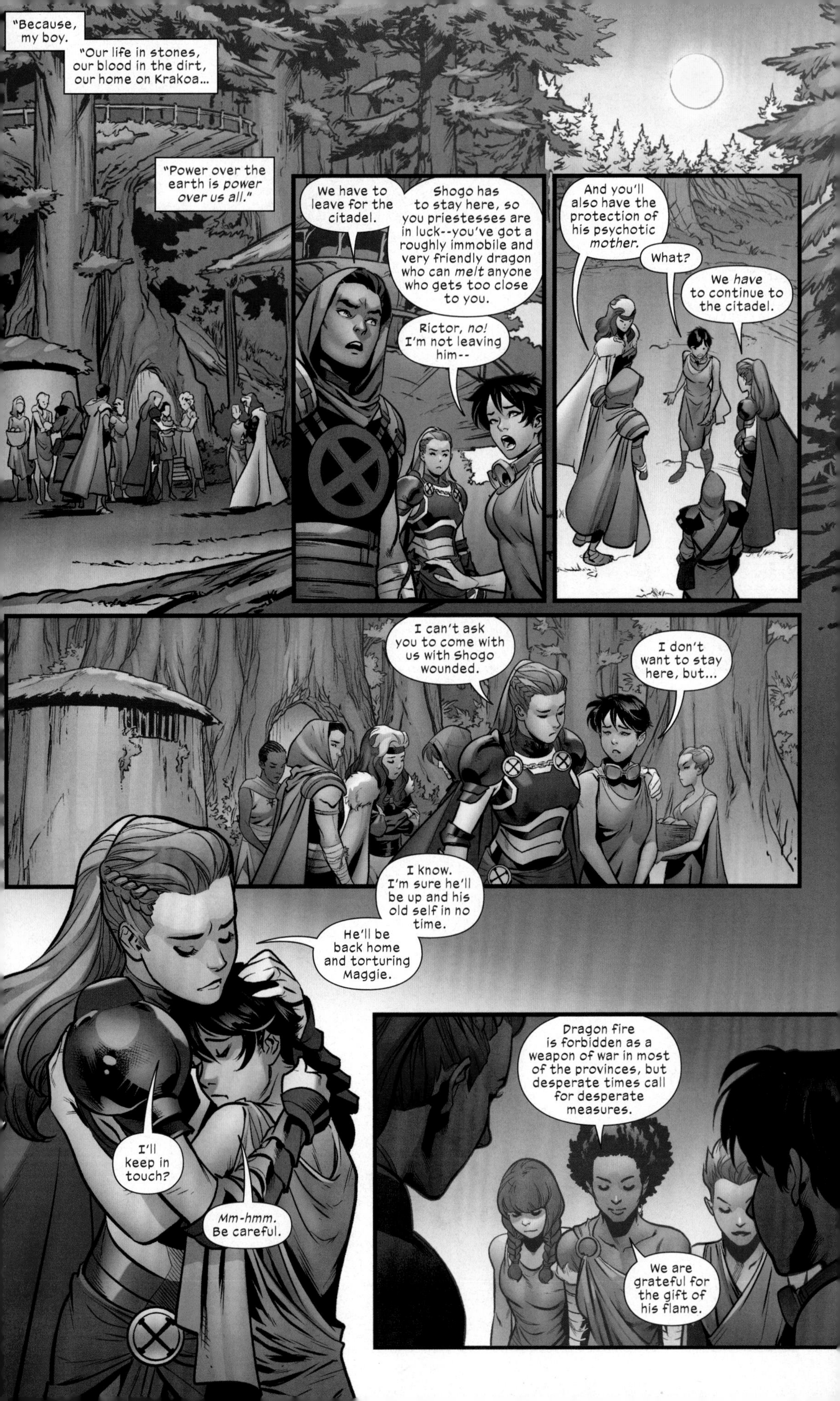
"Because, my boy.
"Our life in stones, our blood in the dirt, our home on Krakoa...
"Power over the earth is *power over us all*."
We have to leave for the citadel.
Shogo has to stay here, so you priestesses are in luck--you've got a roughly immobile and very friendly dragon who can *melt* anyone who gets too close to you.
Rictor, *no!* I'm not leaving him--
And you'll also have the protection of his psychotic *mother*.
What?
We *have* to continue to the citadel.
I can't ask you to come with us with Shogo wounded.
I don't want to stay here, but...
I know. I'm sure he'll be up and his old self in no time.
He'll be back home and torturing Maggie.
I'll keep in touch?
Mm-hmm. Be careful.
Dragon fire is forbidden as a weapon of war in most of the provinces, but desperate times call for desperate measures.
We are grateful for the gift of his flame.

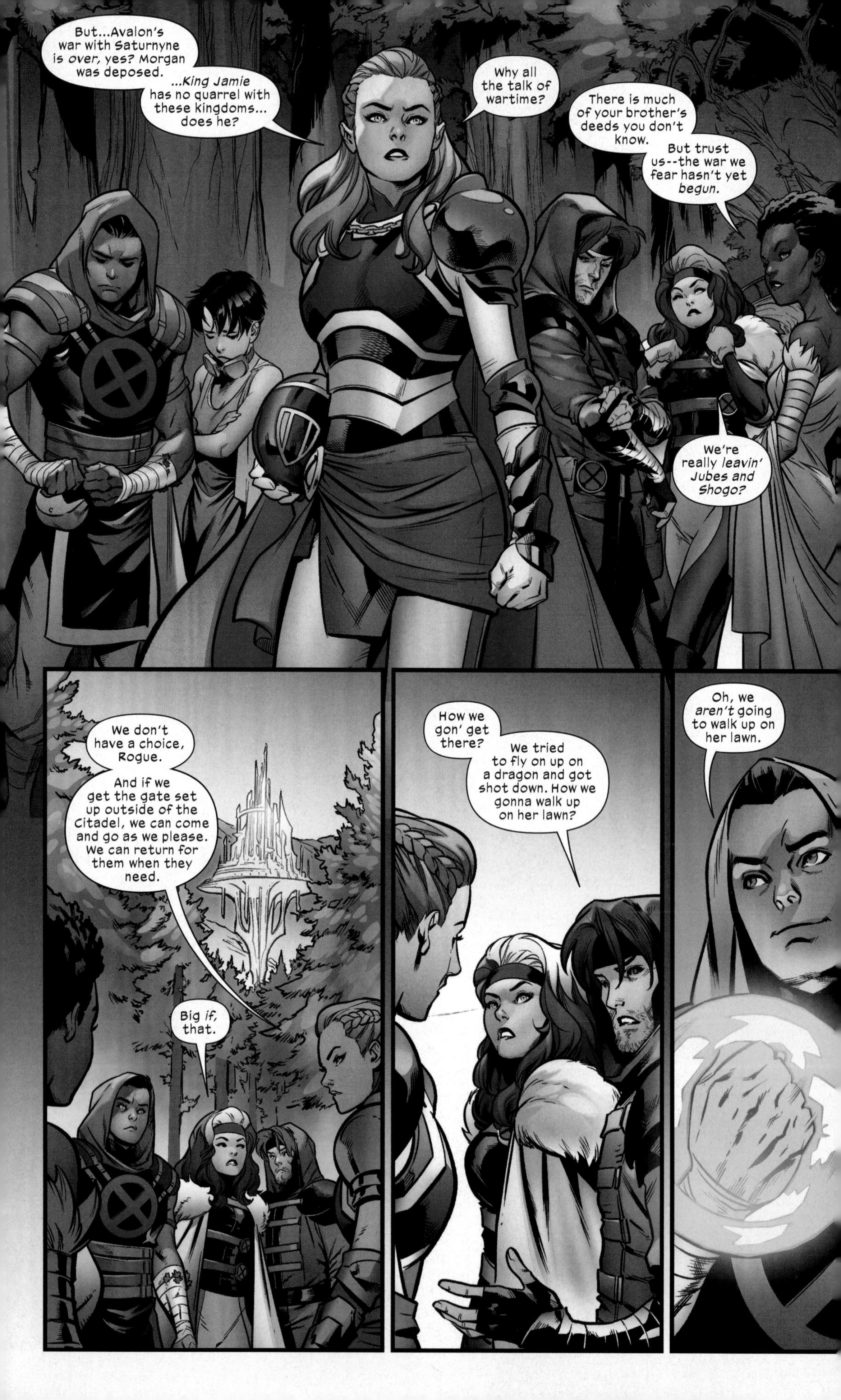

But...Avalon's war with Saturnyne is *over*, yes? Morgan was deposed.
...*King Jamie* has no quarrel with these kingdoms... does he?
Why all the talk of wartime?
There is much of your brother's deeds you don't know.
But trust us--the war we fear hasn't yet *begun*.
We're really *leavin'* Jubes and Shogo?
We don't have a choice, Rogue.
And if we get the gate set up outside of the Citadel, we can come and go as we please. We can return for them when they need.
Big *if*, that.
How we gon' get there?
We tried to fly on up on a dragon and got shot down. How we gonna walk up on her lawn?
Oh, we *aren't* going to walk up on her lawn.

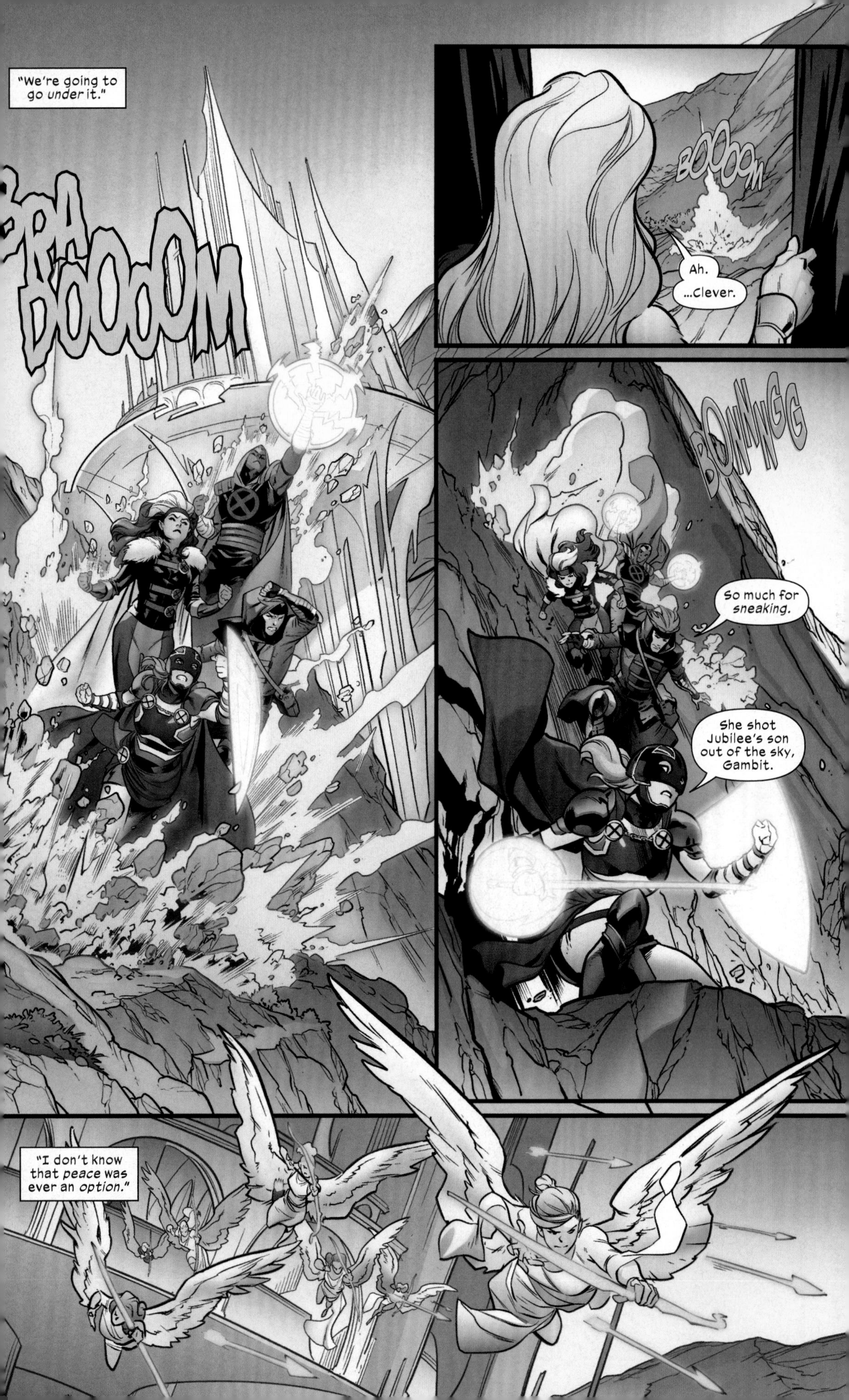
"We're going to go *under* it."
BRA BOOOOOM
BOOOOM
Ah.
...Clever.
BONNNGG
So much for *sneaking*.
She shot Jubilee's son out of the sky, Gambit.
"I don't know that *peace* was ever an *option*."

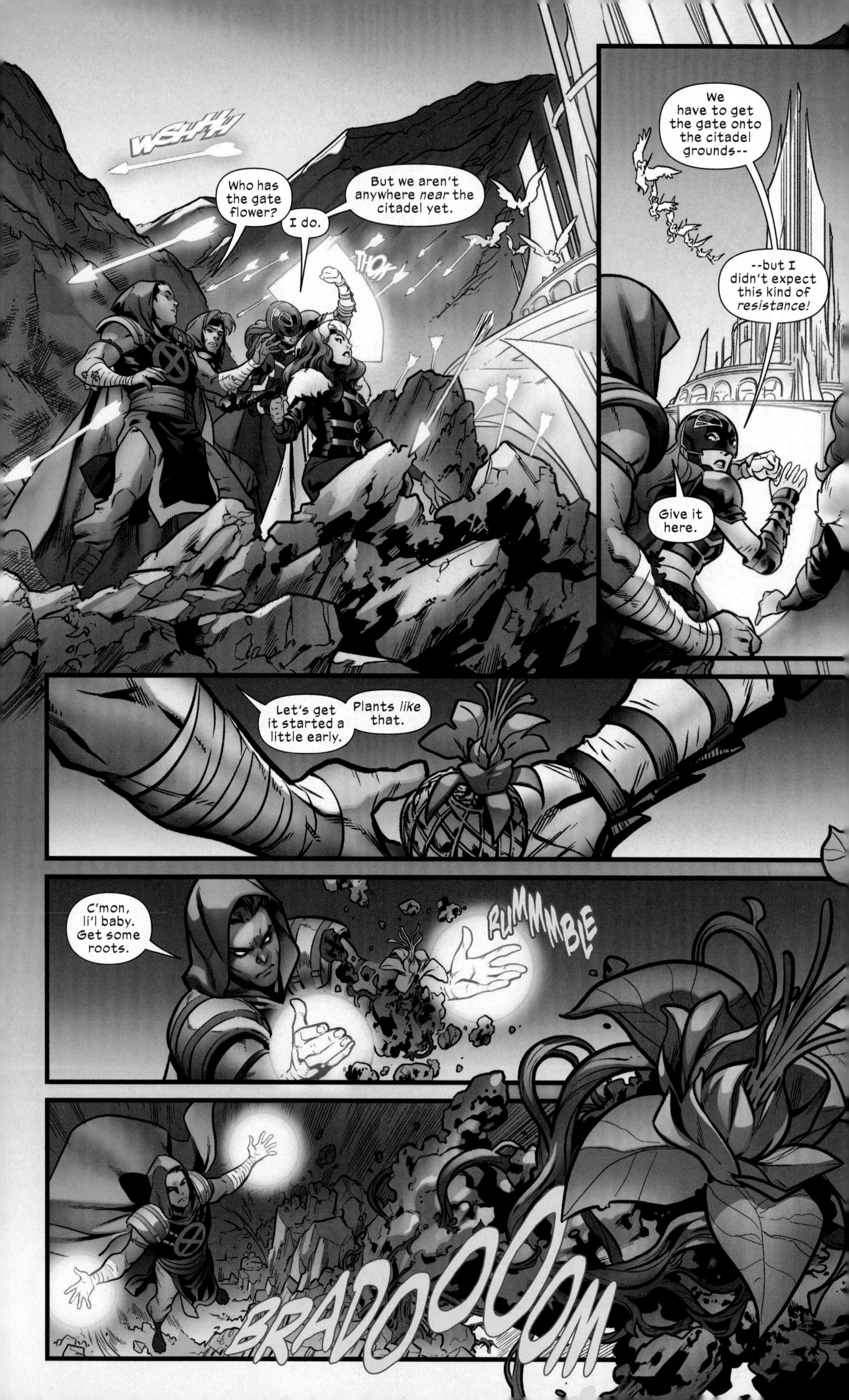

WSHHH
Who has the gate flower?
I do.
But we aren't anywhere *near* the citadel yet.
THOK
We have to get the gate onto the citadel grounds--
--but I didn't expect this kind of *resistance!*
Give it here.
Let's get it started a little early.
Plants *like* that.
C'mon, li'l baby. Get some roots.
RUMMMBLE
BRADOOOOM

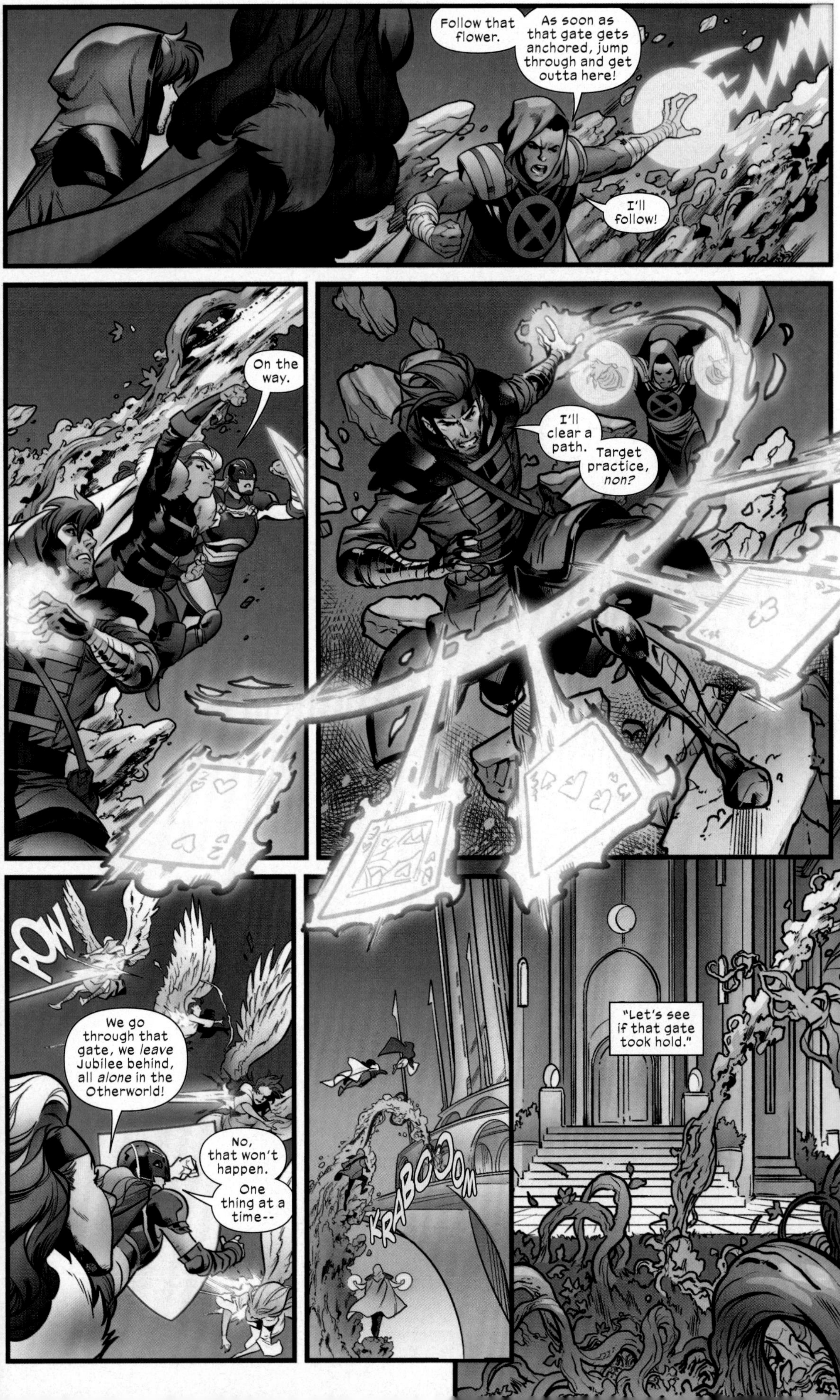
Follow that flower.
As soon as that gate gets anchored, jump through and get outta here!
I'll follow!
On the way.
I'll clear a path.
Target practice, *non?*
POW
We go through that gate, we *leave* Jubilee behind, all *alone* in the Otherworld!
No, that won't happen.
One thing at a time--
KRABOOOM
"Let's see if that gate took hold."

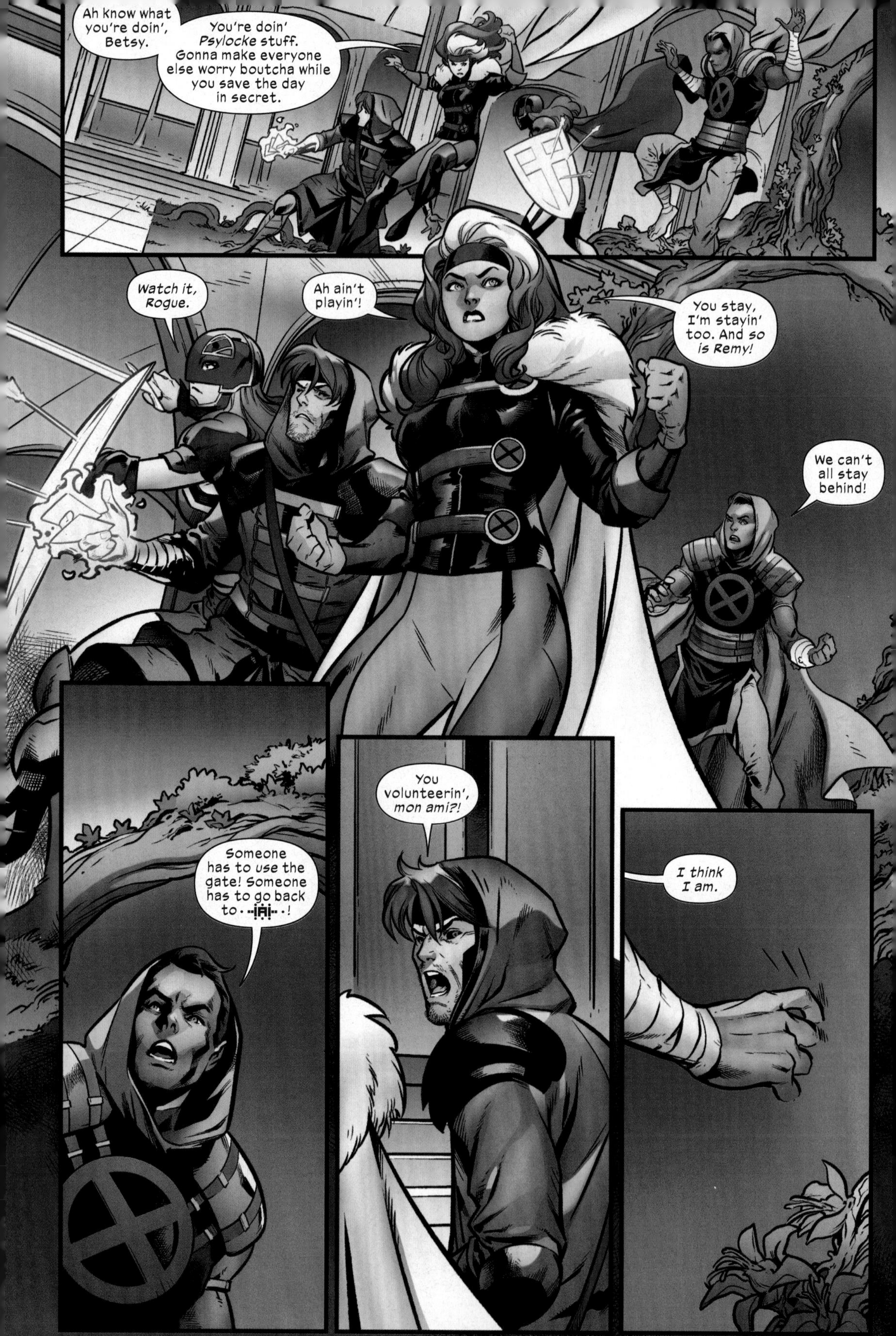
Ah know what you're doin', Betsy.
You're doin' Psylocke stuff. Gonna make everyone else worry boutcha while you save the day in secret.
Watch it, Rogue.
Ah ain't playin'!
You stay, I'm stayin' too. And so is Remy!
We can't all stay behind!
Someone has to use the gate! Someone has to go back to
You volunteerin', mon ami?!
I think I am.

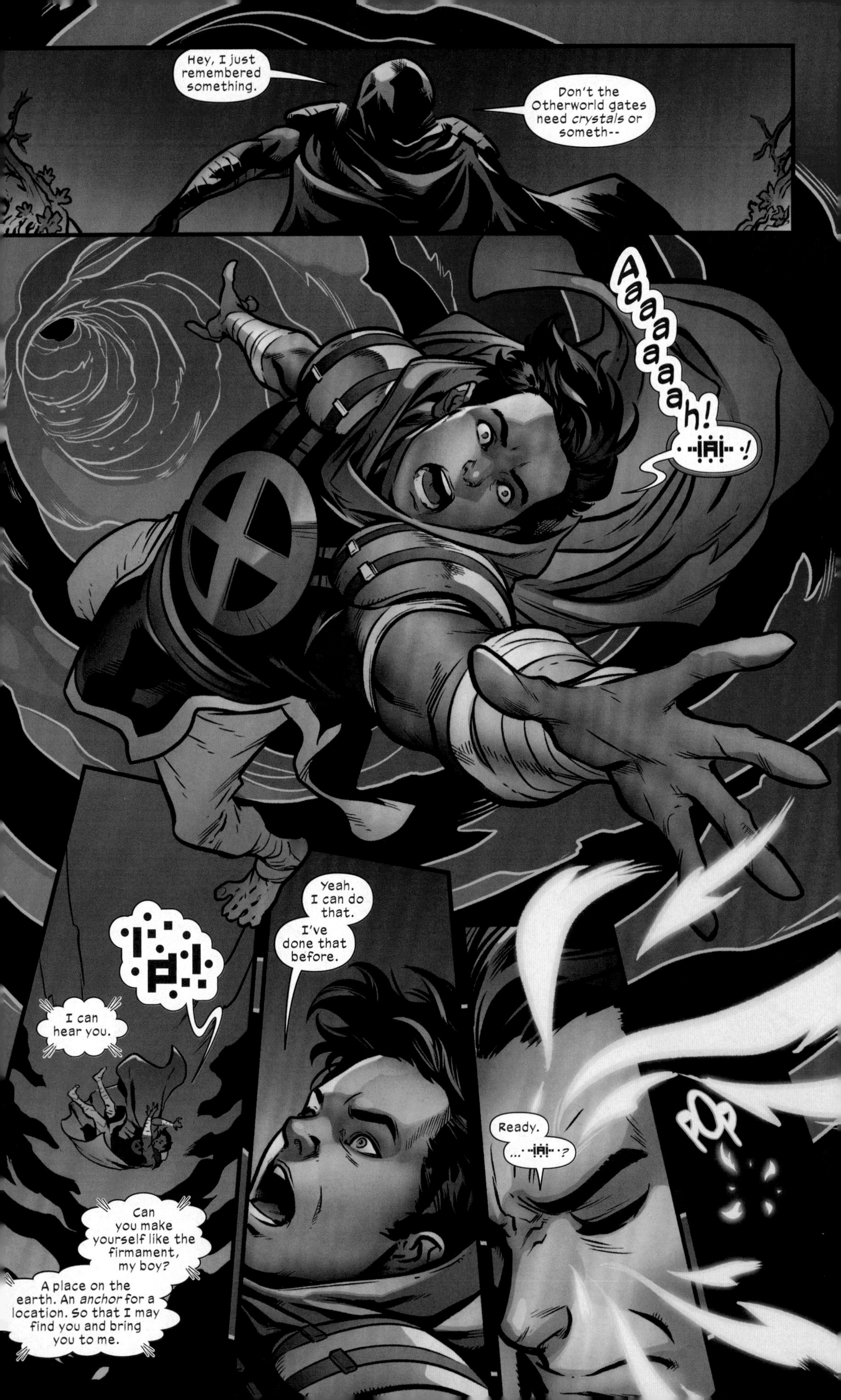

Hey, I just remembered something.
Don't the Otherworld gates need *crystals* or someth--
Aaaaaaah!
Yeah. I can do that.
I've done that before.
I can hear you.
Ready.
POP
Can you make yourself like the firmament, my boy?
A place on the earth. An *anchor* for a location. So that I may find you and bring you to me.

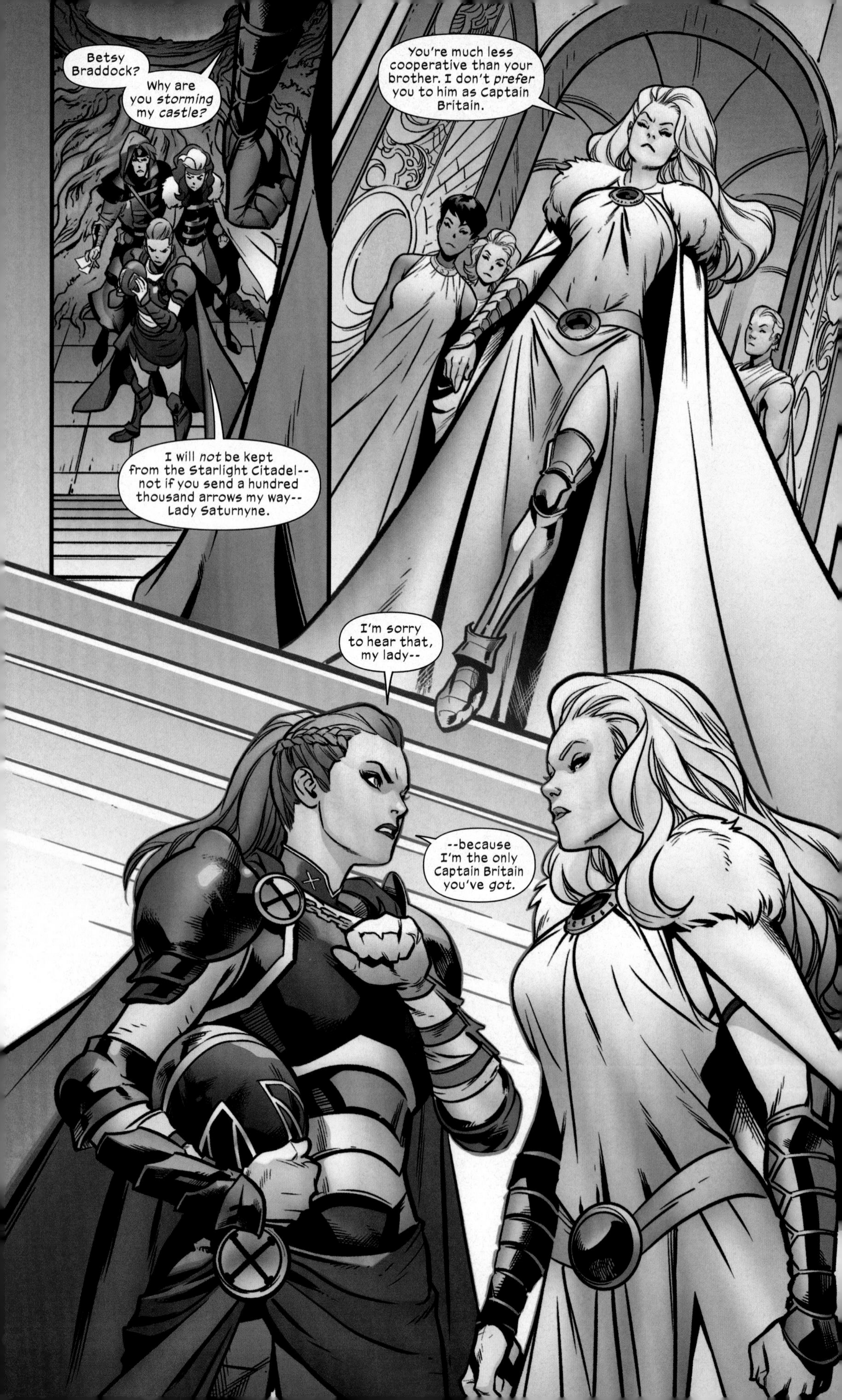
Betsy Braddock?
Why are you *storming* my *castle?*
You're much less cooperative than your brother. I don't *prefer* you to him as Captain Britain.
I will *not* be kept from the Starlight Citadel-- not if you send a hundred thousand arrows my way-- Lady Saturnyne.
I'm sorry to hear that, my lady--
--because I'm the only Captain Britain you've *got.*

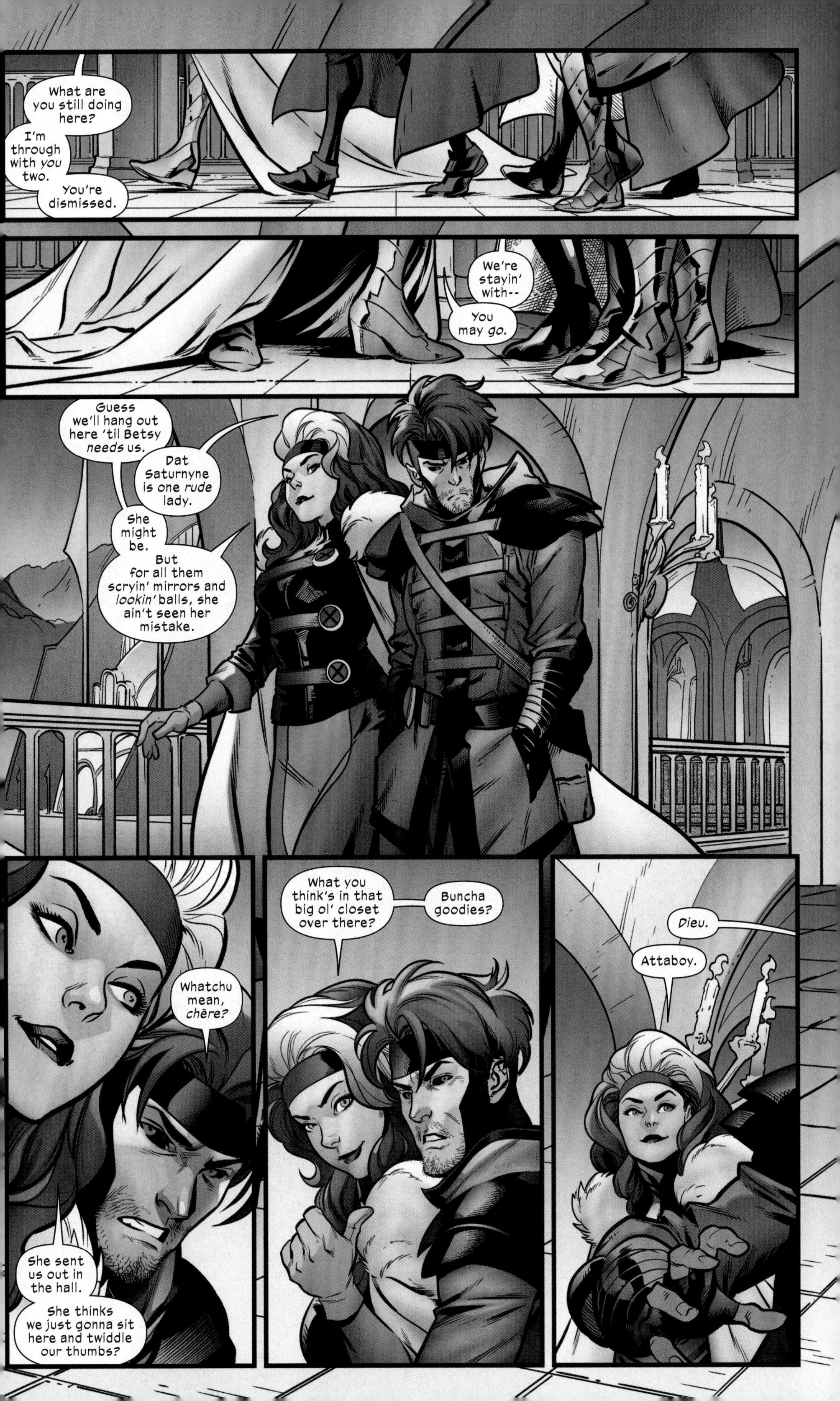

What are you still doing here?
I'm through with *you* two.
You're dismissed.
We're stayin' with--
You may *go.*
Guess we'll hang out here 'til Betsy *needs* us.
Dat Saturnyne is one *rude* lady.
She might be.
But for all them scryin' mirrors and *lookin'* balls, she ain't seen her mistake.
Whatchu mean, *chère?*
She sent us out in the hall.
She thinks we just gonna sit here and twiddle our thumbs?
What you think's in that big ol' closet over there?
Buncha goodies?
Dieu.
Attaboy.

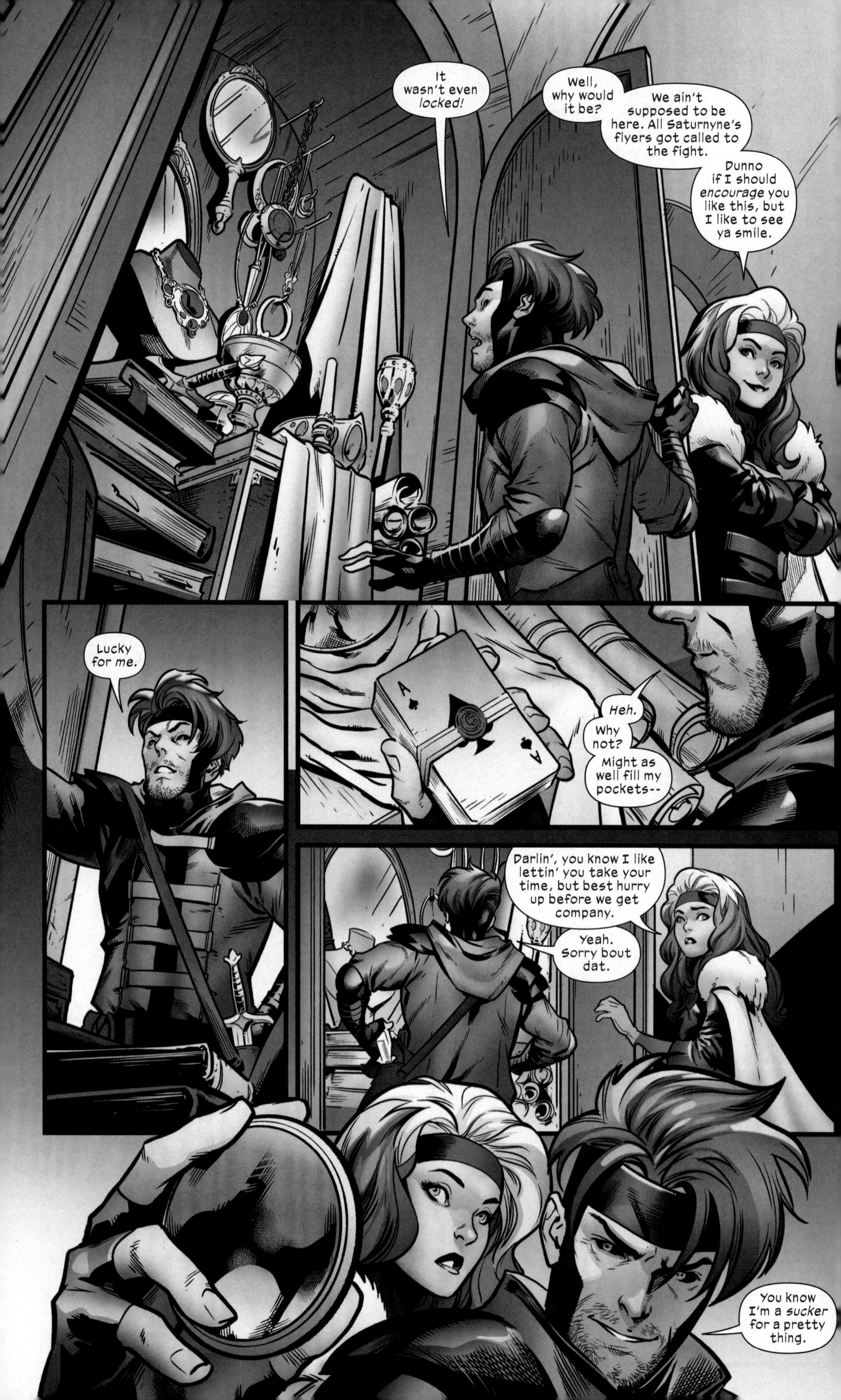
It wasn't even *locked!*
Well, why would it be?
We ain't supposed to be here. All Saturnyne's flyers got called to the fight.
Dunno if I should *encourage* you like this, but I like to see ya smile.
Lucky for me.
Heh.
Why not?
Might as well fill my pockets--
Darlin', you know I like lettin' you take your time, but best hurry up before we get company.
Yeah. Sorry bout dat.
You know I'm a *sucker* for a pretty thing.

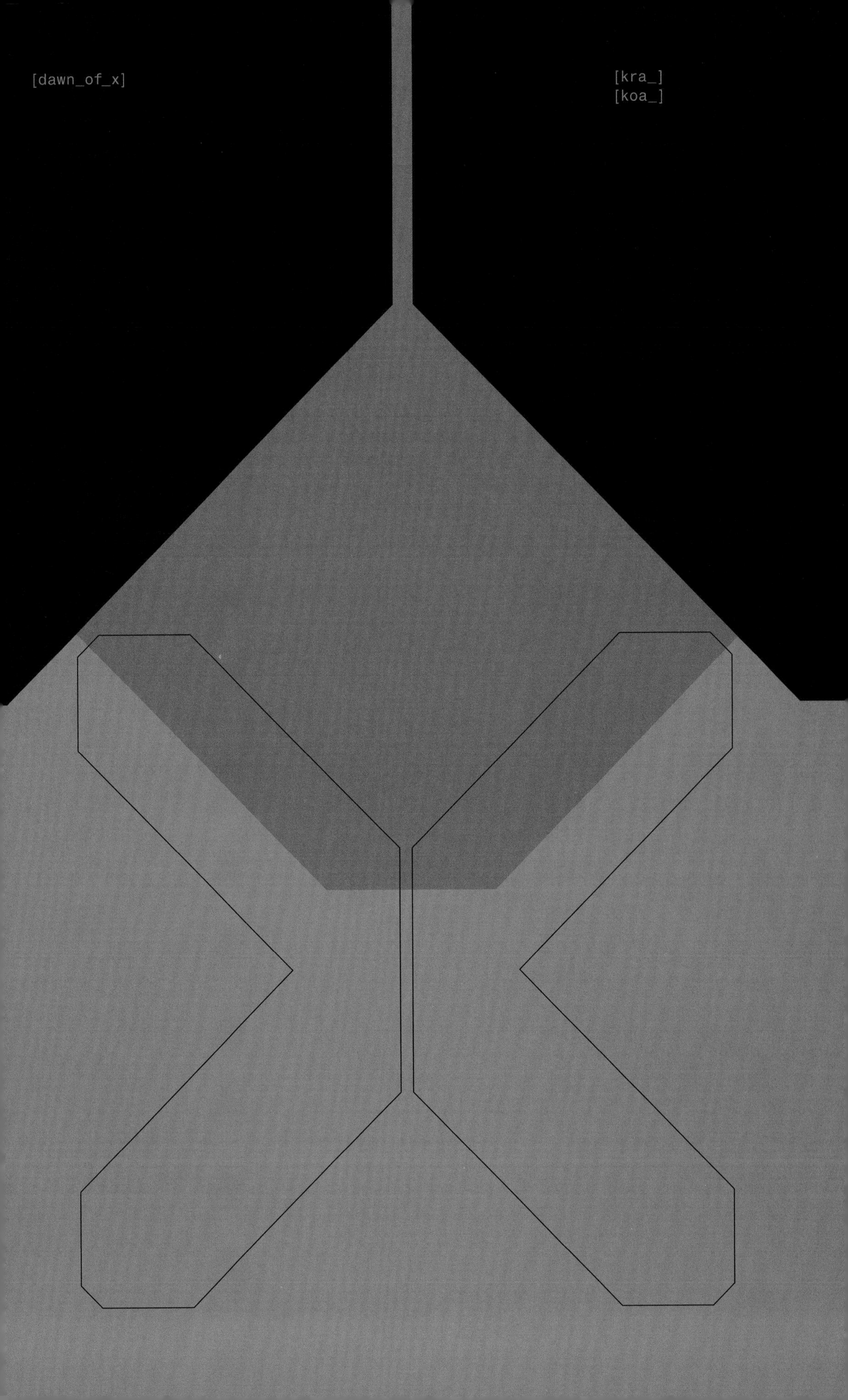
[dawn_of_x]
[kra_]
[koa_]

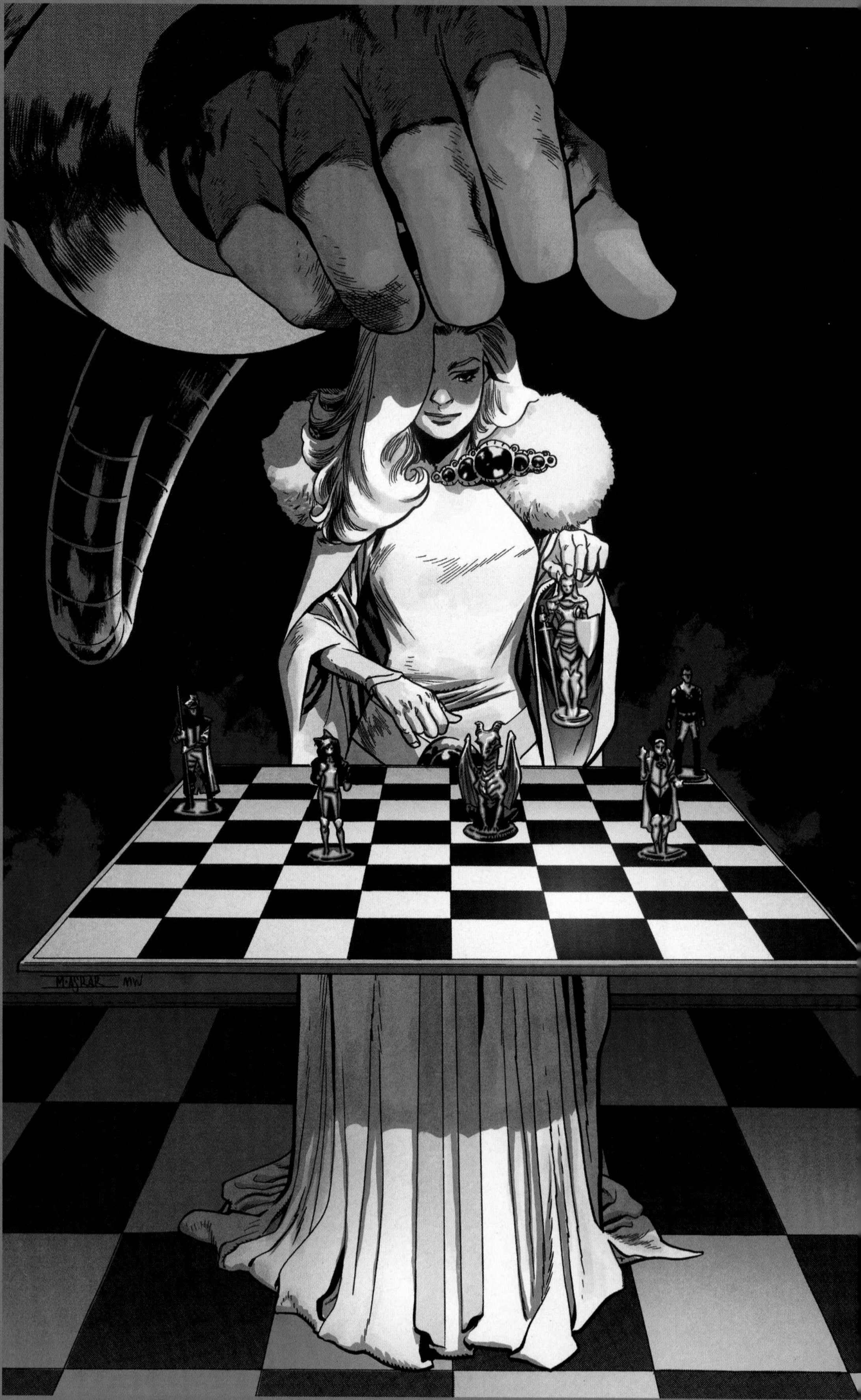
M·ASRAR MW

The Beginning

12

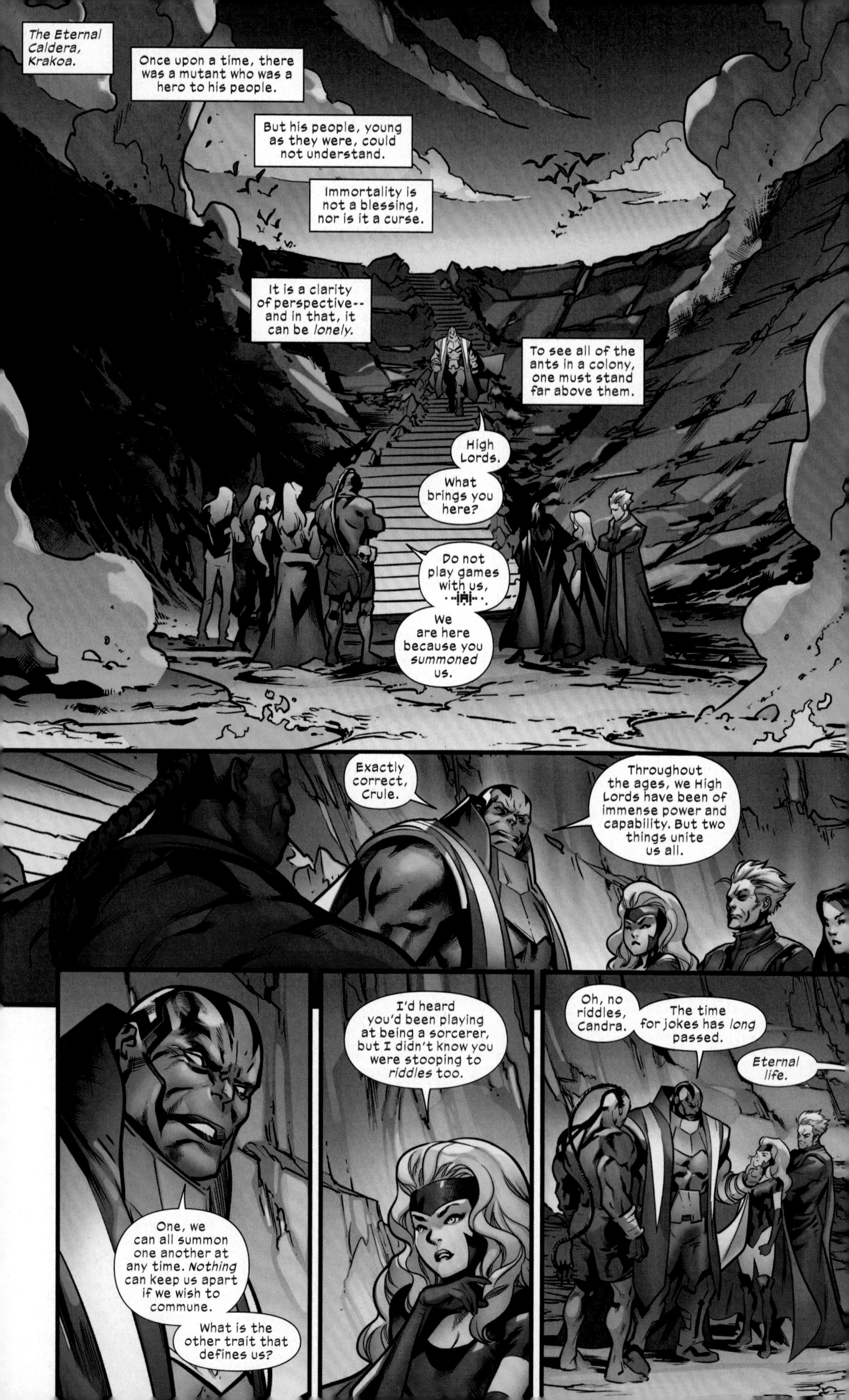
The Eternal Caldera, Krakoa.
Once upon a time, there was a mutant who was a hero to his people.
But his people, young as they were, could not understand.
Immortality is not a blessing, nor is it a curse.
It is a clarity of perspective--and in that, it can be *lonely*.
To see all of the ants in a colony, one must stand far above them.
High Lords.
What brings you here?
Do not play games with us,
We are here because you *summoned* us.
Exactly correct, Crule.
Throughout the ages, we High Lords have been of immense power and capability. But two things unite us all.
One, we can all summon one another at any time. *Nothing* can keep us apart if we wish to commune.
What is the other trait that defines us?
I'd heard you'd been playing at being a sorcerer, but I didn't know you were stooping to *riddles* too.
Oh, no riddles, Candra.
The time for jokes has *long* passed.
Eternal life.

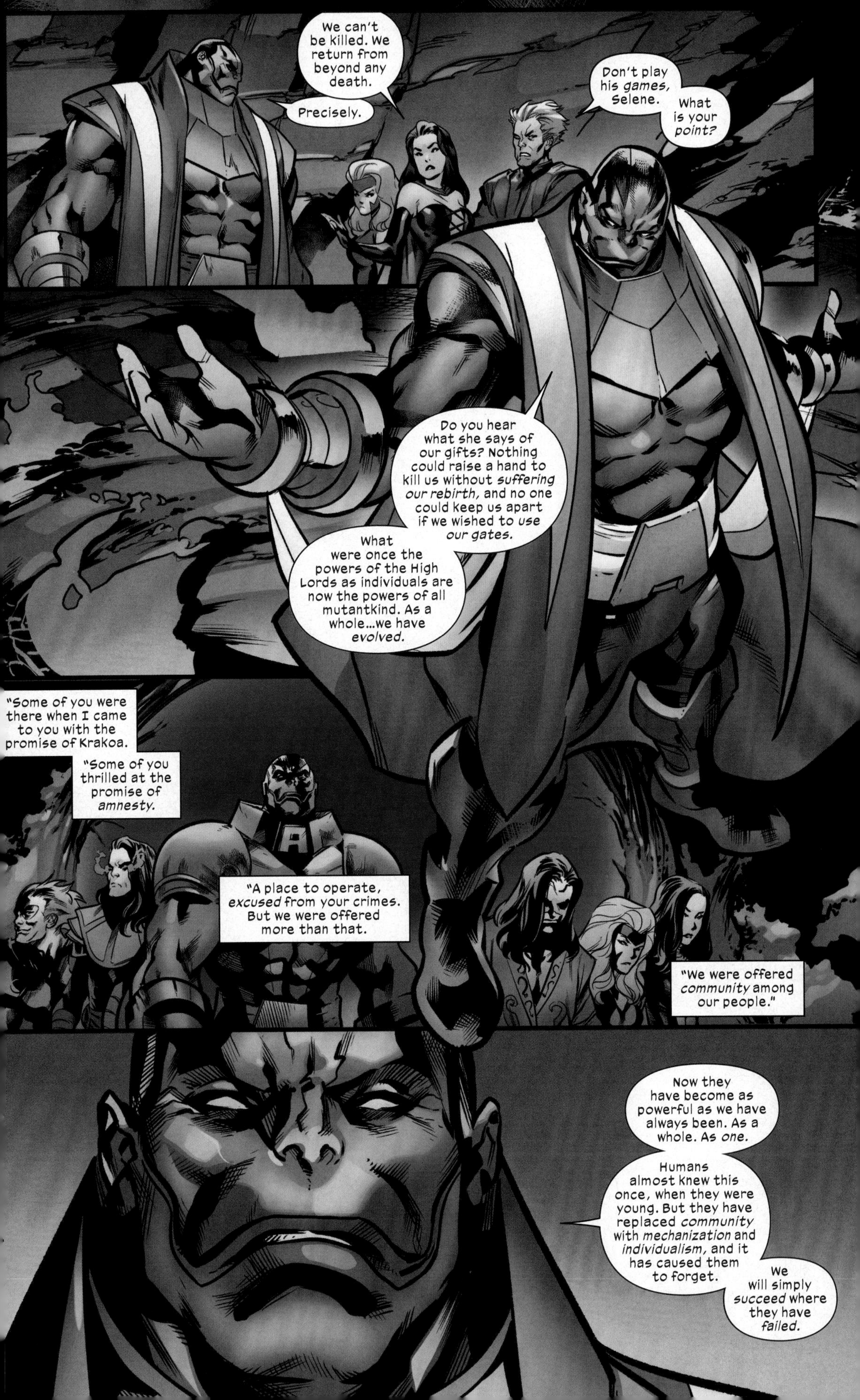

We can't be killed. We return from beyond any death.
Precisely.
Don't play his games, Selene.
What is your point?
Do you hear what she says of our gifts? Nothing could raise a hand to kill us without suffering our rebirth, and no one could keep us apart if we wished to use our gates.
What were once the powers of the High Lords as individuals are now the powers of all mutantkind. As a whole...we have evolved.
"Some of you were there when I came to you with the promise of Krakoa.
"Some of you thrilled at the promise of amnesty.
"A place to operate, excused from your crimes. But we were offered more than that.
"We were offered community among our people."
Now they have become as powerful as we have always been. As a whole. As one.
Humans almost knew this once, when they were young. But they have replaced community with mechanization and individualism, and it has caused them to forget.
We will simply succeed where they have failed.

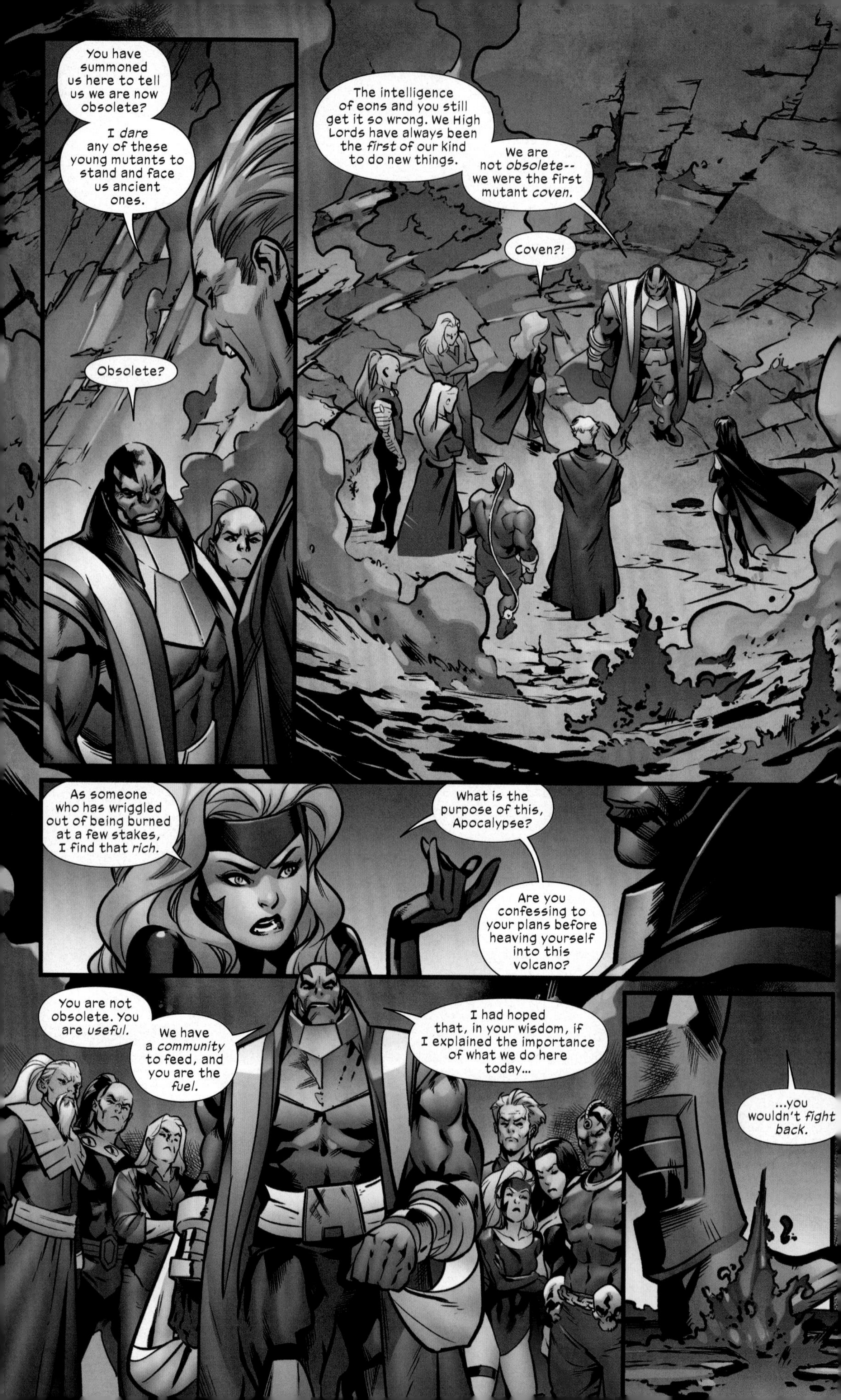
You have summoned us here to tell us we are now obsolete?
I *dare* any of these young mutants to stand and face us ancient ones.
Obsolete?
The intelligence of eons and you still get it so wrong. We High Lords have always been the *first* of our kind to do new things.
We are not *obsolete*-- we were the first mutant *coven.*
Coven?!
As someone who has wriggled out of being burned at a few stakes, I find that *rich.*
What is the purpose of this, Apocalypse?
Are you confessing to your plans before heaving yourself into this volcano?
You are not obsolete. You are *useful.*
We have a *community* to feed, and you are the *fuel.*
I had hoped that, in your wisdom, if I explained the importance of what we do here today...
...you wouldn't *fight* back.

THE HIGH LORDS

THE EXTERNALS

At times believed to be a subspecies or evolved offshoot of mutantdom, it is now believed that the so-called "High Lords" were perhaps an early tendency toward the eventual gifts that mutantkind would come to possess during the pax Krakoa. Much has been supposed of their origin, limitations, and abilities, but it largely remains in the realm of theory. What is not theoretical is their long-term involvement in human politics, finance, and law - they have oft been seen as a sort of "mutant Illuminati."

In addition to the abilities of very old, powerful mutants, their additional External gifts included:

1:: RESURRECTION. High Lords of Mutantdom can be killed, but most possess rapid healing traits, and all return (occasionally in a different form) if they meet true death. Mutants suspected to have External traits have indeed been tested with death, returning, at times, several years later.

2:: COMMUNION. High Lords are always aware of one another, can communicate across great distances, and can come together at will. They are known to possess a shared life force - when one External kills another, their ancient energy is dispersed within the remaining Externals. Additionally, their life force can be contained within a gem, which has been shown to keep it out of the shared energetic loop.

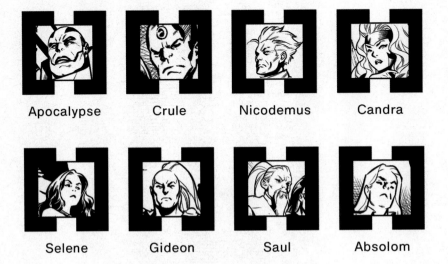

| Apocalypse | Crule | Nicodemus | Candra |
| Selene | Gideon | Saul | Absolom |

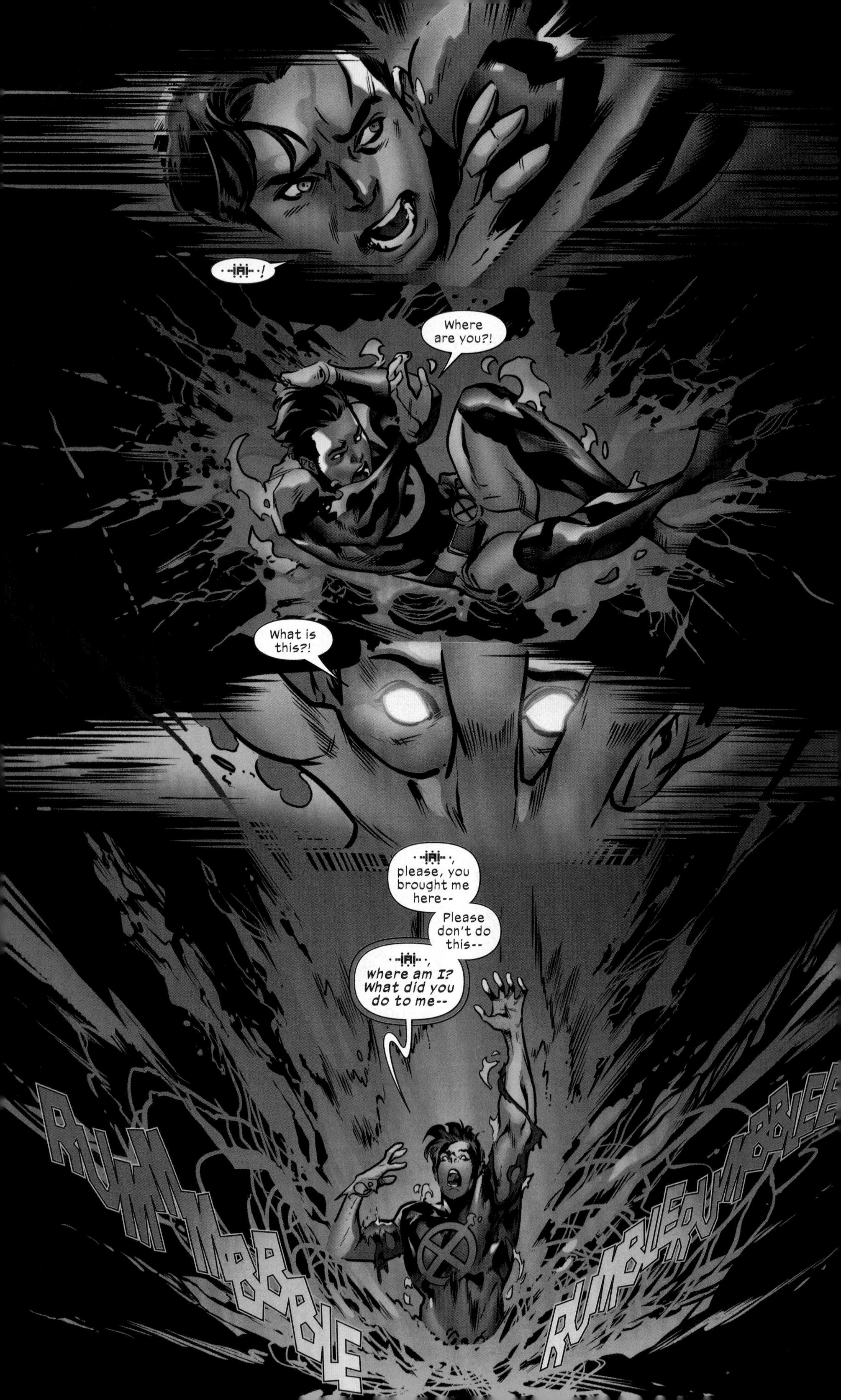
Where are you?!
What is this?!
please, you brought me here--
Please don't do this--
where am I? What did you do to me--
RUMMMBBBLE
RUMBLERUMBLEE

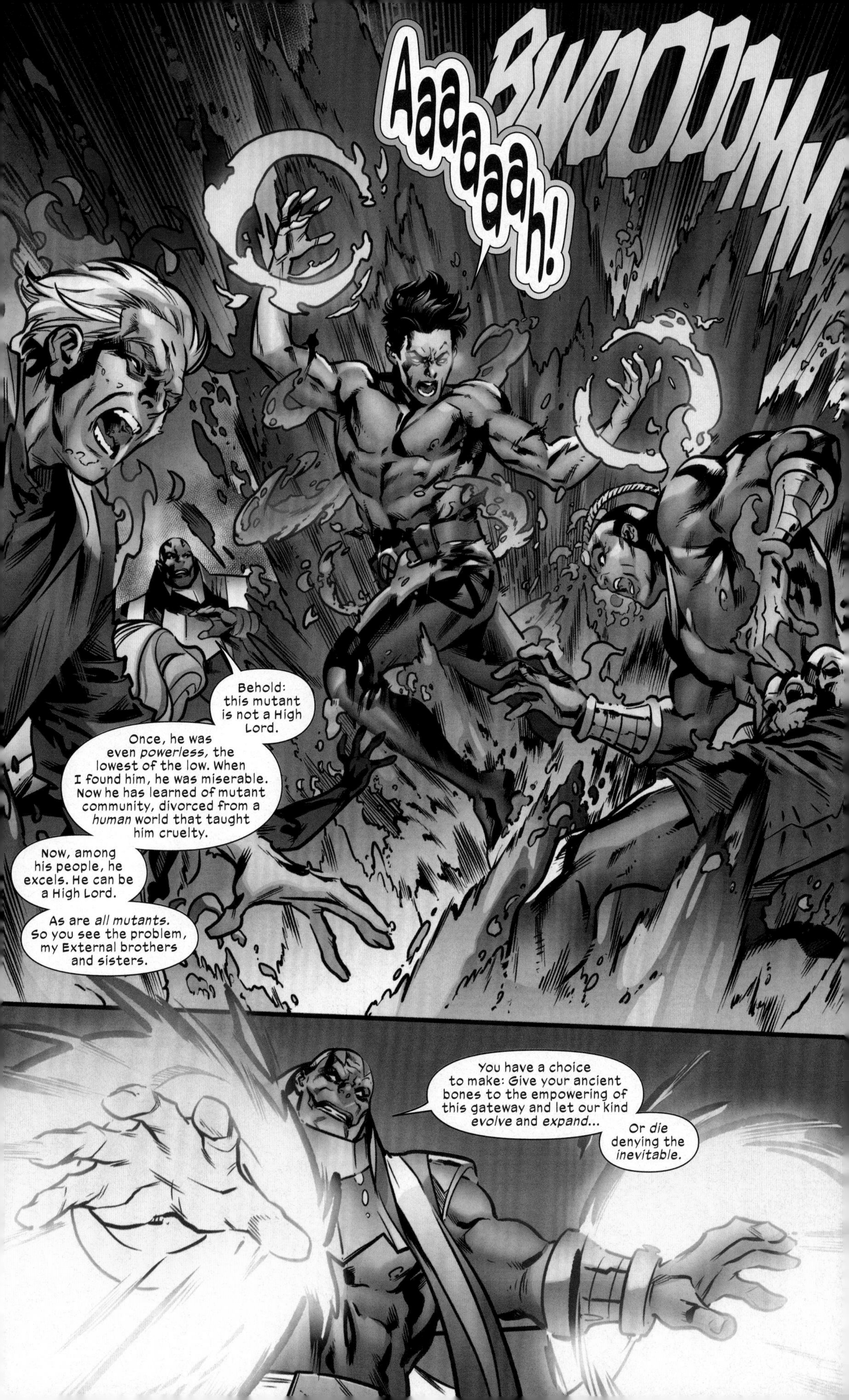
Aaaaaaah!
BWOOOOM
Behold: this mutant is not a High Lord.
Once, he was even *powerless,* the lowest of the low. When I found him, he was miserable. Now he has learned of mutant community, divorced from a *human* world that taught him cruelty.
Now, among his people, he excels. He can be a High Lord.
As are *all mutants.* So you see the problem, my External brothers and sisters.
You have a choice to make: Give your ancient bones to the empowering of this gateway and let our kind *evolve* and *expand*...
Or *die* denying the *inevitable.*

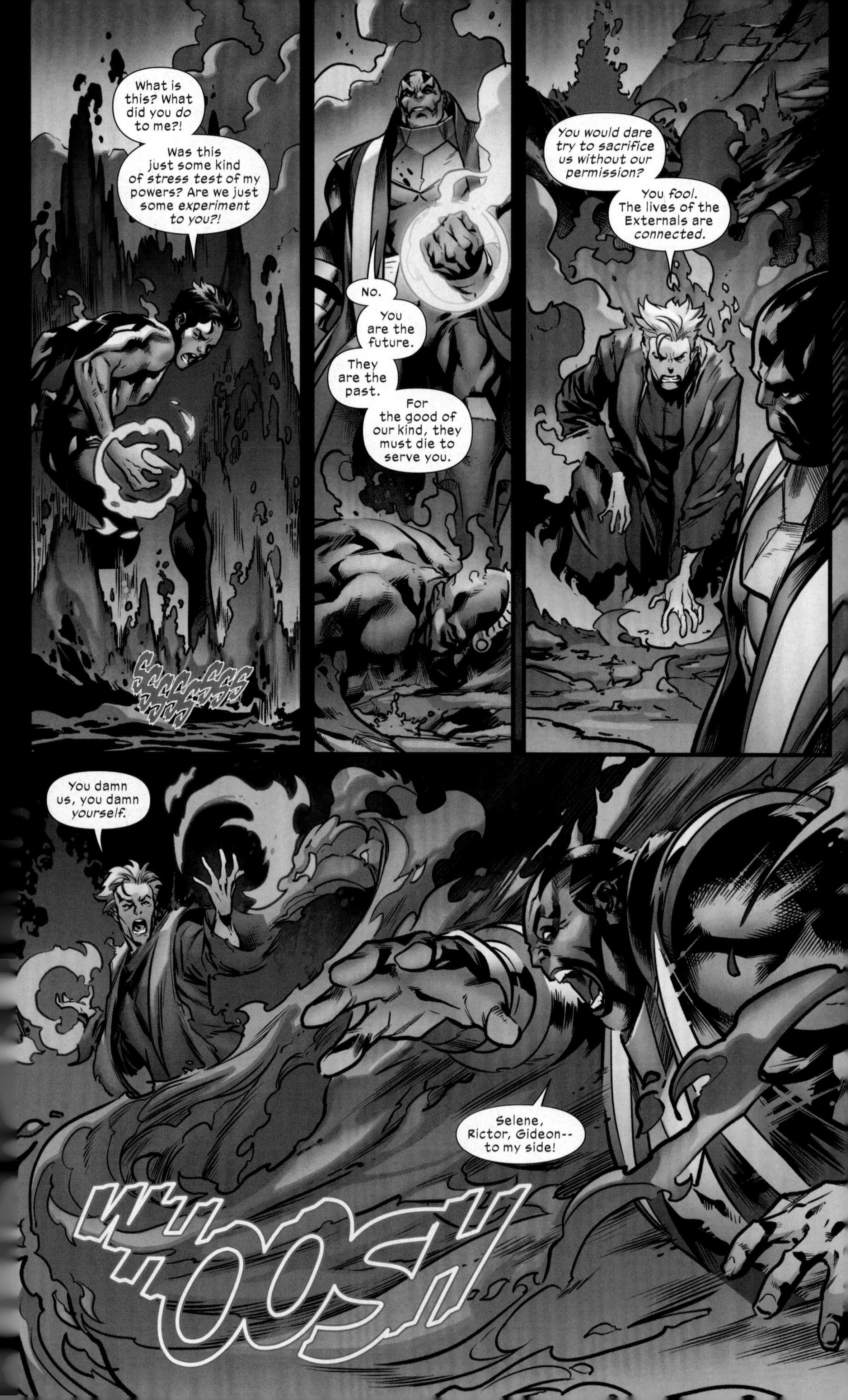
What is this? What did you do to me?!
Was this just some kind of stress test of my powers? Are we just some experiment to you?!
SSSSSS
No.
You are the future.
They are the past.
For the good of our kind, they must die to serve you.
You would dare try to sacrifice us without our permission?
You fool. The lives of the Externals are connected.
You damn us, you damn yourself.
Selene, Rictor, Gideon-- to my side!
WHOOSH

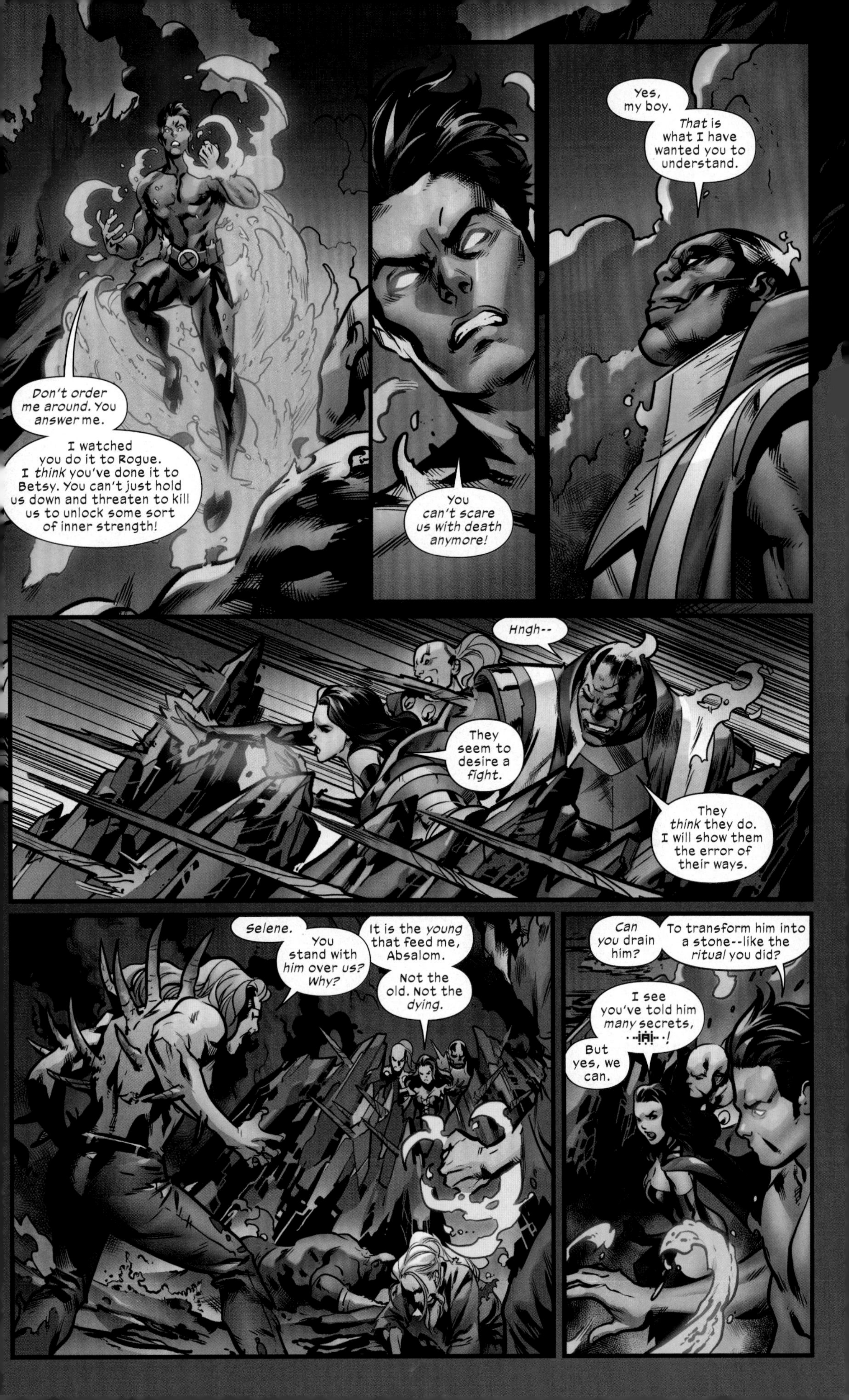
Don't order me around. You answer me.
I watched you do it to Rogue. I think you've done it to Betsy. You can't just hold us down and threaten to kill us to unlock some sort of inner strength!
You can't scare us with death anymore!
Yes, my boy.
That is what I have wanted you to understand.
Hngh--
They seem to desire a fight.
They think they do. I will show them the error of their ways.
Selene.
You stand with him over us? Why?
It is the young that feed me, Absalom.
Not the old. Not the dying.
Can you drain him?
To transform him into a stone--like the ritual you did?
I see you've told him many secrets,
But yes, we can.

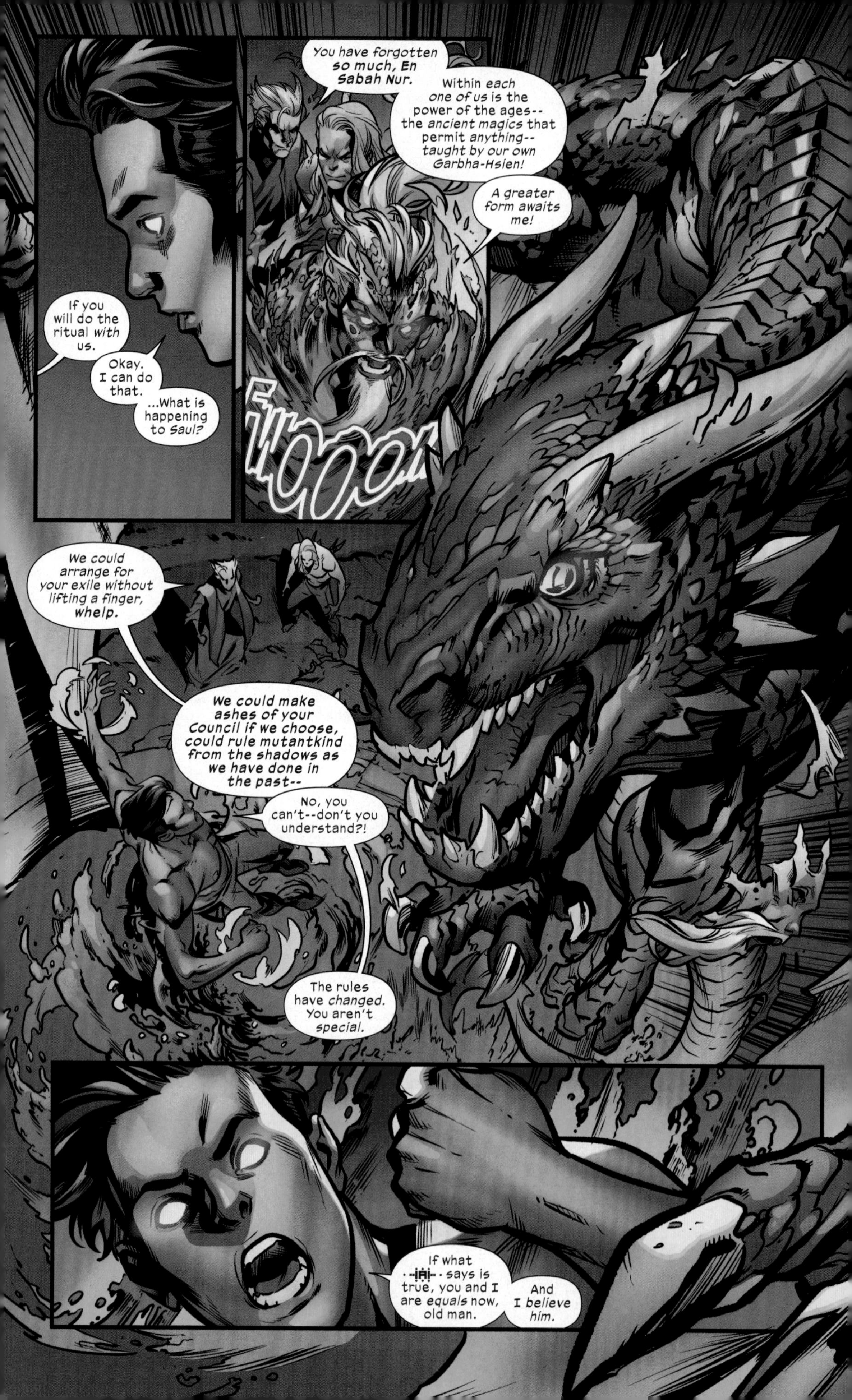
You have forgotten so much, En Sabah Nur.
Within each one of us is the power of the ages-- the ancient magics that permit anything-- taught by our own Garbha-Hsien!
A greater form awaits me!
If you will do the ritual with us.
Okay. I can do that.
...What is happening to Saul?
We could arrange for your exile without lifting a finger, whelp.
We could make ashes of your Council if we choose, could rule mutantkind from the shadows as we have done in the past--
No, you can't--don't you understand?!
The rules have changed. You aren't special.
If what
says is true, you and I are equals now, old man.
And I believe him.

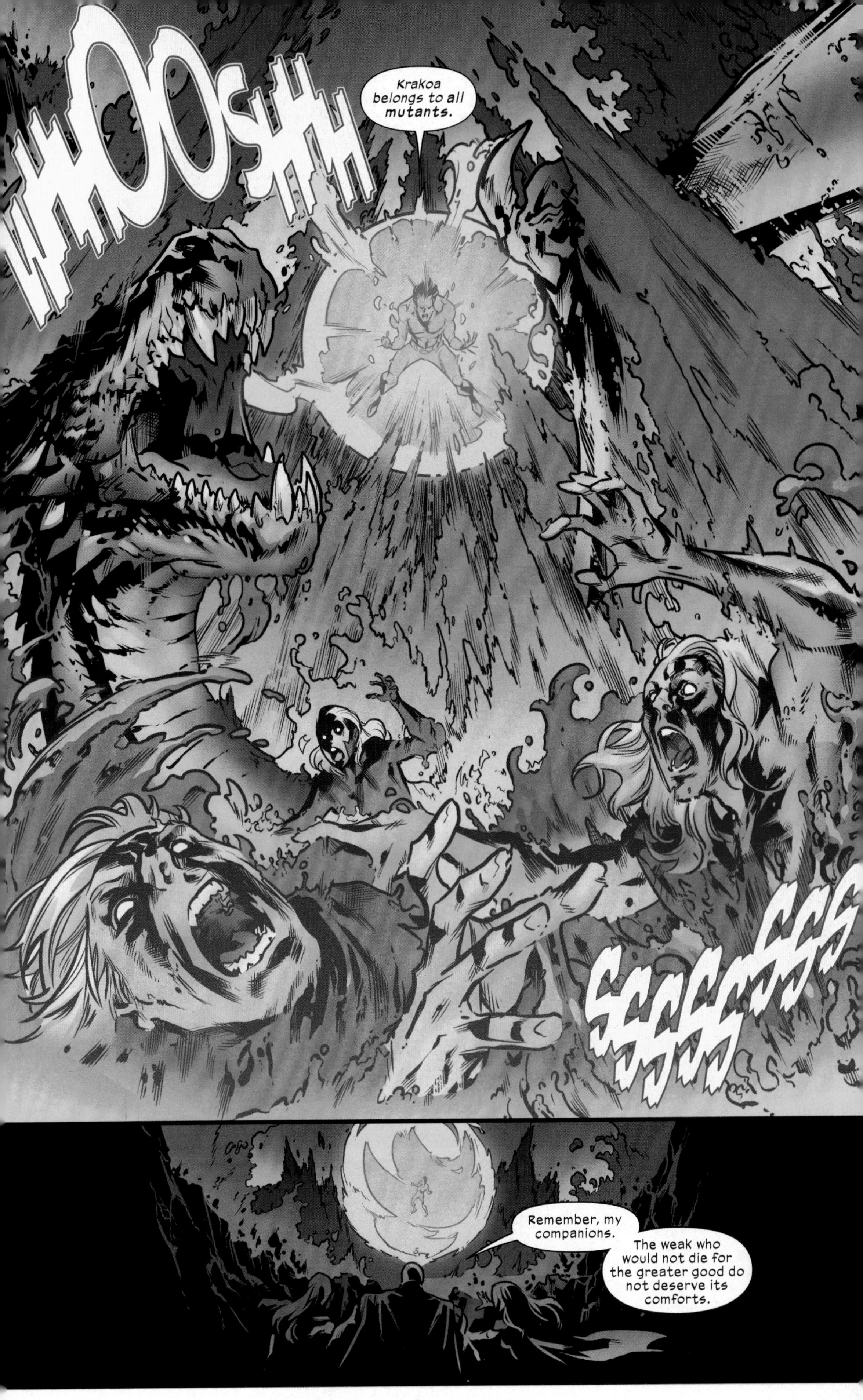
WHOOSHH
Krakoa belongs to all mutants.
SSSSSSS
Remember, my companions.
The weak who would not die for the greater good do not deserve its comforts.

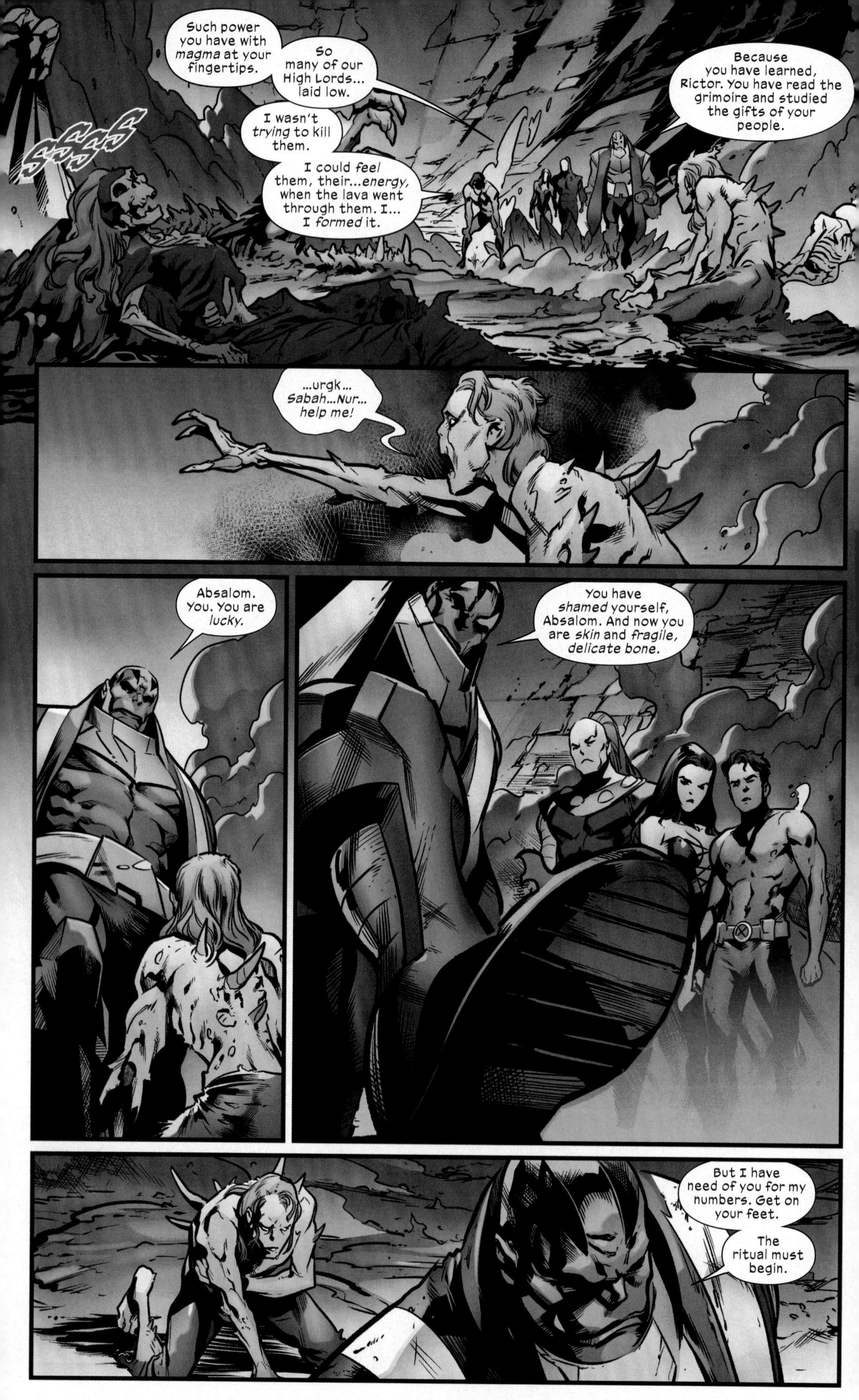
SSSSS
Such power you have with *magma* at your fingertips.
So many of our High Lords... laid low.
I wasn't *trying* to kill them.
I could *feel* them, their...*energy,* when the lava went through them. I... I *formed* it.
Because you have learned, Rictor. You have read the grimoire and studied the gifts of your people.
...urgk... Sabah...Nur... help me!
Absalom. You. You are *lucky.*
You have *shamed* yourself, Absalom. And now you are *skin* and *fragile, delicate bone.*
But I have need of you for my numbers. Get on your feet.
The ritual must begin.

FROM THE GRIMOIRE OF

EX MAGICA: ALMANAC (Fig. 14)

GATE
COMPONENT
COMPONENT
TRANSMUTER
COMPONENT
COMPONENT

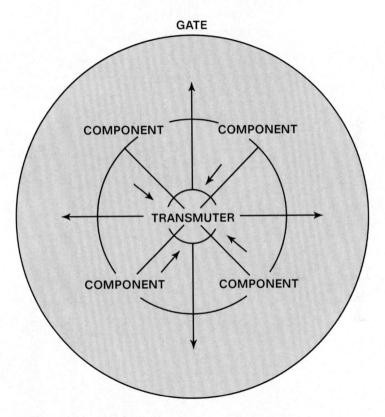

1. :: NEUTRALIZE PHYSICAL COMPONENTS TO FREE UP HIGH LORD LIFE FORCE. ENERGIES WILL TEND TOWARD CENTRAL CONDUIT

2. :: FORCE FLOWS TOWARD SORCERER (EARTH TRANSMUTER)

3. :: SORCERER TRANSMUTES EXTERNAL ENERGIES INTO ROCK CRYSTAL FORMATION (see: *Notes Upon an Ancient Darkness: CANDRA.*)

4. :: ROCK CRYSTAL FORMATION CREATES EMPOWERED EXTERNAL GATE, ALLOWING MASS OTHERWORLD ACCESS AT SPECIFIC DESIRED LOCATION. (For further reading see: EX MAGICA: ALMANAC (fig. 1)

[ava_[0.12]...]
[lon_[0.12]...]

[GRIMOIRE....]

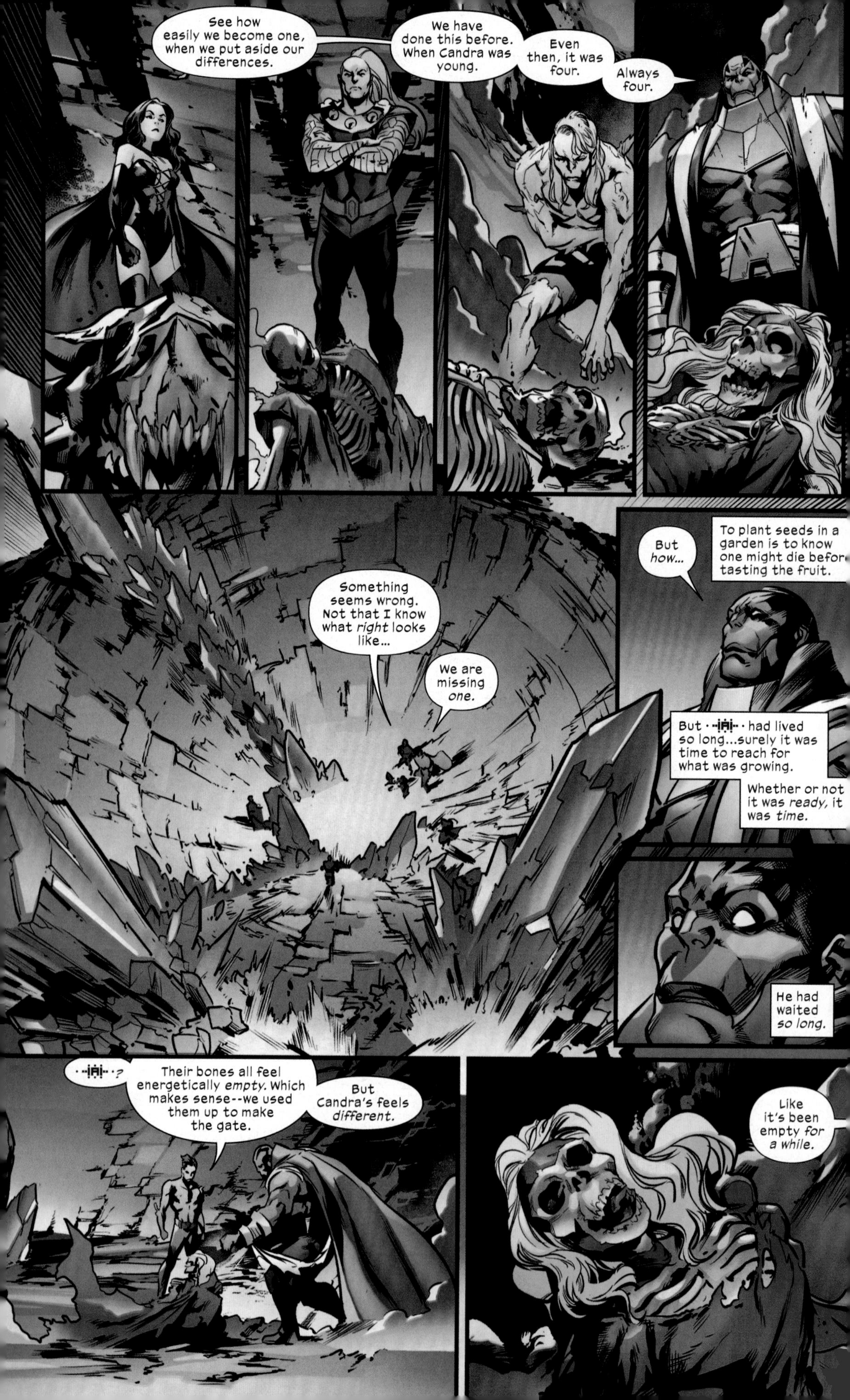
See how easily we become one, when we put aside our differences.
We have done this before. When Candra was young.
Even then, it was four.
Always four.
Something seems wrong. Not that I know what *right* looks like...
We are missing *one.*
But *how...*
To plant seeds in a garden is to know one might die befor tasting the fruit.
But had lived so long...surely it was time to reach for what was growing.
Whether or not it was *ready,* it was *time.*
He had waited *so long.*
Their bones all feel energetically *empty.* Which makes sense--we used them up to make the gate.
But Candra's feels *different.*
Like it's been empty *for a while.*

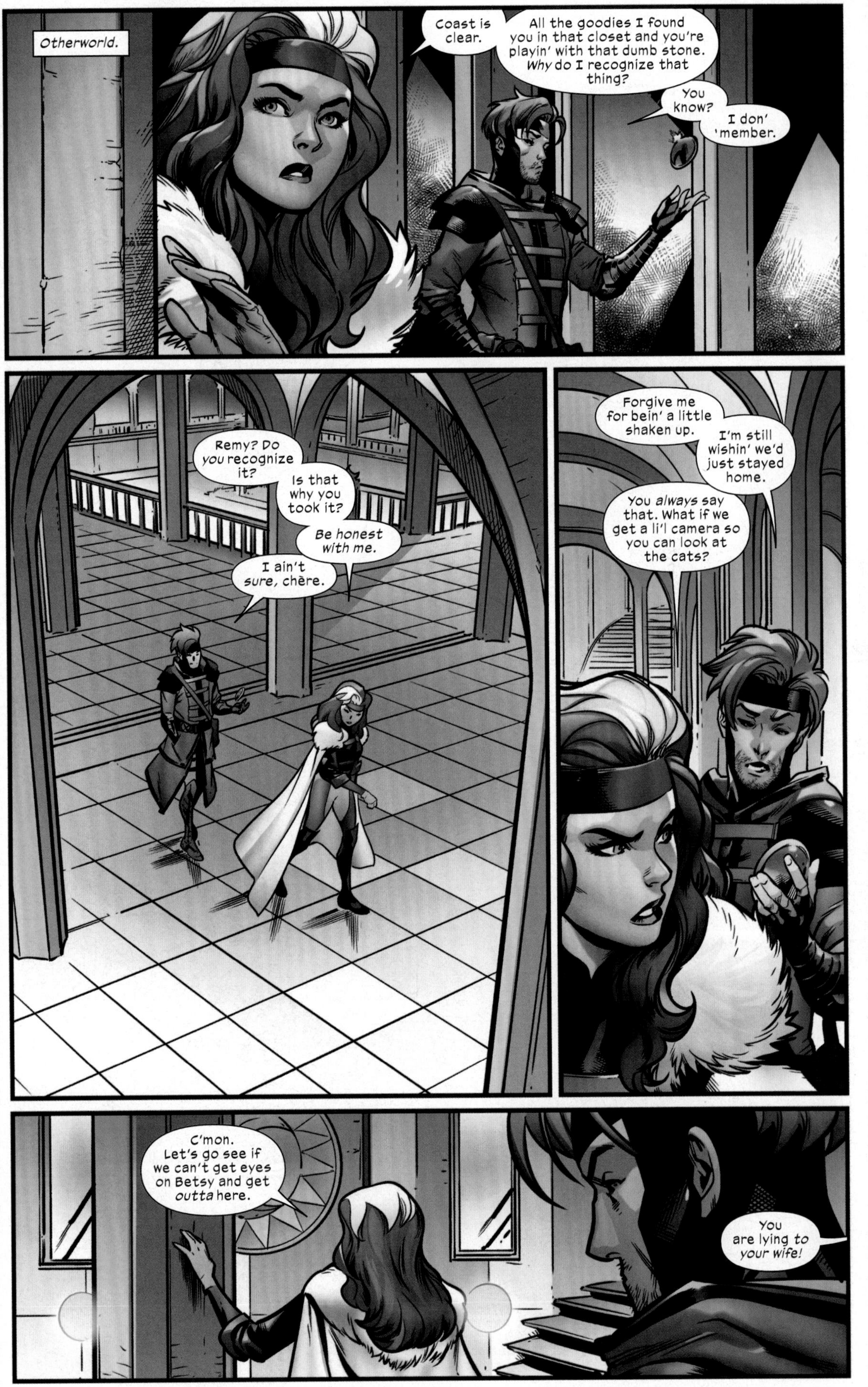
Otherworld.
Coast is clear.
All the goodies I found you in that closet and you're playin' with that dumb stone. *Why* do I recognize that thing?
You know?
I don' 'member.
Remy? Do *you* recognize it?
Is that why you took it?
Be honest with me.
I ain't *sure, chère.*
Forgive me for bein' a little shaken up.
I'm still wishin' we'd just stayed home.
You *always* say that. What if we get a li'l camera so you can look at the cats?
C'mon. Let's go see if we can't get eyes on Betsy and get *outta* here.
You are lying to your wife!

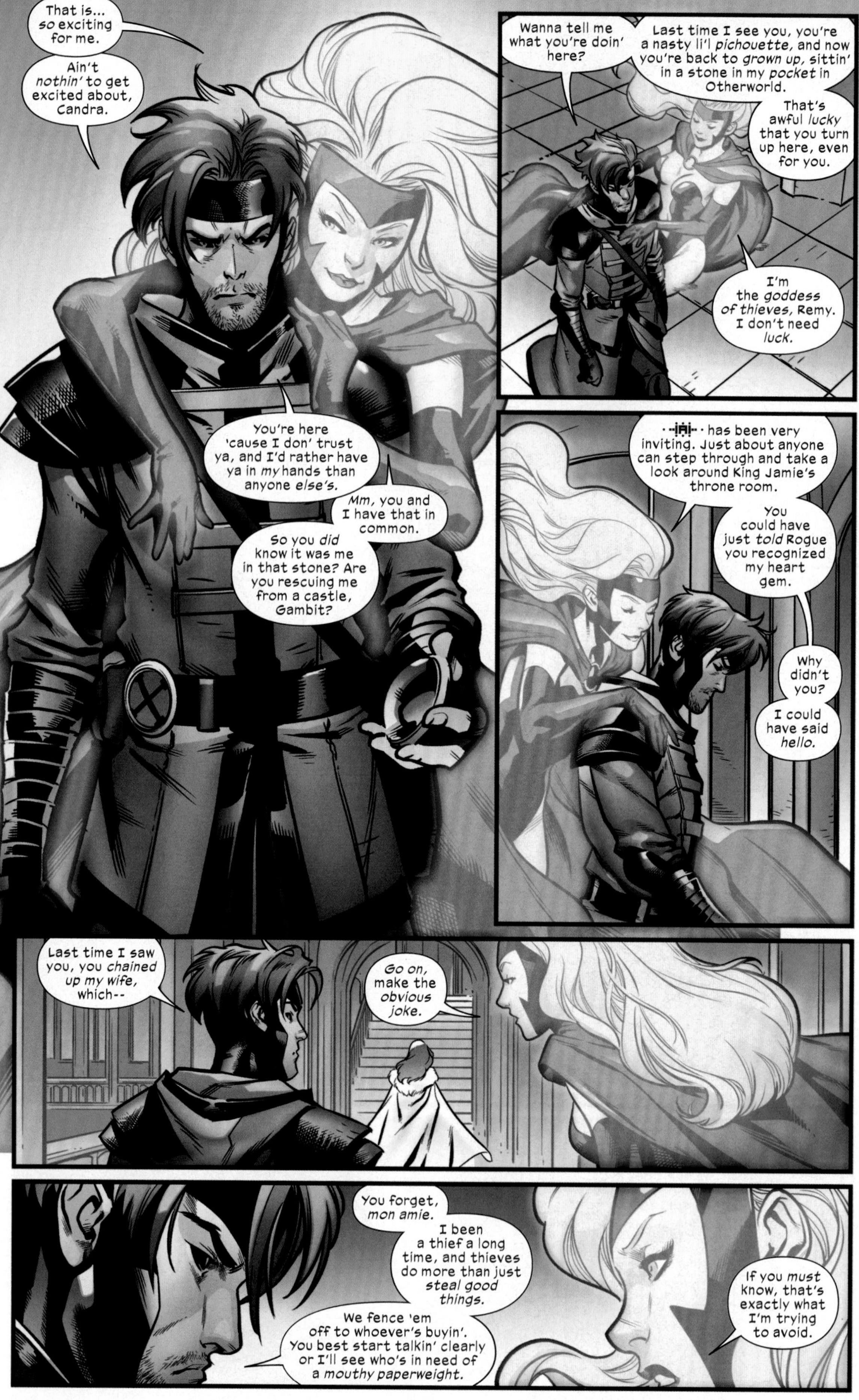
That is... so exciting for me.
Ain't nothin' to get excited about, Candra.
You're here 'cause I don' trust ya, and I'd rather have ya in my hands than anyone else's.
Mm, you and I have that in common.
So you did know it was me in that stone? Are you rescuing me from a castle, Gambit?
Wanna tell me what you're doin' here?
Last time I see you, you're a nasty li'l pichouette, and now you're back to grown up, sittin' in a stone in my pocket in Otherworld.
That's awful lucky that you turn up here, even for you.
I'm the goddess of thieves, Remy. I don't need luck.
has been very inviting. Just about anyone can step through and take a look around King Jamie's throne room.
You could have just told Rogue you recognized my heart gem.
Why didn't you?
I could have said hello.
Last time I saw you, you chained up my wife, which--
Go on, make the obvious joke.
You forget, mon amie.
I been a thief a long time, and thieves do more than just steal good things.
We fence 'em off to whoever's buyin'. You best start talkin' clearly or I'll see who's in need of a mouthy paperweight.
If you must know, that's exactly what I'm trying to avoid.

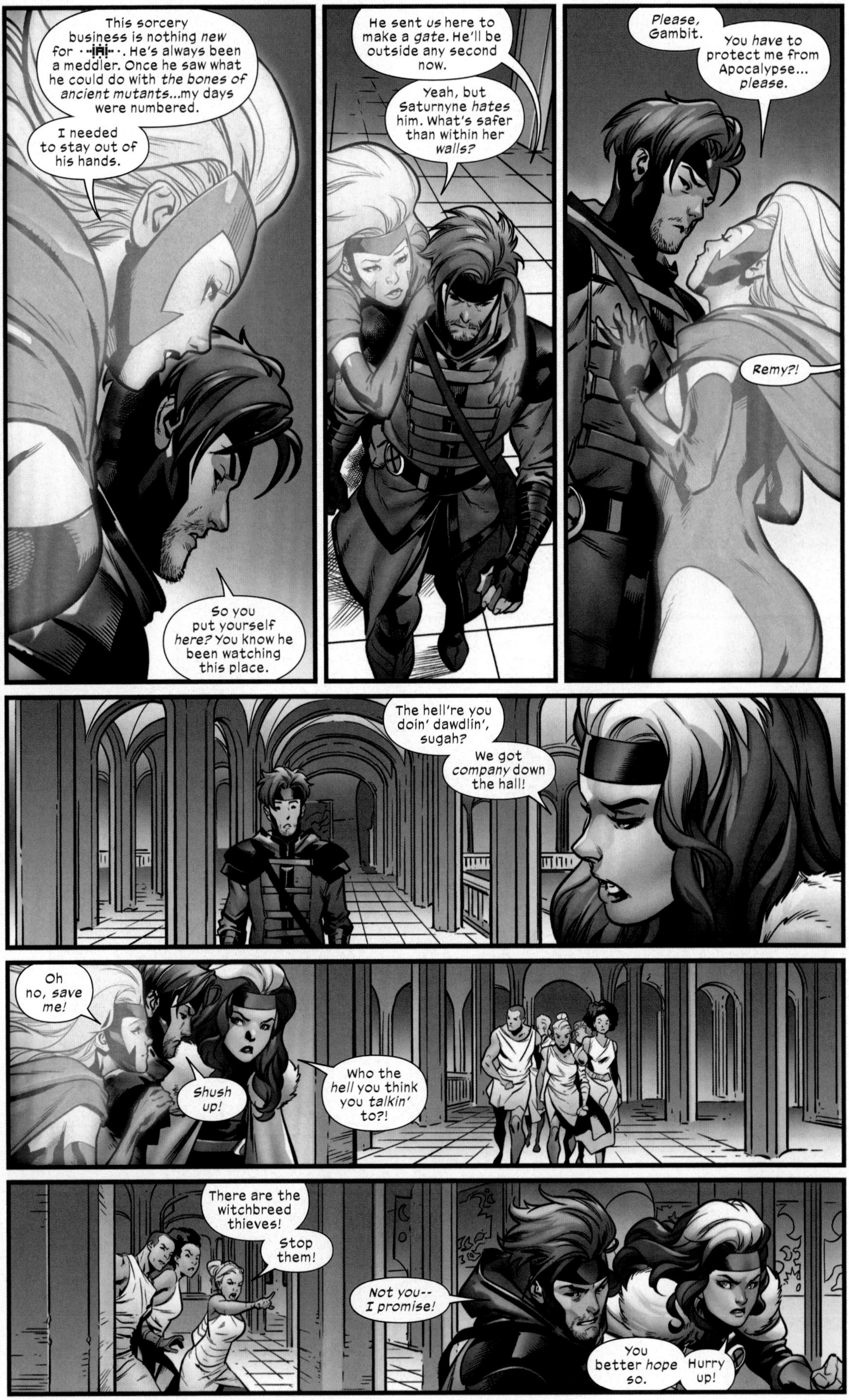

This sorcery business is nothing *new* for . He's always been a meddler. Once he saw what he could do with *the bones of ancient mutants*...my days were numbered.
I needed to stay out of his hands.
So you put yourself *here?* You know he been watching this place.
He sent *us* here to make a *gate.* He'll be outside any second now.
Yeah, but Saturnyne *hates* him. What's safer than within her *walls?*
Please, Gambit.
You *have* to protect me from Apocalypse... *please.*
Remy?!
The hell're you doin' dawdlin', sugah?
We got *company* down the hall!
Oh no, *save me!*
Shush up!
Who the *hell* you think you *talkin'* to?!
There are the witchbreed thieves!
Stop them!
Not you-- I promise!
You better *hope* so.
Hurry up!

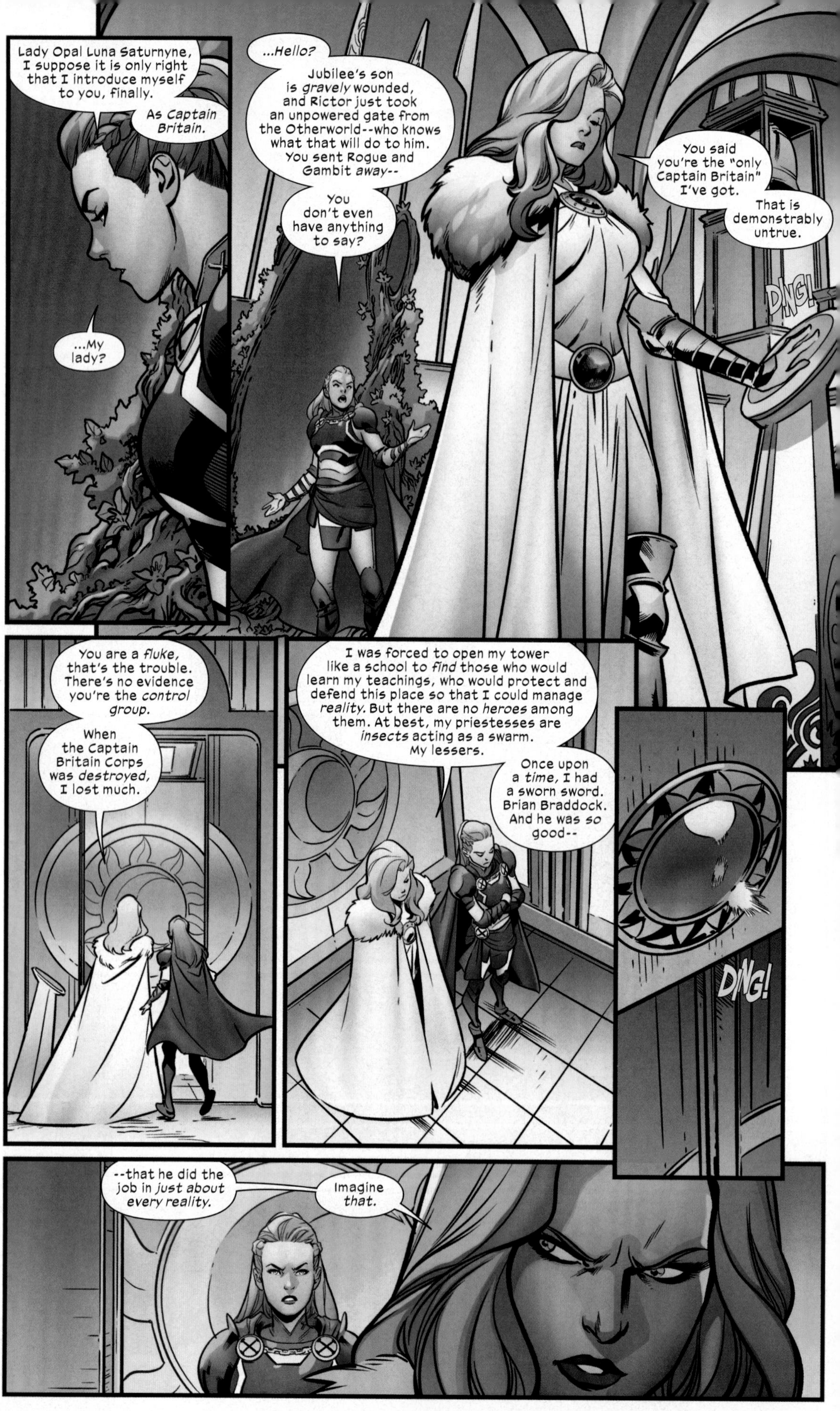
Lady Opal Luna Saturnyne, I suppose it is only right that I introduce myself to you, finally.
As Captain Britain.
...My lady?
...Hello?
Jubilee's son is gravely wounded, and Rictor just took an unpowered gate from the Otherworld--who knows what that will do to him. You sent Rogue and Gambit away--
You don't even have anything to say?
You said you're the "only Captain Britain" I've got.
That is demonstrably untrue.
DING!
You are a fluke, that's the trouble. There's no evidence you're the control group.
When the Captain Britain Corps was destroyed, I lost much.
I was forced to open my tower like a school to find those who would learn my teachings, who would protect and defend this place so that I could manage reality. But there are no heroes among them. At best, my priestesses are insects acting as a swarm. My lessers.
Once upon a time, I had a sworn sword. Brian Braddock. And he was so good--
DING!
--that he did the job in just about every reality.
Imagine that.

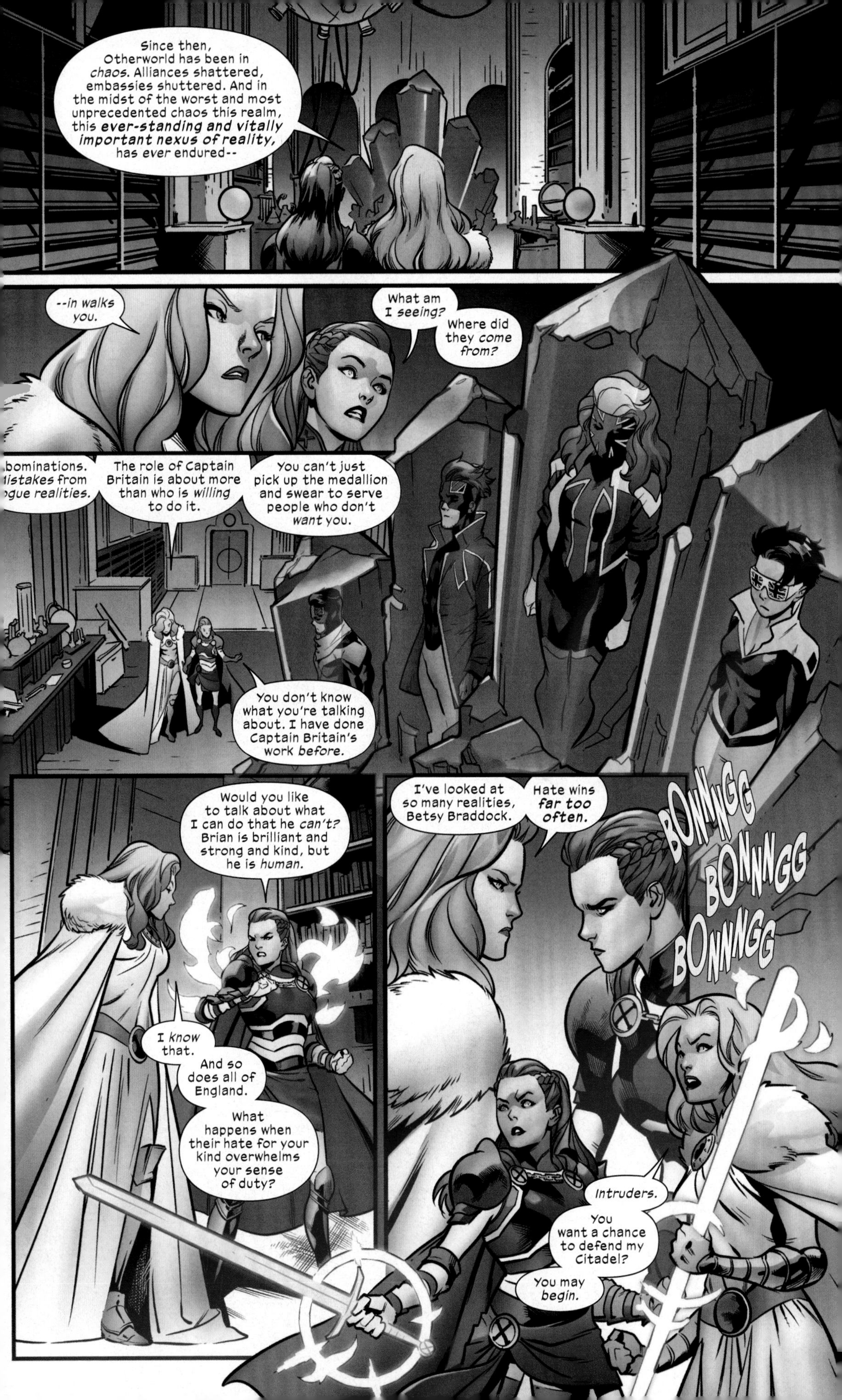

Since then, Otherworld has been in *chaos*. Alliances shattered, embassies shuttered. And in the midst of the worst and most unprecedented chaos this realm, this ***ever-standing and vitally important nexus of reality,*** has *ever* endured--
--in walks you.
What am I *seeing?*
Where did they *come* from?
bominations. *Mistakes* from *gue realities.*
The role of Captain Britain is about more than who is *willing* to do it.
You can't just pick up the medallion and swear to serve people who don't *want* you.
You don't know what you're talking about. I have done Captain Britain's work *before.*
Would you like to talk about what I can do that he *can't?* Brian is brilliant and strong and kind, but he is *human.*
I *know* that.
And so does all of England.
What happens when their hate for your kind overwhelms your sense of duty?
I've looked at so many realities, Betsy Braddock.
Hate wins ***far too often.***
BONNNGG
BONNNGG
BONNNGG
Intruders.
You want a chance to defend my Citadel?
You may *begin.*

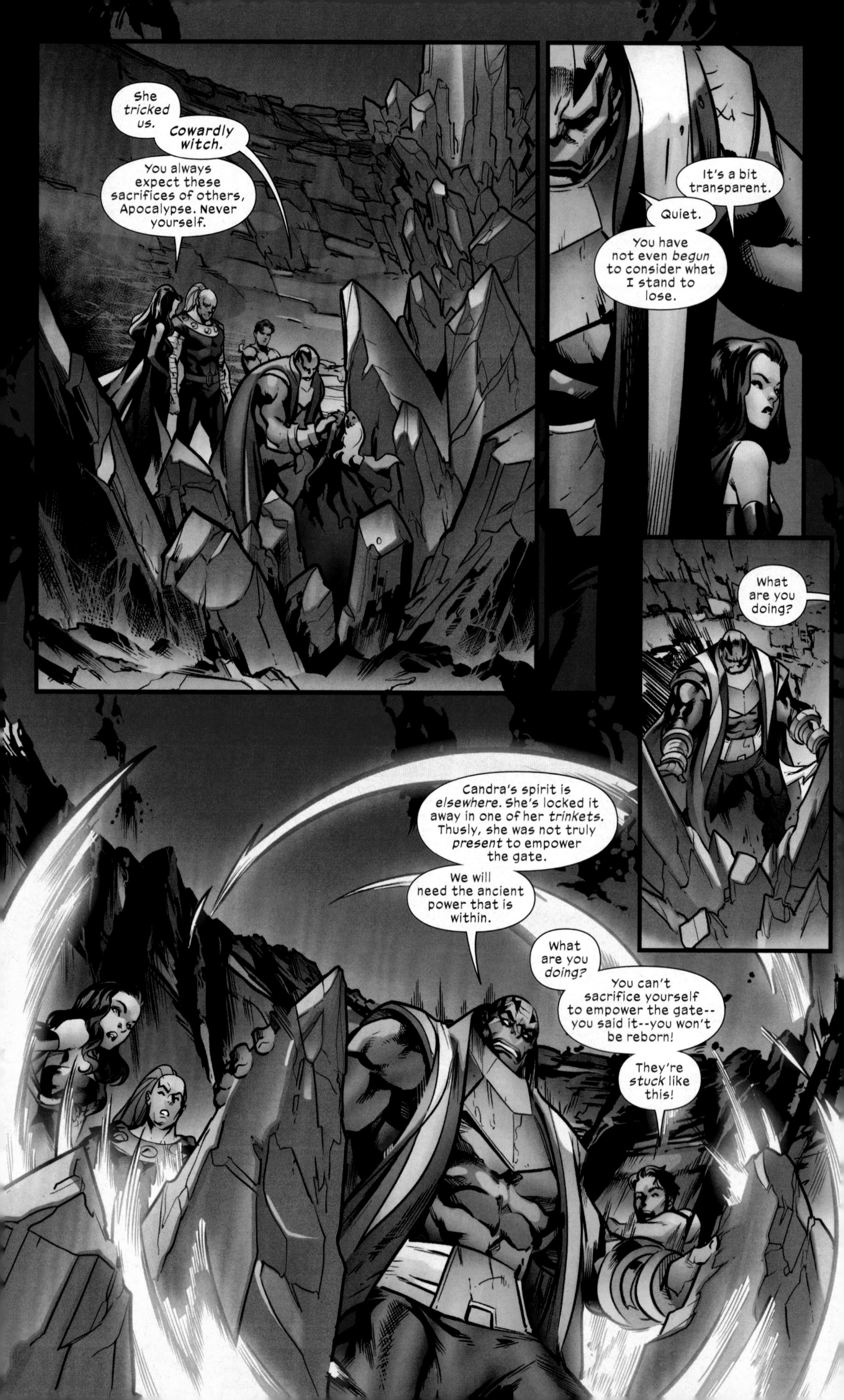
She tricked us.
Cowardly witch.
You always expect these sacrifices of others, Apocalypse. Never yourself.
It's a bit transparent.
Quiet.
You have not even begun to consider what I stand to lose.
What are you doing?
Candra's spirit is elsewhere. She's locked it away in one of her trinkets. Thusly, she was not truly present to empower the gate.
We will need the ancient power that is within.
What are you doing?
You can't sacrifice yourself to empower the gate--you said it--you won't be reborn!
They're stuck like this!

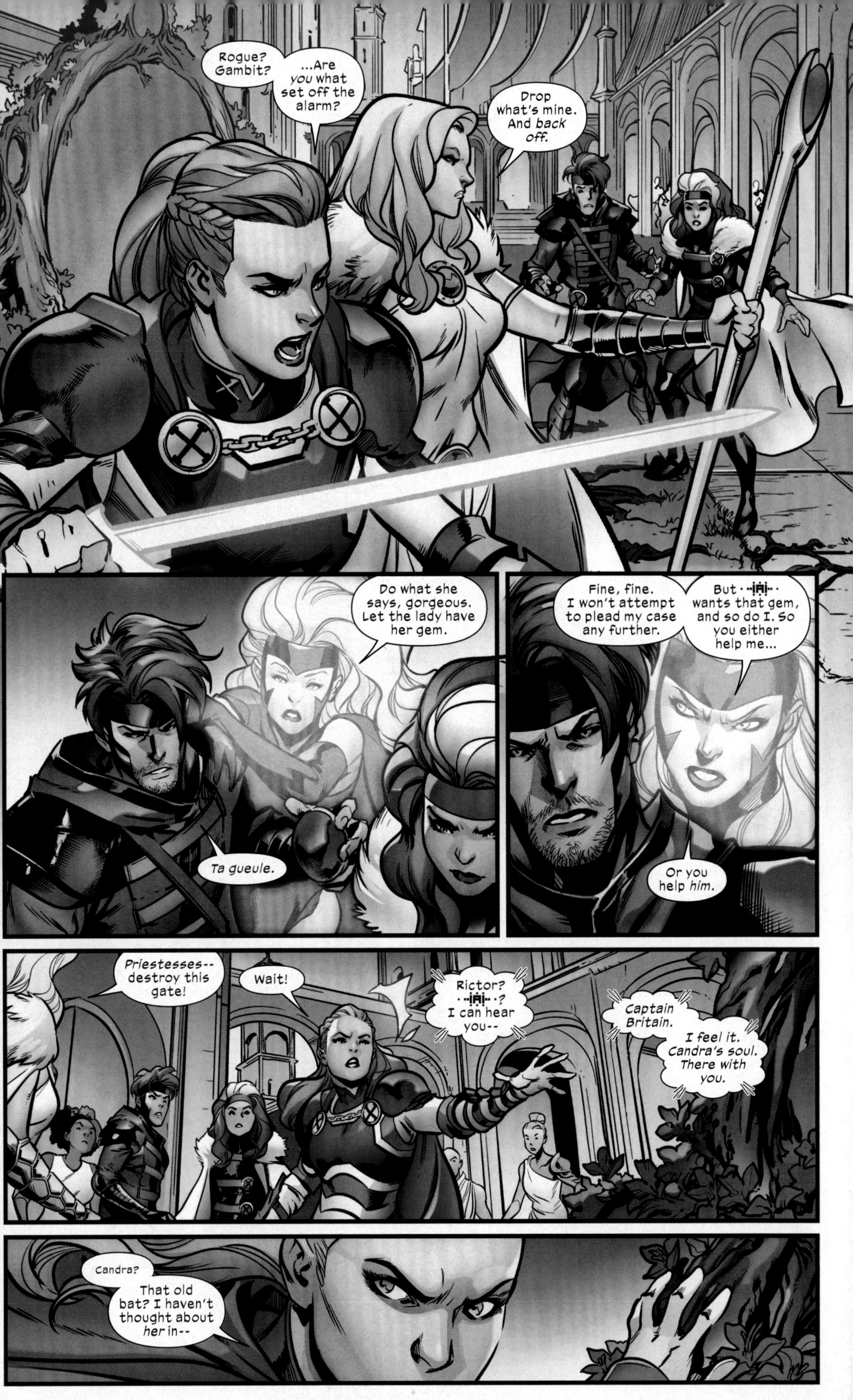
Rogue? Gambit?
...Are you what set off the alarm?
Drop what's mine. And back off.
Do what she says, gorgeous. Let the lady have her gem.
Ta gueule.
Fine, fine. I won't attempt to plead my case any further.
But wants that gem, and so do I. So you either help me...
Or you help him.
Priestesses-- destroy this gate!
Wait!
Rictor?
?
I can hear you--
Captain Britain.
I feel it. Candra's soul. There with you.
Candra?
That old bat? I haven't thought about her in--

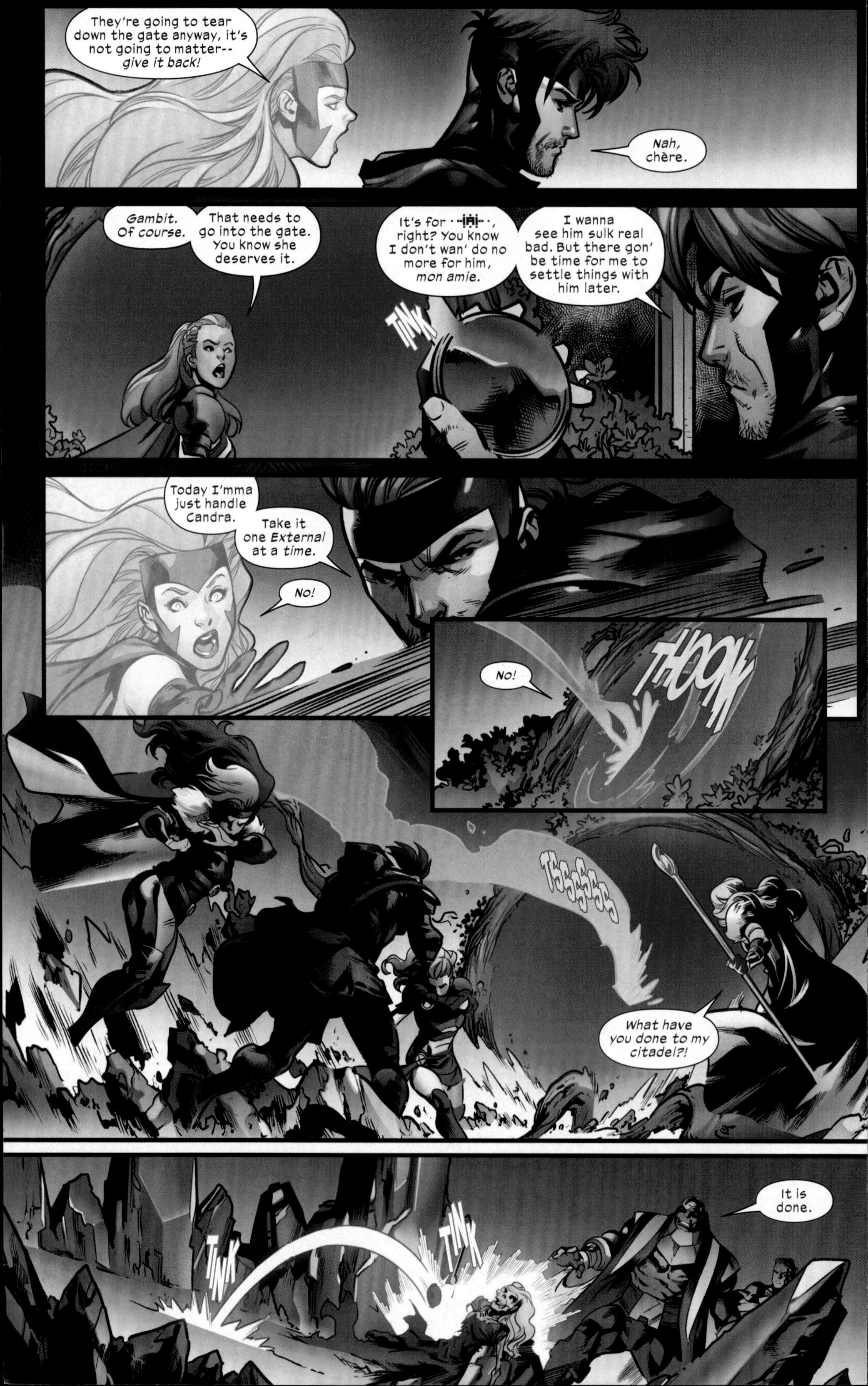
They're going to tear down the gate anyway, it's not going to matter-- *give it back!*
Nah, chère.
Gambit. Of course.
That needs to go into the gate. You know she deserves it.
It's for ··, right? You know I don't wan' do no more for him, *mon amie.*
I wanna see him sulk real bad. But there gon' be time for me to settle things with him later.
TINK
Today I'mma just handle Candra.
Take it one *External* at a *time.*
No!
No!
THOOK
TSSSSSS
What have you done to my citadel?!
It is done.
TINK
TINK

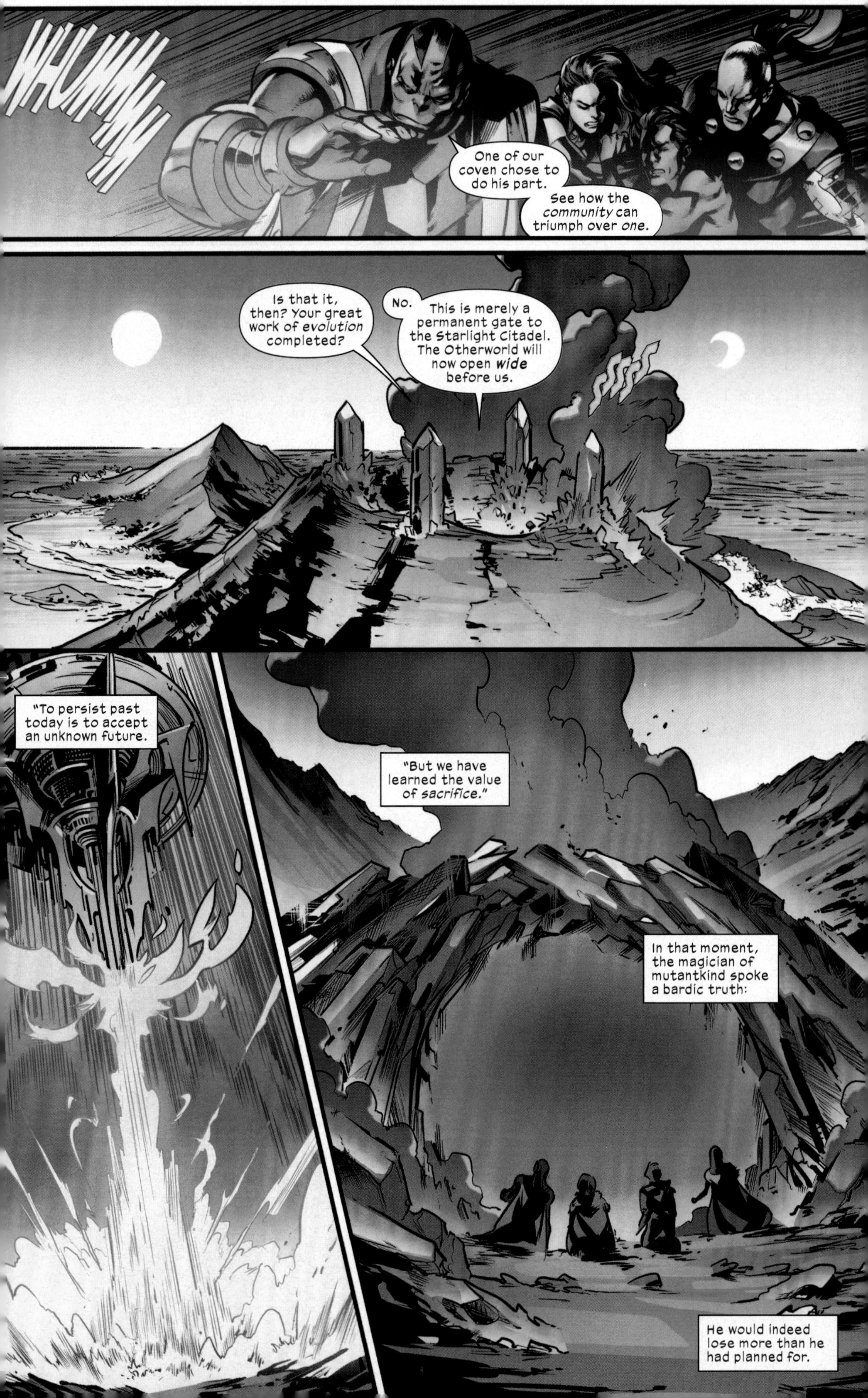
WHUMMM
One of our coven chose to do his part.
See how the *community* can triumph over *one*.
Is that it, then? Your great work of *evolution* completed?
No.
This is merely a permanent gate to the Starlight Citadel. The Otherworld will now open ***wide*** before us.
SSSS
"To persist past today is to accept an unknown future.
"But we have learned the value of *sacrifice*."
In that moment, the magician of mutantkind spoke a bardic truth:
He would indeed lose more than he had planned for.

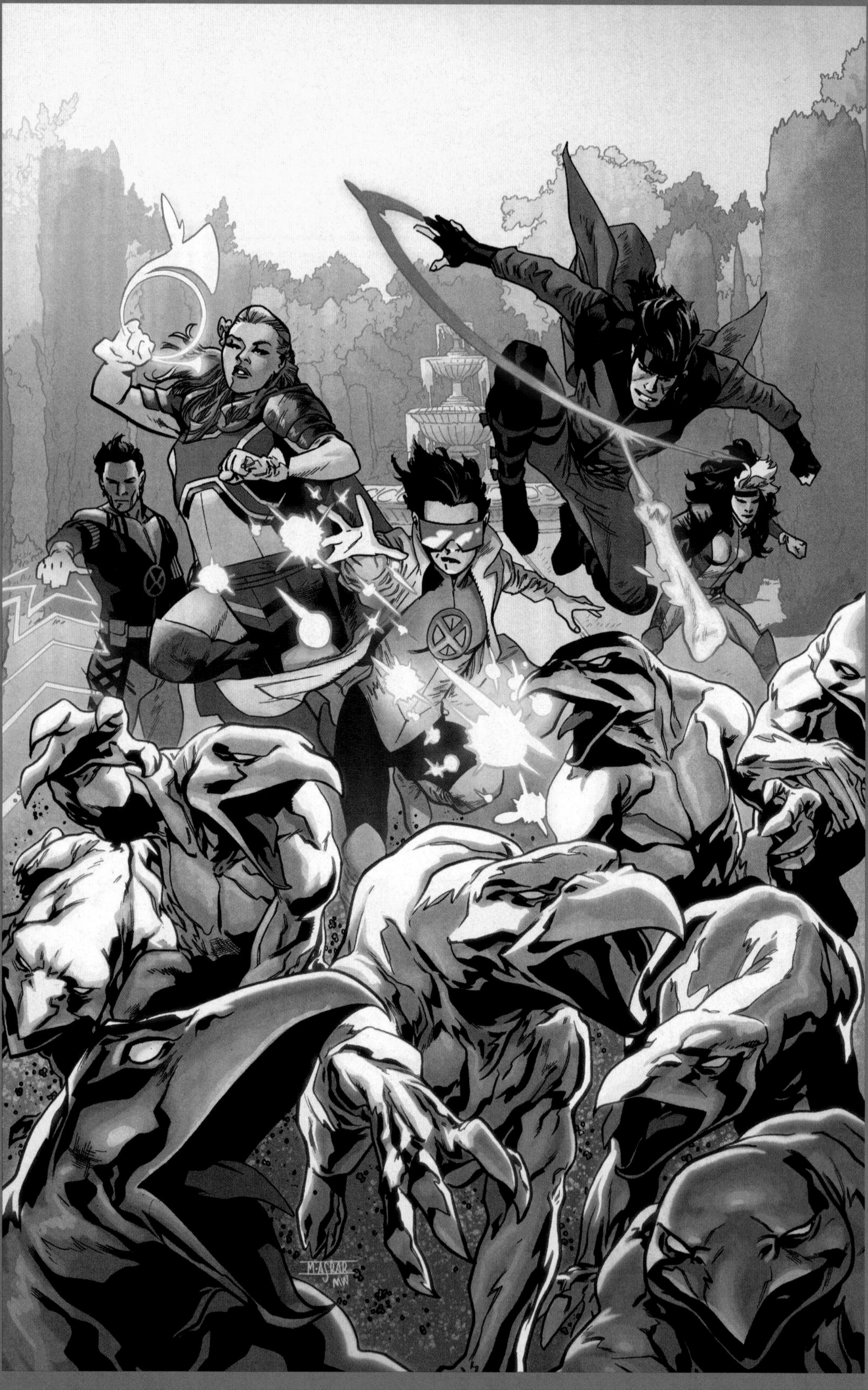
M·ASRAR
MW

Excalibur #7

by Mahmud Asrar
& Matthew Wilson

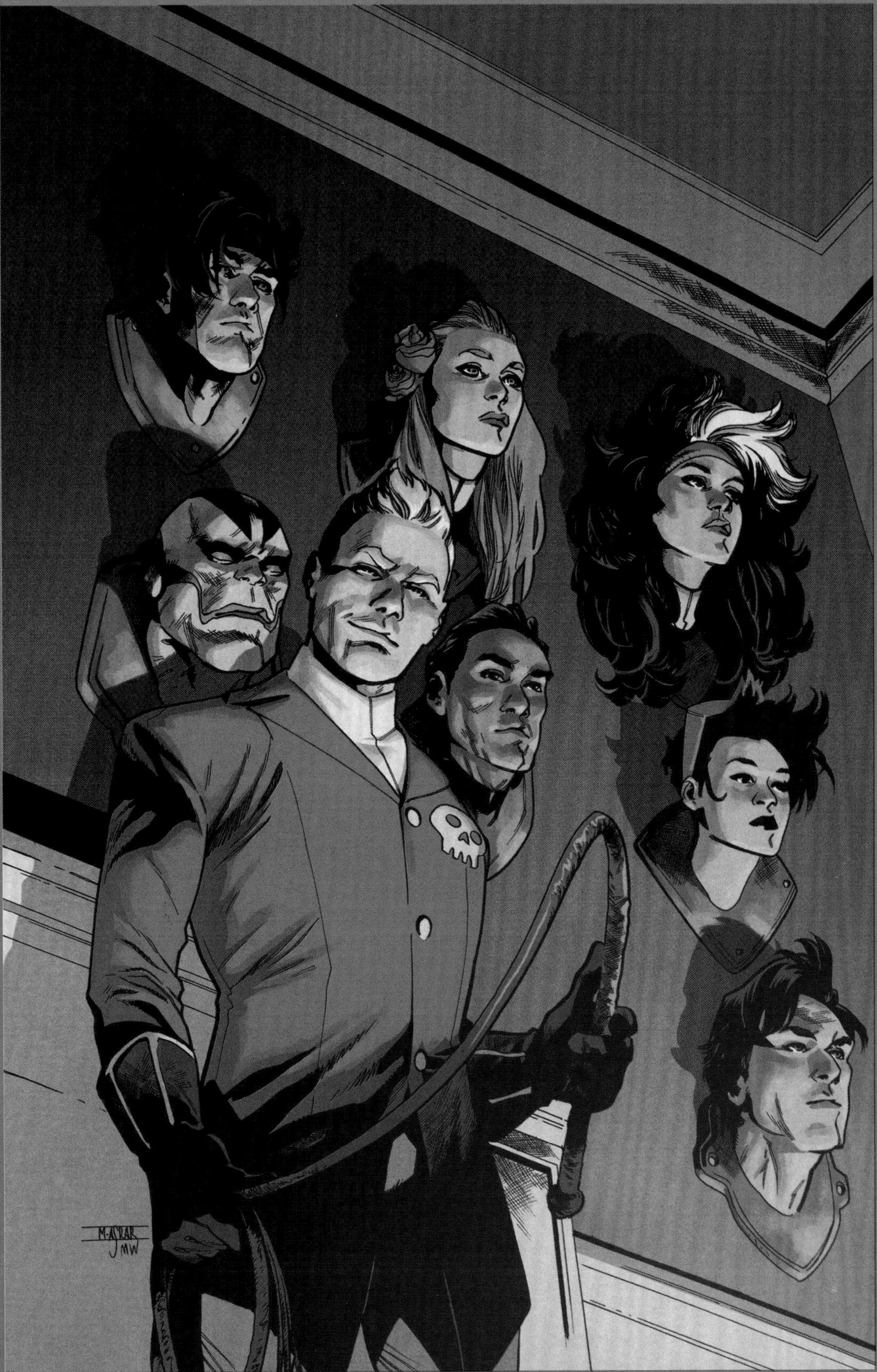
M.ASRAR
MW

Excalibur #8

by Mahmud Asrar
& Matthew Wilson

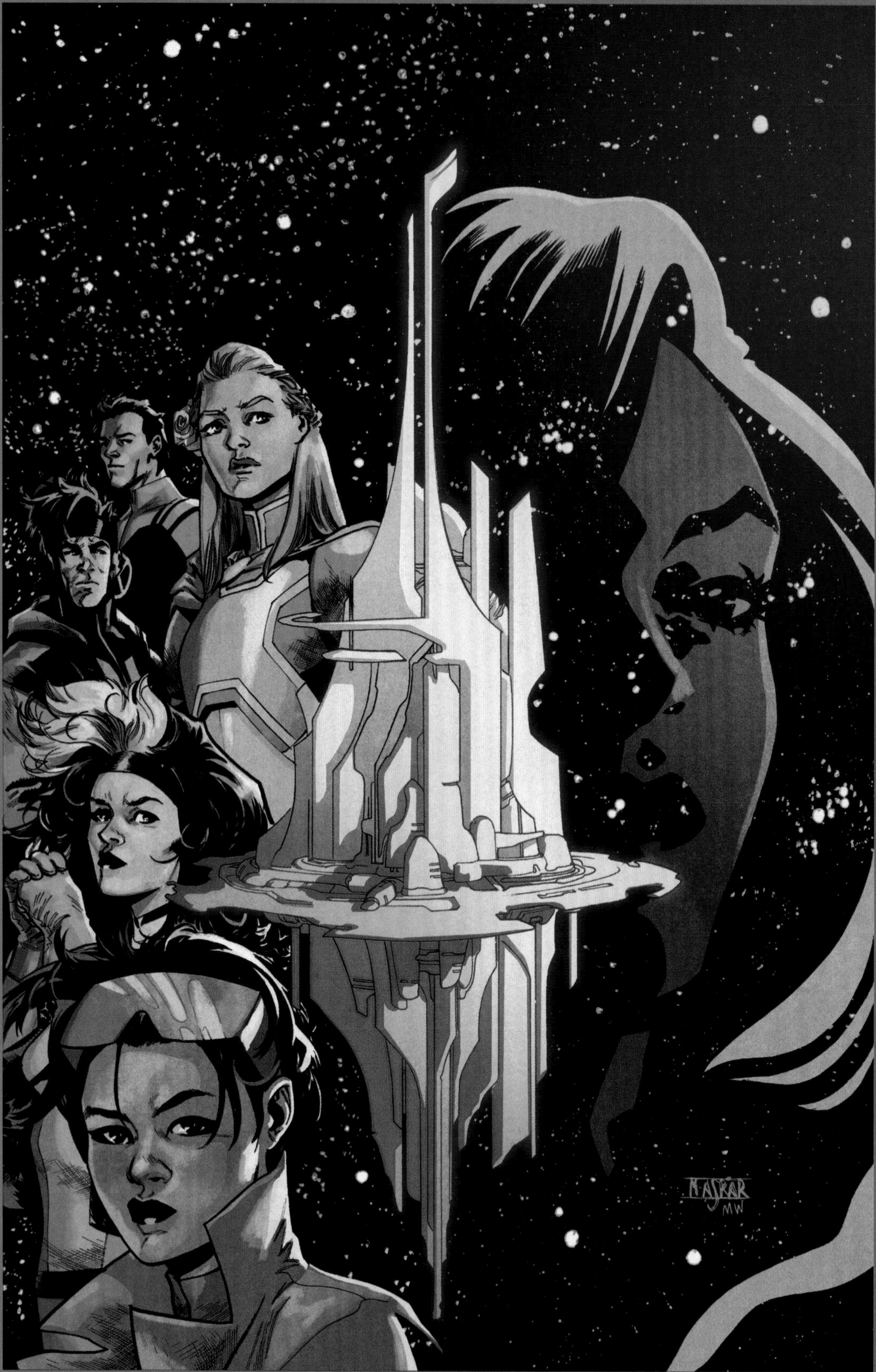
M ASRAR
MW

Excalibur #9

by Mahmud Asrar
& Matthew Wilson

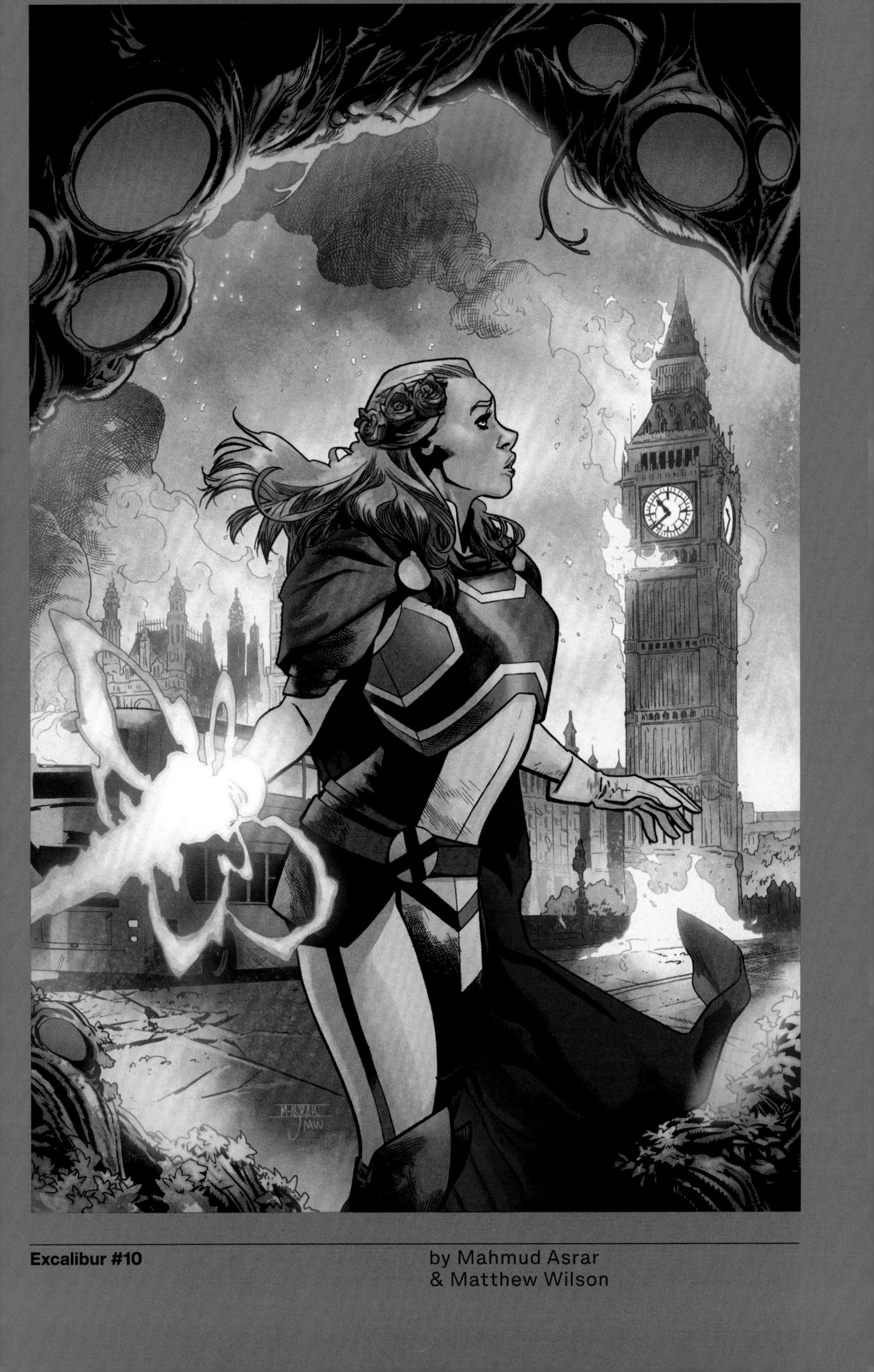

Excalibur #10

by Mahmud Asrar
& Matthew Wilson

Excalibur #11

by Mahmud Asrar
& Matthew Wilson

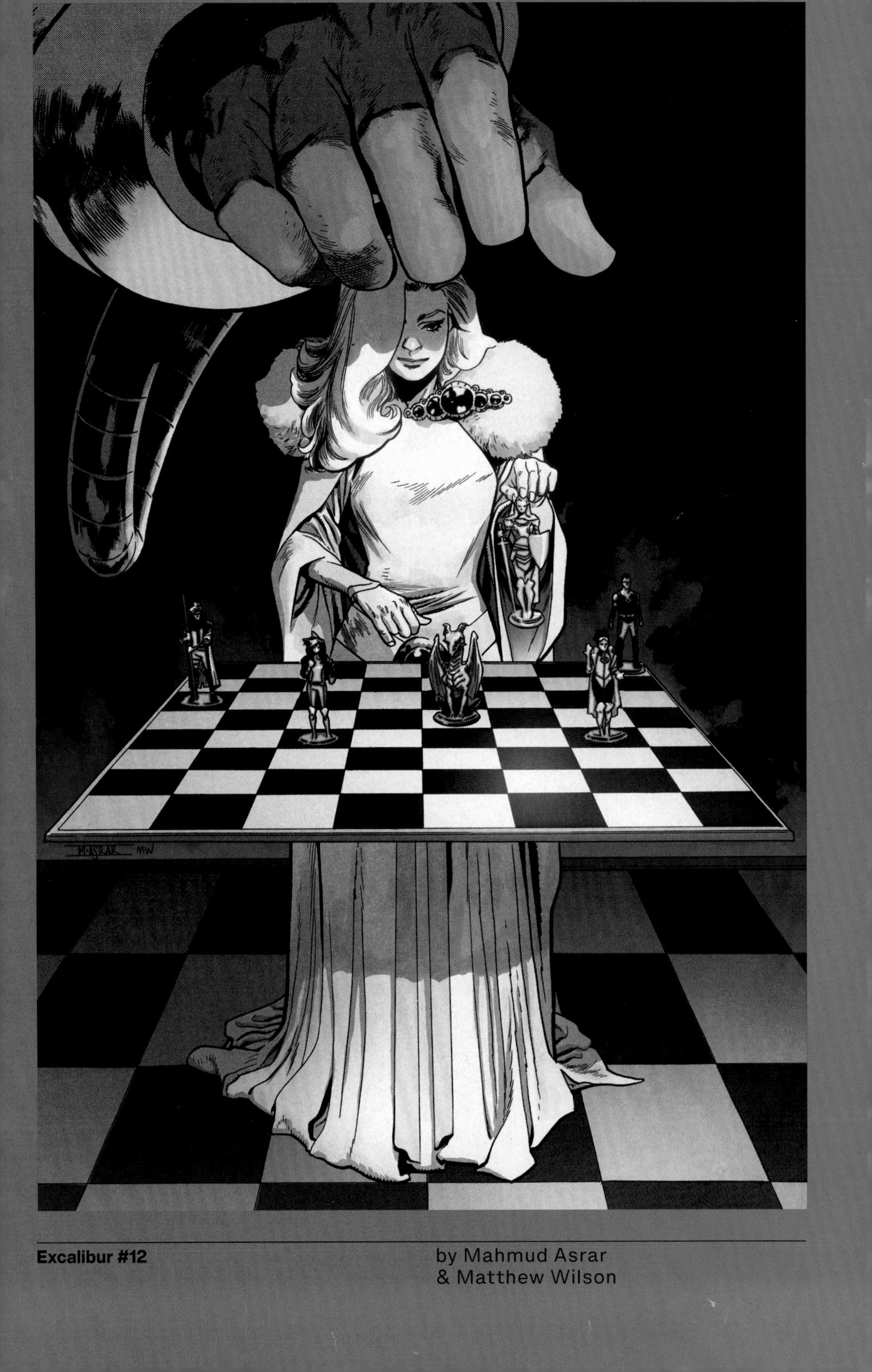

Excalibur #12

by Mahmud Asrar
& Matthew Wilson

Excalibur #7 Gwen Stacy Variant
by Ben Oliver

Excalibur #9 God Loves, Man Kills Variant
by Marcos Martin